DEMOCRATIC MARXISM SERIES

Series Editor: Vishwas Satgar

The crisis of Marxism in the late twentieth century was the crisis of orthodox and vanguardist Marxism associated mainly with hierarchical communist parties, and imposed, even as state ideology, as the 'correct' Marxism. The Stalinisation of the Soviet Union and its eventual collapse exposed the inherent weaknesses and authoritarian mould of vanguardist Marxism. More fundamentally, vanguardist Marxism was rendered obsolete but for its residual existence in a few parts of the world, as well as within authoritarian national liberation movements in Africa and in China.

With the deepening crises of capitalism, a new democratic Marxism (or democratic historical materialism) is coming to the fore. Such a democratic Marxism is characterised in the following ways:

- Its sources span non-vanguardist grassroots movements, unions, political fronts, mass parties, radical intellectuals, transnational activist networks and parts of the progressive academy;
- It seeks to ensure that the inherent categories of Marxism are theorised within constantly changing historical conditions to find meaning;
- Marxism is understood as a body of social thought that is unfinished and hence challenged by the need to explain the dynamics of a globalising capitalism and the futures of social change;
- It is open to other forms of anti-capitalist thought and practice, including currents within radical ecology, feminism, emancipatory utopianism and indigenous thought;
- It does not seek to be a monolithic and singular school of thought but engenders contending perspectives;
- Democracy, as part of the heritage of people's struggles, is understood as the basis for articulating alternatives to capitalism and as the primary means for constituting a transformative subject of historical change.

This series seeks to elaborate the social theorising and politics of democratic Marxism.

Published in the series and available:

Michelle Williams and Vishwas Satgar (eds). 2013. *Marxisms in the 21st Century: Crisis, Critique and Struggle*. Johannesburg: Wits University Press.

Vishwas Satgar (ed.). 2015. *Capitalism's Crises: Class Struggles in South Africa and the World*. Johannesburg: Wits University Press.

Vishwas Satgar (ed.). 2018. *The Climate Crisis: South African and Global Democratic Eco-Socialist Alternatives*. Johannesburg: Wits University Press.

RACISM AFTER APARTHEID

CHALLENGES FOR MARXISM AND ANTI-RACISM

Edited by Vishwas Satgar

WITS UNIVERSITY PRESS

Published in South Africa by:

Wits University Press
1 Jan Smuts Avenue
Johannesburg, 2001
www.witspress.co.za

Compilation © Vishwas Satgar 2019
Chapters © Individual contributors 2019
Published edition © Wits University Press 2019

First published 2019

http://dx.doi.org.10.18772/22019033061

978-1-77614-306-1 (Paperback)
978-1-77614-307-8 (Web PDF)
978-1-77614-308-5 (EPUB)
978-1-77614-309-2 (Mobi)
978-1-77614-359-7 (Open Access PDF)

All rights reserved. No part of this publication may be reproduced, stored in a retrieval system, or transmitted in any form or by any means, electronic, mechanical, photocopying, recording or otherwise, without the written permission of the publisher, except in accordance with the provisions of the Copyright Act, Act 98 of 1978.

This book is freely available through the OAPEN library (www.oapen.org) under a Creative Commons CC-BY-NC-ND 4.0 Creative Commons License. (https://creativecommons.org/licenses/by-nc-nd/4.0/).

The publication of this volume was made possible by funding from the Rosa Luxemburg Stiftung and through a grant received from the National Institute for the Humanities and Social Sciences.

Project manager: Inga Norenius
Copyeditor: Sally Hines
Proofreader: Inga Norenius
Indexer: Margaret Ramsay
Cover design: Hothouse, South Africa
Typesetter: MPS
Typeset in 10 point Minion Pro

CONTENTS

ACKNOWLEDGEMENTS vii
ACRONYMS AND ABBREVIATIONS ix

CHAPTER 1: The Anti-Racism of Marxism: Past and Present 1
Vishwas Satgar

PART ONE: AGAINST RACISM IN THE WORLD 29

CHAPTER 2: The International Indigenous Peoples' Movement:
A Site of Anti-Racist Struggle Against Capitalism 30
Roxanne Dunbar-Ortiz

CHAPTER 3: Emancipation, Freedom or Taxonomy? What Does
It Mean to be African? 49
Firoze Manji

CHAPTER 4: Colonialism, Apartheid and the Native Question: The Case of
Israel/Palestine 75
Ran Greenstein

CHAPTER 5: The Role of Racism in the European 'Migration Crisis':
A Historical Materialist Perspective 96
Fabian Georgi

CHAPTER 6: Hindutva, Caste and the 'National Unconscious' 118
Aditya Nigam

CHAPTER 7: Marxism, Feminism and Caste in Contemporary India 137
Nivedita Menon

PART TWO: AGAINST RACISM IN SOUTH AFRICA 157

CHAPTER 8: The Reproduction of Racial Inequality in South Africa:
The Colonial Unconscious and Democracy 158
Peter Hudson

CHAPTER 9:	Democratic Marxism and the National Question: Race and Class in Post-Apartheid South Africa Khwezi Mabasa	173
CHAPTER 10:	Seven Theses on Radical Non-Racialism, the Climate Crisis and Deep Just Transitions: From the National Question to the Eco-cide Question Vishwas Satgar	194
CHAPTER 11:	Foreign Nationals are the 'Non-Whites' of the Democratic Dispensation Sharon S. Ekambaram	217

CONCLUSION: Vishwas Satgar   237
CONTRIBUTORS   242
INDEX   245

ACKNOWLEDGEMENTS

This volume owes a special debt to the Rosa Luxemburg Foundation. Without that support it would have been impossible to hold a contributors' workshop in South Africa and to ensure the manuscript was completed for publication. The use of the conference venue at their office provided a conducive space for engagement during the contributors' workshop. We are also grateful for the support given by the Co-operative and Policy Centre (COPAC), which played a central role in organising the workshop and inviting contributors and activists from various social movements and community organisations. The support given by the National Institute for the Humanities and Social Sciences has enabled the open access publication of this volume. Moreover, it is important to acknowledge the editorial assistance provided by Jane Cherry from COPAC. Her efforts were crucial for keeping things on track. The input from Sunanda Mathis and Nadia Karodia, working with Jane Cherry, are also appreciated. Special thanks to Professor Michelle Williams for her supportive feedback during this project. Finally, our sincerest appreciation to the team at Wits University Press, particularly Veronica Klipp, Roshan Cader and Corina van der Spoel, for supporting this volume and the Democratic Marxism series.

ACRONYMS AND ABBREVIATIONS

AIM	American Indian Movement
ANC	African National Congress
BIA	Bureau of Indian Affairs
BJP	Bharatiya Janata Party
Cosatu	Congress of South African Trade Unions
CPI	Communist Party of India
CPI(M)	Communist Party of India (Marxist)
CPSA	Communist Party of South Africa
CST	colonialism of a special type
EFF	Economic Freedom Fighters
EU	European Union
FBI	Federal Bureau of Investigation
GDP	gross domestic product
IITC	International Indian Treaty Council
IOM	International Organization for Migration
JNU	Jawaharlal Nehru University
LHR	Lawyers for Human Rights
ML	Muslim League
NASA	National Aeronautics and Space Administration
NGO	non-governmental organisation
OBC	Other Backward Classes
PAIGC	African Party for the Independence of Guinea and Cape Verde
RSS	Rashtriya Swayamsevak Sangh
SACP	South African Communist Party
SAHRC	South African Human Rights Commission
UDF	United Democratic Front
UN	United Nations
UNHCR	United Nations High Commissioner for Refugees
US	United States
WCIP	World Council of Indigenous Peoples
WGIP	Working Group on Indigenous Populations

CHAPTER

1

THE ANTI-RACISM OF MARXISM: PAST AND PRESENT

Vishwas Satgar

There is no scientific basis for race and racism to be a part of social reality. Nonetheless, race as a mode of social categorisation and racism as a form of discrimination, violence and oppression persists in our twenty-first-century capitalist world. W.E.B. Du Bois' prescience in *The Souls of Black Folk* presented us with a notion of the colour-line not just as a problem of the twentieth century, but also a problem that extends into the twenty-first-century world of deep capitalist globalisation. This 'long colour-line' is marked by continuities and discontinuities and systemic racisms, but also contingent and conjunctural shifts engendering new racisms. Today, a new extreme right, neo-fascist white nationalisms, xenophobia, resurgent narrow black nationalisms, continued apartheid-like oppression of Palestine, further dispossessions of indigenous peoples and Islamophobia are all on the rise. The world is faced with an ugly problem, expressed through an over-inflation of racialised thinking and practices, in different historical contexts and places. With their rise and prevalence, these particular racisms and their oppressive impacts need to be understood as a matter of urgency. This volume contributes to this challenge by drawing on Marxist and non-Marxist perspectives, engaging in a dialogue with the historical role of Marxism in the struggle against racism and with movements confronting racism.

South Africa was ruled by one of the most heinous and brutalising racist regimes called apartheid from 1948 to 1994. This institutionalised form of racism had its roots in 350 years of capitalist development involving slavery, colonialism, genocidal violence and segregation. The white privilege entrenched in this society benefited the white minority, despite some disagreeing with apartheid while others were simply 'unaware' of this racist reality. However, apartheid engendered resistance from the national liberation movements in South Africa, the global anti-apartheid movement and popular forces that played a vital role in confronting and ending this regime. The resistance to apartheid was built on a dream of a non-racial, non-sexist, egalitarian and democratic society. Yet, the promise of non-racial politics in advancing fundamental transformation and deepening democracy has stalled. Obscene levels of inequality, high unemployment, deepening public debt, rampant corruption, creeping authoritarianism, weakening of democratic institutions, and growing signs of state failure express the profound degeneration of African National Congress (ANC)-led national liberation politics. In this context, nation building and hegemonic nationalist narratives have dissipated. Instead, there is a resurgent Black Consciousness, narrow populist Africanist nativism, white nationalism, xenophobic state practices and growing race-based polarisation. The many racisms of contemporary South Africa come under scrutiny in this volume.

In the current fragmentation of South African politics and ideologies, Marxism has been the target of various attacks. Africanists argue that Marxism is a foreign ideology with its genealogy in Europe and it is ultimately the product of white thought. For them, Marxism is racist. The other attack confronting Marxism is from the champions of identity politics. It is argued that difference is the master category to understand 'whiteness' and 'blackness'. This critique suggests that all Marxists are about class reductionism and hence blind to understanding race and racism. In the South African context these attacks are rather polemical, crude and based on caricature. What both critiques refuse to recognise is that Marxism has contributed immensely to South African emancipation from racism and its intellectual itinerary speaks for itself. From theories of racial capitalism, colonialism of a special type, articulations of modes of production to studies on ideology, social history, national question debates and studies on the making of apartheid, there is a powerful Marxist body of thought that is explicitly against racism and cannot be ignored. Class in this body of work has been intrinsically connected to race and gender.

However, recognising Marxism's positive role in South African history does not mean that Marxism does not have to be self-reflexive to understand its limits and shortcomings. Today, Marxism is non-hegemonic in the South African academy and in broader society given the unravelling of the anti-racist national liberation project and the rise of the post-structural turn among many in the intelligentsia. Part of Marxism's history that needs to be confronted is the fact that there are dogmatic Marxisms, with a formulaic approach to social reality, that do not appreciate the importance of non-Marxist radicalism and anti-capitalism and do not want to engage in dialogue. Such Marxisms are against the materiality of identity formation in social processes. The world today has many Marxisms, including ecological Marxisms, cultural Marxisms, Marxisms sensitive to the affective life of people, Marxist feminism and anti-racist Marxisms. There are also Eurocentric Marxisms, Marxisms that are not explicitly anti-racist, and Marxisms that do not have an adequate understanding of systemic and conjunctural racisms and contemporary oppressions. These latter Marxisms are challenged in this volume.

The issue of South African Marxism and its location in anti-racist struggles was a theme in volume 1 of the Democratic Marxism series. This is taken further in this volume. In this chapter, I interrogate the charge that Marxism is racist. The chapter seeks to find an answer to this question, recognising that there is more than one Marxism, which was an important theme in volume 1 in the series. The starting point for this chapter is to understand the relationship between racism and Marx's thought. This journey is not to valorise Marx or defend his ideas against all odds. Rather, it is to set the historical record straight by looking at his work for its insights and weaknesses. It is important to understand Marx's own thinking on race in order to ascertain the relevance of Marx's ideas in the twenty-first century. After engaging Marx's thought, the chapter then critically scrutinises the extent to which Marxisms in the twentieth century were part of anti-racist struggles. Again, this is important in order to understand the varied and complex history of Marxisms. The chapter locates some of the current themes in Marxist theorising on race and racism. By engaging current Marxist ideas, the chapter goes beyond an essentialising binary of 'white Marxism'/'black Marxism', while mapping some of the current frontiers of racist/anti-racist struggle in order to clarify the location of Marxism in these struggles. Finally, the chapter provides an overview of the various chapters in the volume, in terms of the offerings made to struggles against racism and its various intersections in the world and in South Africa.

BEYOND THE EUROCENTRIC MOMENT IN MARX

Karl Marx (1818–1883) was marked by the European Enlightenment (c.1720–1820) and the pseudo-scientific racist milieu of nineteenth-century Europe, which was bent on colonising every part of the world. The civilising mission of Christian expansion of the Columbian project (1492) was replaced by a more sophisticated racialised supremacy in the social world in which Marx was living. For Edward Said in *Orientalism* (1979), Marx is a racist Orientalist alongside John Stuart Mill, Lord Balfour and other luminaries of western imperial thought. Said (1979: 2) charges Marx for thinking ontologically and epistemologically, like many others who constructed the 'Orient'/'Occident' distinction. He suggests Marx's notion of the Oriental mode of production or despotism was also utilised by Balfour when describing Egypt (Said 1979: 32). In the main, for Said, Marx was a Eurocentric thinker and deeply racist in how he understood and viewed the non-western world.

Said's indictment of Marx has been extended to Marxism in general and there is a resonance of this critique in the present among post-colonial and postmodern thinkers. This is a view anchored in a geographic essentialism, which means that if you are located in the west you will only see and understand the rest of the world through a western supremacist optic. Ironically, Said himself was sitting in the western academy when ruminating about Orientalist modes of thought in the 1970s. Moreover, Said's critique of Marx's Orientalism is rather crude and over-generalising. It does not take into account the departures, discontinuities and even shifts in the overall body of Marx's thought. Given the vast corpus of Marx's work and the scope of his thought, there is an epistemological evolution in it that cannot be ignored and that has to be engaged with for a more nuanced view.

In this regard, Gilbert Achar (2013: 82–88) makes an important clarifying intervention. First, Achar argues that Marx's Orientalism has to be separated from his Eurocentric orientation. On the former, Marx clearly went beyond an Orientalist view of essentialising peoples and cultures when he broke with historical idealism. Second, Achar makes an important distinction between *epistemic* Eurocentrism and *supremacist* Eurocentrism. The former definitely appeared as a moment in Marx's understanding of non-European societies, particularly India. This has to do with the knowledge limitations faced by Marx as an outside observer of these societies and the fact that he had to rely on the observations of others from Europe, including ethnocentric accounts of these societies, without also having any experience of these societies. Moreover, Achar further clarifies that Marx was certainly not a supremacist believing in the ethnocentric superiority of the west. In fact, Marx was a firm critic of the bourgeois thought of the west.

Let us return to the *epistemic* Eurocentrism in Marx. Marx leaves his epistemic Eurocentrism behind as his theoretical understanding of capitalism and his practice of working-class solidarity develops. First, he leaves behind a teleological view of history in which the rest is the mirror image of the west. This kind of teleological thinking was a residue from Hegel, which Marx abandons. Instead, Marx complexifies his understanding of the history of capitalism and racism and he then goes beyond a unilinear approach to social change and the transition beyond capitalism. In *Capital*, Marx observes through the category of primitive accumulation the role of colonialism and slavery in the making of capitalism. He locates racism in the originary moment of capitalism.

Marx ([1867] 1976: 915) observes in *Capital, Volume I*:

> The discovery of gold and silver in America, the extirpation, enslavement and entombment in mines of the indigenous population of that continent, the beginnings of the conquest and plunder of India, and the conversion of Africa into a preserve for the commercial hunting of blackskins, are all things which characterize the dawn of the era of capitalist production. These idyllic proceedings are the chief moments of primitive accumulation.

In the *Communist Manifesto* (1848), Marx works with a spatio-temporal approach that is epistemologically Eurocentric. Its spatial logic is about capitalism advancing through and radiating outwards from western centres across the world. In a temporal sense this is unilinear and imbricated in a teleological approach to history in which western colonialism will usher in a common modernity. In an extremely original study, Kevin Anderson (2010) draws on Marx's journalism, mainly for the *New York Tribune*, his unpublished 1879–1882 notebooks, *Grundrisse* (1857–1858), the French edition of *Capital* (1872–1875) and his writings on non-western and pre-capitalist societies, to examine Marx's approach to temporality. He finds that while Marx in the 1840s had a unilinear historical view tinged with an ethnocentrism in which non-western and pre-capitalist societies would be integrated and modernised through colonialism and the world market, Marx's views later evolve. Through

Anderson's (2010: 154–195) reading we learn about two important and crucial complexities in Marx's theory of history: (i) Marx moves away from his understanding of places like India as caught up in despotic rule but rather he finds an alternative historical path of development specific to these societies. In particular, he begins to understand the historical specificity of Asiatic forms of land ownership based on their own social organisation. He appreciates the distinctiveness and difference between Asian and western European history. (ii) Marx becomes increasingly critical of the role of colonialism and its deleterious impacts on non-western societies. He also begins to posit alternative and multilinear paths beyond capitalism. His embrace of the possibility of a non-capitalist path through the Russian commune is important in this regard.

As Marx develops his understanding of capitalism – as a basis of both his theory of historical materialism and his theory of capitalism – he anchors it in two important premises.[1] Capitalism, with its expansionist logic, is a system operating on a world scale and even in its uneven advance, at different rates, is universalising. Capitalism seeks to prevail in various spatio-temporal contexts in a manner that ensures its imperatives and values for accumulation are realised. This, of course, does not necessitate the complete subordination of all cultural relations to achieve its requirements. At the same time, capitalism engenders resistance to meet human well-being and needs. In this context, Vivek Chibber (2014: 76) refers to an *antagonistic interdependence* that develops in the capital-labour relation, which means that the squeeze on production costs, including wages, engenders different forms of context-specific resistance. While labour relies on capital for the sale of labour power, capital is constantly trying to ensure a maximum appropriation of surplus value. For Marx, this struggle against capitalism for human well-being is a universal. The point about these universals is that they are central to understanding the world of capitalism in order to overcome it. In addition, as universals they do not negate particularity as part of a dialectical whole. This places Marx in an insurgent space in relation to the west and capitalism, while affirming his commitment to the emancipation of humanity. Marx is not a white, northern racist waiting to expunge the fragment, the particular, and other valid universals that advance the struggle for human emancipation.

Building on the previous argument, through Marx's practical solidarity with workers, including his involvement in the International Working Men's Association (co-founded by Marx in 1864), he came to appreciate the importance of working-class unity in national and international struggle. This was more than a theoretical imperative and universal, as contained in the *Communist Manifesto*, but was also informed by his understanding of how the working class was actively divided by capital, including through racist and colonial social practices. For instance, Marx wrote a great deal about the American Civil War (1861–1865) and its aftermath. In these writings, he advanced various anti-racist positions: he took a strong stand for the abolition of slavery, insisting that white labour in the US and Europe had to oppose slavery, was critical of Lincoln's slowness to abolish slavery, advocated for an alliance among abolitionists, white farmers in the Midwest and African Americans, and after the civil war he supported calls for full citizens' rights to be given to African Americans (Anderson 2010: 79–115).

In his writings on the Irish struggle against British colonialism, Marx makes the connections between ethnic-based racism, the role of colonialism and the importance of an emancipatory liberation struggle. Marx makes the links between class, race and nationalism. Through his historical materialist analysis, Marx also recognises how capital divides workers, and the role of ideological forces, such as the media and religion, in fostering ethnic and racial divides. Anderson (2010: 149–150) cites Marx's insightful perspective on these issues:

> And most important of all! All industrial and commercial centers in England now have a working class split into two hostile camps, English proletarians and Irish proletarians. The ordinary English worker hates the Irish worker as a competitor who forces down the standard of life. In relation to the Irish worker, he feels himself to be a member of the dominant nation and, therefore, makes himself a tool of his aristocrats and capitalists against Ireland, thus strengthening their domination over himself. He harbors religious, social and national prejudices against him . . . This antagonism is kept artificially alive and intensified by the press, the pulpit, the comic papers, in short by all the means at the disposal of the ruling class. This antagonism is the secret of the powerlessness of the English working class, despite its organization. It is the secret of the capitalist class's maintenance of its power. And the latter is fully conscious of this.

Looking at Marx's positions on the various struggles (such as the struggle against slavery in the US and the struggle of Irish workers against British colonialism), together with much of his lesser-known writings, there is ample evidence to suggest that Marx went beyond his own Eurocentricism. Moreover, his writings demonstrate that Marx changed his mind as he gathered more evidence and developed a deeper understanding of the world, colonialism and capitalism's role in it.

MARXISM AGAINST RACISM IN THE TWENTIETH CENTURY

The record of Marxism against racism in the twentieth century as expressed through colonialism, imperial wars, fascism, national chauvinism and apartheid is mixed and complicated. Three principal problems stand out that complexify Marxism's engagement with racism and its theoretical and practical resistance to racism. First, Marx's epistemic Eurocentrism before 1853 also found its place within some Marxisms. These Marxisms imbibed the teleological assumptions of lineal Eurocentric modern progress, which expressed itself as veneration of the 'forces of production', catch-up 'socialist modernisation', and, in Soviet and Chinese practice, state capitalism that was essentially a copy of western capitalism. Theories of transition did not escape this kind of episteme. Stalin's coercively industrialised Soviet Union, and in more contemporary terms, Chinese authoritarian state capitalism, married to an ethnocentric nationalism, best exemplifies this kind of degenerate, limited and productivist Marxism. These Eurocentric Marxisms reproduced the worst features of western Eurocentricism and modernity: wage exploitation, alienation, techno-centred violence, exclusive ethno-nationalism and the eco-cidal domination of nature.

The second problem with Marxism's relationship to anti-racism in the twentieth century relates to how Lenin's conception of the national question and the right to self-determination was transplanted into other international struggles. Dogmatic Marxism–Leninism, controlled and influenced heavily by the Soviet Union, merely transmitted Lenin's thesis into complex societies. Essentially, dogma was the basis of translating these concepts and formulas. This had important consequences for theory but also for how strategy was developed and alliances were forged. In South Africa, for instance, after the formation of the Communist Party of South Africa in 1921, various Communist Party leaders sought to mechanically apply Lenin to South African conditions. Various versions of racial and ethnic balkanisation were elaborated in their writings to take forward the notion of the right to self-determination. This was despite the formal adoption of the Black Republic Thesis in the late 1920s, which orientated the party around the African majority and the need to connect African nationalism and the struggle for socialism (see Mabasa in this volume).² Moreover, in places like Bolivia, with powerful indigenous forces, the Bolivian Communist Party, also tied to the Soviet Union, turned its back on a dialogue with the indigenous movements (see Dunbar-Ortiz in this volume). These are examples of how translating dogmatic Leninist formulations provide a Sovietised imprint on local conditions and complexified the indigenising of Marxism.

The third problem with Marxism's relationship to anti-racism in the twentieth century centres on the issue of class reductionism. For many dogmatic Marxists, class was a primary analytical and strategic category; nothing else was important.³ Such an abstract approach to class fails to appreciate the materiality of social relations in actually existing societies. For instance, in South Africa the lived experience of race is the lived experience of class and the lived experience of class is race. Class and race are inseparable given the racist history of South Africa's capitalist development and despite new dynamics of capitalist accumulation in contemporary South Africa. Further, for dogmatic class perspectives with overly structural understandings, racism and even gender oppression were considered aberrations or epiphenomena in the class struggle and would only be resolved after the socialist revolution. These colour- and gender-blind Marxisms produced a closure that had serious consequences for the identity of Marxism, for left organisations and for alliance building. This class reductionism became the typical hallmark of dogmatic sectarianism. Moreover, race and gender oppressions for some Marxists could only be explained as expressions of the structural realities of class and the 'laws of motion of capitalism'. The distinctiveness and interconnections of other relations of oppression were not taken seriously analytically, which meant racialised nationalisms, racialised and gendered social structures and historical forms of racism and patriarchy where occluded. The same critique would also apply to those who merely give primacy to race.

Despite these theoretical challenges for Marxism in the twentieth century regarding race and racism, the divisions within Marxist-inspired movements also contributed to variegated impacts by these movements in the struggles against racism. A brief mapping suggests the following:

- *Social democratic parties* took workers and labour movements into an ethnicised First World War, were implicated in managing colonialism, fought fascism, embraced an exclusionary nationalism as the basis of the western welfare state (see Georgi in this volume), in the US context supported US imperialism, segregation and ghettoisation of African Americans, embraced a racialising neoliberalism (after abandoning Marxism) as the basis of a unified Europe, and supported national liberation and anti-apartheid struggle. In Sweden, for instance, important solidarity developed with the ANC. However, many social democratic parties embraced a neoliberal 'third way' social democracy and have further embraced Euro-American hegemony centred on the US imperial centre.[4] The Americanisation of Europe, with all its racialising assumptions, has become central to a neoliberalised Europe. In short, social democratic parties in Europe have a mixed record both within and across countries.

- *Marxist–Leninist parties* were born out of the Russian Revolution and through the Third International (1919–1943) turned their back on jingoistic nationalisms of the social democratic parties that took countries into the First World War. Many of these parties had difficulties finding their own way in their national contexts, given ties to Moscow. However, in Europe many of these parties, such as in Italy and France, played a crucial role in the anti-fascist resistance. The Communist Party of the USA fought actively against racism and Jim Crow segregation. In Africa, Marxist–Leninist parties fought against colonialism, such as in Mozambique and Angola, and in South Africa, the Communist Party played a crucial role in the struggle against apartheid. In the case of the latter, many Marxist-inspired movements, labour organisations and activist groups also played an important role in the global anti-apartheid movement. However, in places like India, such parties have not built powerful anti-caste movements (see Nigam and Menon in this volume), and in Mozambique and Angola, neoliberalised vanguard elites have unleashed a new postcolonial racialising logic on their societies. Like the social democratic parties, Marxist–Leninist parties also have a mixed record.
- *Revolutionary nationalist movements* emerged in anti-colonial struggles and formed the Non-Aligned Movement (NAM) in 1961. Many had a powerful Marxist influence and ideological impulse. The NAM took a stand against western imperial racism and colonialism. These countries (such as India and Tanzania) provided support to national liberation and anti-colonial movements, contributed to the call for a New International Economic Order, and the voice of the 'darker nations' inspired Third

World Solidarity.[5] However, movements such as India's Congress Party and South Africa's ANC have not transformed the coloniality, racist and exclusionary structures of their societies. In the larger African context, the national liberation movements were defeated by imperialism and their own weaknesses, and have ended up abandoning a radical pan-African unity. Many have become conscripts of Afro-neoliberalism and have advanced a racialising logic of the globalised market (Satgar, 2009). Moreover, Bandung-based Third World solidarity has died and in its place the Brazil, Russia, India, China and South Africa (BRICS) bloc is producing a new racialised hierarchy in the global South. In short, western supremacy and the Euro-American imperial centre has prevailed, reproducing a new global apartheid. The revolutionary nationalist movements have all reached a point of exhaustion and degeneration.

As this brief accounting demonstrates, the practices and effects of Marxist-inspired political movements have varied and complex histories. The histories show contradictory positions in relation to race and racism, often allowing chauvinistic nationalisms to come to the fore. Thus, Marxisms in the twentieth century, despite strong anti-racist political commitments in most instances, did not provide an effective anti-racist mooring in theoretical orientation and practice. That is our challenge in the twenty-first century, as we elaborate a non-Eurocentric Marxism in struggles and as part of questioning the racist assumptions of Euro-American modernity.

BEYOND 'WHITE MARXISM' AND 'BLACK MARXISM': MARXIST THEORISING OF ANTI-RACISM AND RESISTANCE TODAY

In today's trenches of popular struggle, identity politics looms large. This is not to argue against the importance of identities, but in its extremes it tends to racialise *difference* in problematic ways. In the encounter with some brands of identity politics, Marxism has bifurcated into a 'white Marxism' and a 'black Marxism'. This racially defined binary is absurd if it is used to understand the vast canon of Marxism but, more substantively, it produces a racially essentialised approach to Marxism suggesting there is a Marxism for different racial groups. This is contrary to the universals of Marxism, particularly the challenge of building across race, gender, ecological and class solidarities to resist capitalism.

This is not to deny the importance of a 'strategic essentialism' to construct solidarities among peoples of a particular race group. However, such particularism also has dangers that can easily veer off into chauvinisms if such solidarities are not politically constructed and guided by emancipatory values.

Part of the reason for the popularity of white Marxism/black Marxism has to do with the problems (epistemic Eurocentrism, dogmatic formulas and class reductionism) discussed above that have plagued some Marxisms in their approach to race, theoretically and in practice. However, despite these problems not all Marxisms can be painted with the same brush and also collapsed into white Marxism. As a slogan, white Marxism is over-generalised and lacks appreciation of the rich diversity in Marxisms. It erases those Marxisms that are conscious about race and racism and which have been engaged in anti-racist struggles, including Marx's own post-Eurocentric Marxism. Another reason for the white Marxism/black Marxism binary has to do with the work of Cedric Robinson and his book *Black Marxism* (1983). Robinson was a black nationalist writing about Marxists in the early 1980s. In this text, he essentialises racism as a European problem; a problem of European civilisation shaped by a racialising ideology (Robinson 1983: 9–29). Thus, for Robinson, capitalism is essentially about an ideologically determined racial capitalism. The logic of this argument is that if you fix the racial ideology capitalism is fine. This idealistic understanding of the origins of racism in the west are not convincing. Yes, a racialised capitalism did emerge from the west, but the history is much more complex and relates to contingencies of specific historic social relations, ideological structures and practices that have engendered racism/anti-racism. Moreover, the making of capitalism in other parts of the world, say contemporary India, China or South Africa, also requires an understanding of its racialising relations of oppression, logics and practices. Robinson's essentialist and reductive understanding of racism in the west occludes this.

Robinson reads the black Marxists in a way that sets them up against solidarity among white and black workers.[6] This is a racialising reading and takes away from the actual commitments of W.E.B. Du Bois and C.L.R. James, for instance, to working-class solidarity across the colour-line for human emancipation. Finally, his text rejects Marxism as a Eurocentric ideology and in its place he argues for an idealised Black Radical Tradition, based on a mythical common black identity (Robinson 1983: 167–175). This is not to suggest that Robinson's highlighting of the Haitian revolution and other crucial moments of black resistance, in the course of modern history, is unimportant. Rather, polarising

Marxism into racial binaries is counterproductive and ignores the fact that post-Eurocentric Marxists are alive to these moments and forms of resistance.[7] It is part of a decolonised dialectic. Moreover, Robinson's argument is based on a selective reading of the Marxist canon and fails to appreciate Marx's own commitment to understanding race, class and nationalism and his own anti-racism highlighted above. Inadvertently, Robinson's work feeds into an anti-Marxism.

Many Marxists and Marxisms in the twenty-first century are engaged with the challenge of confronting racism and have a more self-reflexive approach to Marxist theory.[8] In terms of the theorising today on racial oppression and historical racisms, various pathways are being pursued, producing a fruitful body of work.[9] The literature is too vast to be covered extensively here, but a few essential themes will be highlighted.

First, *analysing race and racism*: in general, Marxists conscious of racial oppression have understood that race has no scientific basis, but is socially constructed. In historicising racism, these Marxists have located this phenomenon in the structural dynamics of the making of capitalism, including slavery and various forms of colonialism (Scott 2002). Marxists have also recognised that despite the structural or systemic basis of historical racism, racisms are also conjunctural. Racism is constituted by various social forces in the context of particular class projects. Beyond this, Marxists differ on other aspects of theorising and analysing racism. Robert Miles and Malcolm Brown (2003) locate racism as interdependent with nationalism. They situate it within ideological signification practices, within processes of racialisation, linking class relations and immigration. Racism and racialisation have exclusionary material effects within the capitalist mode of production and in particular conjunctures. They also recognise that racism is a moral and political question and through signification practices its meanings shift over time. This approach has been criticised for being too ideology centred; however, the counter-response from Miles and Brown (2003: 3–10) is that their ideological definition is minimalist and ideology is not the problem but its content.

Another approach to analysing race and racism, from a historical materialist perspective, is David Camfield's work. Camfield (2016: 43) challenges the racism-as-ideology approach by arguing that a theory of racism did not precede the existence and practice of racism and also it is crucial as a methodological premise for understanding racism as a distinctive relation of oppression in human activity. In this approach, the emphasis on oppression brings out the systemic or structural impact of racism. It highlights the distinct harm done and this is not necessarily reducible to a relationship linked to social production. In addition, such racial oppression does not have to be consciously perpetuated. Privilege is also crucial in this analytical approach, as a very specified concept, to understand advantage relative to the conditions of the oppressed in their relationship with a dominant group within the relations of oppression. In short, this approach recognises that racism as a distinct relation of oppression exists simultaneously with class, at an individual level of identity but also in terms of larger objective social processes. Racism as a relation of oppression is about a new ontology within historical materialism.

Second, *race, oppression and intersectionality*: the concept of intersectionality emerges from feminism as a juridical intervention, with the promise of theory building, meta-theoretical implications and of course concrete implications for struggles. Analytically, it strives to equalise struggles against various oppressions and provides focal points for convergence. Marxist feminists have engaged the notion of intersectionality from different angles. One view does not embrace intersectionality because it fails to make the connection with its material grounding, capitalism, and hence operates at a discursive level and strategically promotes a multiplicity of social identities and social divisions (Aguilar 2015). Ultimately, intersectional approaches cannot explain the oppressions they describe because of a lack of structural grounding. Instead, a historical materialist optic is suggested to think about class, gender and race. Such an approach is critical of shallow postmodern approaches to intersectionality that merely focus on a liberal individual subject immersed in varied intersecting relations (race, class, gender, region, etc.) and how this forms individual identity. Instead, a historical materialist approach looks at how intersecting relations reproduce oppression and exploitation. This serves as a basis to understand collective oppression and the need for solidarities. A crucial example is a study of migrant domestic workers in their relationships with the state, their employers, reproductive work and capitalism. Ultimately, the condition of paid domestic work is racialised in ways comparable to slavery, in which the sale of labour power and the sale of the self is happening simultaneously.[10] Another Marxist–feminist approach is sympathetic to intersectionality, but recognises its analytical ambitions may not be fulfilled, given the complex social phenomena it seeks to straddle. In this regard, Joan Acker (2006) theorises an approach to class as gendered and racialised and provides another historical materialist approach that is more conscious of racial and gender oppression, while recognising the salience of class. Similarly, Himani Bannerji (2005: 145) rejects an approach to intersectionality that reduces it to a simple arithmetic exercise of adding race together with class and gender. Instead, she also argues for a more socially composite conception of class that has intrinsic to it gender and 'race', while rejecting a stratificatory and aggregation conception of intersectionality.

Third, *further development of post-Eurocentic Marxisms*: developing post-Eurocentric Marxisms is not new and has its roots in the indigenising of Marxism in various contexts, based on the national point of departure, as part of international struggles for a socialist world.[11] For instance, Marxisms in Africa have been shaped by resisting colonialism, apartheid and globalisation.[12] Samir Amin (1989) has been one of the foremost Marxists consciously elaborating a post-Eurocentric Marxism. He has incisively challenged the racist historical myth of a Eurocentric Europe, emerging out of its own genius from Greece, to Rome, and then to contemporary modernity. This Eurocentric historical trajectory is challenged by his conception of world systems history, which shows the interconnections between Greece, the periphery, and the Ancient civilisations in the pre-capitalist world. In addition, his commitment to theorising radical delinking and fostering solidarities of the South against US imperialism has been consistent in all his work over many decades.

George Ciccariello-Maher (2017) has also broken ground in foregrounding the challenge of decolonising the dialectic. His most recent intervention has been to draw on Georges Sorel, Frantz Fanon and Enrique Dussel to provide a decolonised conception of the people as part of capturing the heterogeneity of resistance struggles in Venezuela and Latin America more generally. Through this intervention, he articulates a new relationship between race, class, nation and popular identity. Moreover, a post-Eurocentric Marxism has also been affirming its place in the academy in the context of its offerings and engagements with Postcolonial Studies. This has been an uneasy relationship, given that Postcolonial Studies positioned itself as part of the post-structural turn and also as part of the disavowal of Marxism (Lazarus and Varma 2009). Despite Marxism's insurgent presence in Postcolonial Studies, it has made a contribution to the challenge of unthinking Eurocentrism, rethinking modernity and has posed challenges to theory (Bartolovich and Lazarus 2002).

In practice the anti-racism of Marxism is also located at the frontiers of various struggles in the twenty-first century. Some of these struggles include:

- *Challenging a racialising neoliberalism and the new right wing*: neoliberalism as a class project is implicated in remaking global accumulation, the state and social structures through marketisation. Power has been ceded to corporations. The inequalities of neoliberalisation have reinforced historical patterns of racialisation and have further entrenched racial divides. Moreover, as an ideology of US imperial hegemony, it has entrenched a Euro-American supremacy in social relations across the world; it is the continuity of western capitalist modernity premised on a racialised hierarchy of knowledge and power. In this context Marxists have analysed how neoliberalism has been constituted as a class and imperial project; they have identified its imperialising mechanisms, spotlighted how racialising logics prevail in processes of neoliberalisation, identified the fragmenting of worker and popular solidarities, highlighted the rise of racialised immigration regimes, assessed the conditions giving rise to and orientating racialised ethno-nationalisms and new right-wing forces, including the emergence of a new fascism in the world, and have mapped emerging resistance.[13] These interventions have implications for left analysis, debates and for anti-racist resistance.

- *Advancing indigenous resistance*: the rise of the indigenous descendants of aboriginal populations has also been expressed in global politics over the past few decades. In the 1960s and 1970s, Native Americans began organising politically and asserting claims for self-determination, building networks across various countries and continents (see Dunbar-Ortiz in this volume). At the same time, an ascriptive politics of identity and demands for recognition came to the fore. For example, the World Council of Indigenous Peoples secured non-governmental organisation (NGO) status in the US. By the 1980s and 1990s, various strategies were used to secure legal decisions in favour of indigenous rights and claims in Canada, Australia and Nordic countries. Within the multilateral system, this became even more pronounced with the following: the International Labour Organization Convention No. 169 of 1989 concerning indigenous and tribal peoples in independent countries, the UN Year of the Indigenous Peoples in 1993 and the subsequent decade dedicated to Indigenous Peoples (1995–2004). This produced the UN Draft Declaration on the Rights of Indigenous Peoples and the opening of the UN Permanent Forum on Indigenous Issues in New York in 2002. Today, radical indigenous movements are advancing anti-capitalist systemic alternatives in the context of resisting a new wave of dispossessions due to fracking, oil pipelines, mega development projects and expanding industrial agriculture. This has engendered an encouraging dialogue between Marxists and indigenous movements, as part of rethinking climate justice politics and democratic eco-socialism (Satgar 2018). Indigenous intellectuals themselves have also called for a dialogue with Marx and Fanon to deepen resistance to capitalism (Coulthard 2014).

- *Racist America and Black Lives Matter*: the US is a deeply racist society for historical reasons related to genocidal violence against indigenous peoples, its own colonial expansions, slavery, Jim Crow segregation, racialised immigration regimes, white nationalism and its imperial role in the world. Contemporary US racism has been highlighted through the brutal police shootings of African Americans and the counter-resistance by #BlackLivesMatter. For one of the leading black intellectuals in the US, Ta-Nehisi Coates (2017), who grasps the historical dynamics of race and class in the making of the US, Marxists need to think carefully about the depth of white supremacy in US society and how it impacts on black and white working-class solidarity.[14] This is shared by the Marxist labour historian David Roediger (2017) in his work on the 'wages of whiteness' and in his analysis of the challenges facing class and race solidarity. Roediger's interventions, in the very polarised race-versus-class debates in the US, point us in the direction of white supremacy being integral to the logic of capital. Other leading Marxists have highlighted how the 'black problem' has amounted to incarcerating the problem in the prison-industrial complex.[15] This, in turn, spawned powerful activist campaigns to abolish prisons. Marxists have also opened up an important debate on transforming #BlackLivesMatter into a movement for black liberation and have argued for solidarities to be constituted with the working class (Taylor 2016).

- *Against Islamophobia and solidarity with Palestine*: post-9/11 Islamophobia, with its racist stereotypes, racial profiling and incendiary rhetoric in the context of the never-ending war on terror has become central to imperial politics. Samuel P. Huntington's (1997) 'clash of civilisations' narrative also fed into this homogenising perspective of the Muslim other. This racialising of the Oriental other is not new. Even more than Said, Marxists have been grappling with the racism of Orientalising for a long time (Achar 2013). For example, in the same year that Said's book was published, a Marxist, Bryan Turner, released his path-breaking book on Orientalism entitled *Marx and the End of Orientalism* ([1978] 2014).[16] In it he provides a devastating critique of the idealist epistemology, ethnocentricism and evolutionary view of development underpinning the Orientalist tradition. Marxists today have critiqued over-Islamisation, the evacuation of historical complexity, the vulgarity of Islamophobia discourses and have highlighted the historical commitment of Islam to secularism in its own past (Al-Azmeh 2002). At the same time, Islamophobia has also been harnessed to the cause of 'Israeli apartheid'. It has been used to isolate and vilify the Palestinian cause. In this context, Marxists have responded on various fronts. Achar (2013: 10–35) has called for distinguishing fundamentalism as well as for a Marxist sociology of religion to understand religions in the world, including the nuances of Islam. Others have located the Arab-Israeli conflict in the context of global dynamics and the contingencies of US imperial power, including the remaking of the Middle East after 9/11, highlighting the shifts in hegemonic Zionism as a political ideology from labour to liberal and now to religious Zionism.[17] Central to these perspectives have been normative analyses in support of the Palestinian cause and Intifada.

- *Decolonising the university*: the university as a site of struggle has emerged sharply in the post-apartheid context led by students. In 2015, students at the University of Cape Town targeted the statue of Cecil John Rhodes and demanded its removal as part of recognising the need to confront the coloniality of the university: its theories, epistemologies, understandings of ways of being and culture that affirmed Eurocentrism despite the end of colonialism. This has intellectually strengthened the tide for the decolonial turn vis-à-vis the knowledge systems in South African universities. This volume, and the Democratic Marxism series it is part of, is an intellectual response to the decolonial and de-imperialising challenge (which refers to shifting citizens of the global North to appreciate the contribution of the global South on its own terms). This series stakes out a place alongside more Africanist understandings of this challenge (Ndlovu-Gatsheni and Zondi 2016). The Democratic Marxism series recognises that African Marxists such as Amilcar Cabral, Fanon, Ruth First, Govan Mbeki and Amin, to name a few, have theoretically, epistemologically and methodologically been engaged with challenging colonialism, settler colonialism and apartheid. The task is to build on this within the university-society nexus and elaborate further this post-Eurocentric Marxism that affirms the history of Africa and the global South; critique new modes of imperial control and situate the new crisis tendencies and oppressions of capitalism within Africa and beyond; identify the new subjects of anti-capitalist resistance, such as workers, the precariat, the permanently unemployed, African peasant women farmers, indigenous peoples, Dalits and more facing exploitation, dispossession, commodification and eco-cidal violence; develop new forms of global solidarity and renew a twenty-first-century socialism based on democratic and people-driven systemic alternatives.

In this volume, there is a further elaboration of historical racisms and the anti-racist challenges facing Marxism. The volume elaborates a post-Eurocentric Marxism, in dialogue with some Marxisms and against other Marxisms that are blind to racism and other oppressions. What follows is an overview of the chapters in this volume on racism after apartheid. These chapters are addressed to the progressive public and more generally to all those committed to fighting racism.

AGAINST RACISM IN THE WORLD

Roxanne Dunbar-Ortiz, in chapter 2, provides a crucial insight into how the Columbian project of 1492, premised on the Christian Doctrine of Discovery, has been used historically to justify conquest, dispossession and genocidal violence against indigenous peoples over the past 500 years. Despite the deep racial prejudice and Eurocentrism at the heart of this doctrine, recourse to this racialised dimension of capitalist ideology did not die even in the twentieth century, particularly in liberal republics like the US, which has consistently attempted to undermine treaty rights of indigenous peoples. Today, in the context of fracking and the extension of gas pipelines, a racist rationality is still being used against indigenous peoples. Dunbar-Ortiz highlights the hidden experience and struggles of indigenous peoples to protect their treaty rights within the UN multilateral system but also recognises the important contribution the dialogue between a non-Eurocentric Marxism and indigenous resistance has played in the struggle against a racialised capitalism. Not only does she provide a historical perspective on Marxist-indigenous intellectual engagement and its continued relevance, but she also stresses the increasing relevance of the right to historic land claims as part of the right to self-determination and indigenous radical nationalism attempting to go beyond capitalism.

In chapter 3, Firoze Manji examines the dehumanisation and racist brutalisation of human beings in Africa through exploring the question: what does it mean to be an 'African'? While he historicises the valences of this marker, by tracing the etymology of this category and through locating it in the historical development of racial capitalism, slavery, colonialism and liberalism, he explores this question in dialogue with the thought of Cabral, one of Africa's leading Marxist thinkers. Cabral, as a Marxist, appreciated the importance of universals in the struggle against capitalism; thus he refused to separate Africa and Africans from the universal humanism of the world. Moreover, Cabral maintained an unwavering commitment to affirming African subjectivity as part of the struggle against colonial oppression. It is through this struggle for fundamental transformation and freedom that a profoundly political African identity, history and agency were affirmed. Manji shows how in the postcolonial period, through neocolonialism, 'development' and Africa Rising master narratives, Africans have lost the connection to an emancipatory conception of themselves and as a result have denied themselves genuine freedom. Manji argues for a deeply political conception of being African, consistent with the interventions of Cabral, to avoid the pitfalls of essentialist and taxonomic identity politics.

Ran Greenstein, in chapter 4, interrogates the analytical purchase of utilising the category of settler colonialism to understand Israel/Palestine. Greenstein convincingly shows variegated conditions and trajectories that such a category tries to encapsulate but fails to do. Ultimately, he shows the limits and political pitfalls of understanding Israel/Palestine in such an analytical frame and theoretical model. Instead, he affirms an analytical approach that validates historical specificity, general analytical concepts with predictive value and engaging in selective comparisons to affirm commonalities and differences. Through this approach, he provides a compelling analysis of Israel/Palestine as a case of 'apartheid of a special type'. While conceptually recognising the apartheid character of Israel/Palestine, Greenstein goes further to ground this in a comparative analysis with South Africa. A strong case is made to understand the particularities of an ethno-nationalist and Jewish democracy in Israel but conjoined to the militarisation of Palestine, as distinctive from South Africa. The modes of politics and structural dynamics, particularly the racialised class structure of apartheid society and working-class solidarity, which played a crucial role in South Africa's liberation struggle, is not analogous to the Israel/Palestine context. Greenstein nonetheless stakes out important possibilities for progressive alignment and resistance inherent in both the analytical tracks of 'settler colonialism' and 'apartheid of a special type'. He thinks rigorously against the grain of Israel's racialised oppression and domination of Palestine.

Fabian Georgi, in chapter 5, analyses the European 'Long Summer' or migration crisis of 2015/2016, centred on the movement of thousands of human beings through dangerous ocean and border crossings in desperate attempts to reach Europe. Georgi utilises a historical materialist approach to the migration regime and the spectre of a conjunctural racism. He grounds this in a relational understanding of racial oppression and the border regime. This avoids reducing racism to ideology, while locating it in a matrix of praxis-driven discourse influenced by structural conditions. Racism is understood as a distinctive relation of oppression not reducible to class and capitalist relations of production. This analytical approach yields two rich and textured levels of analysis. The first situates the conjunctural rise of right-wing racism in Europe as a backlash to the emergence of a post-migrant society and shifts among neoliberal fractions of capital wanting a more open border to meet labour market requirements. This social struggle also plays itself out at the level of the border regime. Georgi's second level of analysis examines the dynamics of racism in European society, which the right wing seeks to organise into a new racial project. Georgi goes beyond economic reductionism to understand, in a sophisticated manner, the depths of European racism and at the same time opens up important ways of grappling with the challenges of anti-racist struggle in contemporary Europe. He calls for direct anti-racism, internationalism and a new class politics.

In chapters 6 and 7, Aditya Nigam and Nivedita Menon deal with caste in India but from different perspectives: a perspective on the agential autonomy of Dalits (a militant self-description by those in the lowest rungs of the Hindu caste order); and from a feminist perspective. Generally speaking, caste is understood as a racialised phenomenon imbricated with discrimination and dehumanisation. It is perceived as racial oppression relationally and ideologically. Such arguments have been made in India itself, and even by activists and movements from lower caste communities at the 2001 World Conference Against Racism. From this perspective, India is a deeply racist society, organised through a historically entrenched caste hierarchy. However, can caste hierarchies and social relations be conflated with race? Or is caste a distinctive relation of oppression? How does caste articulate with gender, labour, sexuality and ecology as part of a discriminatory social order? Indian Marxism is challenged by these questions. Moreover, India is also ruled by fundamentalist and proto-fascist forces engendering a politics of hate against lower castes and Muslims as part of realising a pure 'Hindu India', premised on mythologised understandings of history and dogmatic conceptions of religious scripture. These dynamics are shaping caste and anti-oppression politics, while also challenging left-wing understandings of caste, both historically and conjuncturally.

In chapter 6, Aditya Nigam argues against understanding caste as race and foregrounds the crisis of the modern Indian self and its failings to address the caste question. He argues that caste constitutes the 'national unconscious' of modern India, while revealing the limits of Marxist engagements with the caste question. All of this is complexified in the conjuncture of a rising Hindu proto-fascism, on the one hand, and, on the other hand, a Dalit resurgence. In chapter 7, Nivedita Menon brings a feminist lens to her perspective on the specificity of caste oppression. She explores the materiality of caste and its relations along two axes. First, feminist debates directly engaging Marxism and caste relations; and second, concerns among feminists in terms of sexuality, sex work and ecology and its articulation with caste. She compellingly argues that these feminist and caste concerns need to be taken seriously by Indian Marxism.

AGAINST RACISM IN SOUTH AFRICA

The second half of the book turns its focus to South Africa. In chapter 8, Peter Hudson provides a theoretical analysis of the colonial unconscious as the basis to understand the racism of white capital in South Africa. His argument is novel and path-breaking. Hudson sets up his analysis against what he calls the 'inertia theory' of the democratic breakthrough, which seems to blame colonialism for the present but yet cannot account for how it works, except as a residual historical outcome. Hudson develops an approach to the colonial problematic using a psycho-analytical lens emphasising how the colonial conscious is repressed after 1994, but yet structures the social practice of white capital. The link in this regard is how capitalism brings colonialism into the democratic present. Moreover, Hudson emphasises that the unconscious is also history as a trans-individual and impersonal practice of signification that produces meaning and subjectivity. Put differently, the unconscious is relationally structured practice that sustains and accounts for lived experience. It is ultimately history but also social practice. Through an engagement with Fanon, he makes the link between the capitalist unconscious and the colonial unconscious. A final move connects the colonial unconscious and liberal capitalism. This mode of theorising reveals racist colonial practices inhabiting a post-apartheid capitalism, and continuing to structure the political economic order. Racism in contemporary capitalism, together with its patterned inequalities, is far from dead.

Khwezi Mabasa, in chapter 9, provides a novel and incisive engagement with the national question approach in South Africa. He works with three moves. First, Mabasa stakes out a space beyond liberal race-relations theory, with its reductive emphasis on race and racism as expressions of irrational thought, essentialist black nationalist positions and the anchor thesis of national question ideology: colonialism of a special type. In terms of the latter, he delivers a powerful critique of its numerous theoretical, analytical and strategic pitfalls. Second, he brings forth a democratic Marxism engagement with the national question perspective in South Africa. He argues for harnessing its strengths, namely its emphasis on historical specificity, the significance of different forms of revolutionary agency, the dialectical relationship between race and class and its emphasis on historicising the systemic and conjunctural expressions of racism. Mabasa reminds us that racism is never static and it has to be understood with greater rigour than it is in the classical Marxist tradition.

In chapter 10 Vishwas Satgar demonstrates the importance of non-racialism as an anti-racist practice, but as '*radical non-racialism*' and located in a framework in which the eco-cide question (the destruction of conditions that sustain life) is more important than the jaded and discredited national question approach of ANC-led national liberation politics. He affirms the importance of retrieving the connection between the critique of capitalism and racial oppression as the basis for radical non-racialism. Crucial also are three more important arguments for radical non-racialism to find its place in South African politics but elaborated as a set of theses in his chapter. The first argument is its uncoupling from official ANC non-racialism given its co-option into 'rainbowism', race relations and shallow processes of de-racialising South African capitalism, which is immersed in deep globalisation. Moreover, the degeneration of the ANC, the crisis of legitimation of the Zuma era due to rampant corruption, and failed transformation further discredits non-racialism as a crucial principle. Rescuing radical non-racialism in this context is crucial. The second argument is to recognise the connection between radical non-racialism and a people's history of struggle. Such a history of struggle has been silenced and subsumed in ANC mythology, but has to be challenged as part of renewing popular and class struggles. The final argument is to challenge the old framing of the national question in South Africa as outdated, with its additive model of oppressions and racialised hierarchies of solidarity. What is proposed is a conception of the Democratic Eco-Socialist Project to sustain life and advance the deep just transition, now, in the context of the existential threat of corporate-induced climate change. This also means rethinking the ecological relations that have been part of constituting an eco-cidal South African capitalism and the importance of building a red–green alliance based on radical non-racialism.

Sharon S. Ekambaram, in chapter 11, spotlights the xenophobic practices of the post-apartheid state. Her core argument emphasises departures from the promises of the South African constitution as it relates to migrants, immigrants and refugees. The constitutional obligations of the state are being undermined by deeply reactionary and xenophobic shifts in policy. As a frontline activist involved with Lawyers for Human Rights, she provides a historical and conjunctural perspective on the rise of xenophobia. She brings into view the geopolitical shifts that have taken place post the cold war and which have reframed perceptions of the political value of refugees, the origins of racialised conceptions of the black African and the conjunctural racism of neoliberalism. The empirical thrust of her chapter examines the rise of xenophobia in the post-apartheid context, the failed asylum system and the negative policy shifts against refugees. Ekambaram argues strongly against foreign nationals being treated as the new 'non-whites' of the post-apartheid democratic dispensation. Her appeal is for a new anti-racist solidarity, constituting mass power, to defend the rights of foreign nationals.

NOTES

1 Chibber (2014) highlights the centrality of these universals for Marx's and Engels's thought.
2 See the writings of Lionel Forman in Odendal and Forman (1992).
3 This has continued into the twenty-first century among some Marxists. In an edited volume titled *Marx and Other Four-Letter Words*, which introduces key Marxist concepts, there is not a single chapter on race and racism/anti-racism. The chapter on class by McLaverty (2005) does not take race and racism into consideration.
4 See Vitalis (2015) for an analysis of the racialising dynamics of US foreign policy and international relations.
5 Prashad (2007, 2012) provides a crucial analysis of 'darker nations', including the rise and decline of these nations in the twentieth century as part of 'Third Worldism'.

6   Actually this approach to reading Marxists who happen to be 'black', in a way that turns them against the 'Eurocentric western Marx', has reached its zenith in Afrocentric literary studies. A good example in this regard is Mpofu (2016), who, in his reading, turns Ngugi wa Thiong'o into a post-Marxist Africanist.
7   A case in point is C.L.R. James who wrote extensively about the Haitian revolution in his brilliant book the *The Black Jacobins* (1989).
8   In many ways, the engagement with race is similar to the feminist movements' engagement with gender. The outcome of these engagements enriches the Marxist canon immensely.
9   In the 1980s, the work by Stuart Hall and the Centre for Contemporary Cultural Studies pioneered a non-reductionist historical materialist approach to race. Marxist feminists are also leading the way in terms of theorising anti-racism today. See the excellent collection by Bakan and Dua (2014). See also Carter (2009).
10 In this regard, Aguilar (2015) refers to the research done by Anderson (2000).
11 In Glaser and Walker (2007) there is a useful overview of this itinerary and how Marxism found roots in different national contexts in the twentieth century.
12 See Camara (2008) on the development of Marxism in Africa and the African diaspora. He demonstrates how Marxism has taken on board black specificities while standing firm against racism. See also Mayer (2016) on the development of Nigerian Marxism.
13 In this regard, see Amin (2014) and two issues of the Socialist Register edited by Panitch and Leys (2002) and Panitch and Albo (2015). See also the chapter by Reed (2016).
14 Coates' (2015) award-winning book explores the perils of black male existence in the US.
15 In this regard, see Davis (2016) and Gilmore (2007) on the prison industrial complex and the importance of abolishing prisons. Gilmore was a participant in this current book project, including the contributors' workshop, but unfortunately she fell ill and could not contribute a chapter on this topic.
16 Maxine Rodinson (2015) first published his essays, articles and papers in 1981, which documents the role of Marxist politics since 1958 in Muslim history and society. His work was also crucial in reclaiming the field of Islamic studies from Orientalism.
17 See Ehrlich (2002, 2015). In the latter article he focuses on the hegemonic right in Israel.

REFERENCES

Achar, G. 2013. *Marxism, Orientalism, Cosmopolitanism*. Chicago: Haymarket Books.
Acker, J. 2006. *Class Questions: Feminist Answers*. Lanham, MD: Roman and Littlefield Publishers Inc.
Aguilar, D.D. 2015. 'Intersectionality'. In *Marxism and Feminism*, edited by S. Mojab. London: Zed Books, pp. 203–220.

Al-Azmeh, A. 2002. 'Postmodern obscurantism and the 'Muslim question'. In *Fighting Identities: Race, Religion and Ethno-Nationalism*, Socialist Register 2003, edited by L. Panitch and C. Leys. London: Merlin Press, pp. 28–50.
Amin, S. 1989. *Eurocentrism*. London: Zed Books.
Amin, S. 2014. 'The return of fascism in contemporary capitalism', *Monthly Review*, 66 (4): 1–13.
Anderson, B. 2000. *Doing the Dirty Work: The Global Politics of Domestic Labour*. London: Zed Books.
Anderson, K. 2010. *Marx at the Margins: On Nationalism, Ethnicity and Non-Western Societies*. Chicago: University of Chicago Press.
Bakan, A.B. and Dua, E. 2014. *Theorizing Anti-Racism: Linkages in Marxism and Critical Race Theories*. Toronto, Buffalo and London: University of Toronto Press.
Bannerji, H. 2005. 'Building from Marx: Reflections on class and race', *Social Justice*, 32 (4): 144–160.
Bartolovich C. and Lazarus, N. (eds). 2002. *Marxism, Modernity and Postcolonial Studies*. Cambridge: Cambridge University Press.
Camara, B. 2008. *Marxist Theory, Black/African Specificities and Racism*. Lanham, MD: Lexington Books.
Camfield, D. 2016. 'Elements of a historical materialist theory of racism', *Historical Materialism*, 24 (1): 31–70.
Carter, R. 2009. 'Marxism and theories of racism'. In *Critical Companion to Contemporary Marxism*, edited by J. Bidet and S. Kouvelakis. Chicago: Haymarket Books, pp. 431–452.
Chibber, V. 2014. 'Capitalism, class and universalism: Escaping the cul-de-sac of postcolonial theory', *Socialist Register*, 50: 63–79.
Ciccariello-Maher, G. 2017. *Decolonizing Dialectics*. Durham, NC, and London: Duke University Press.
Coates, T.N. 2015. *Between The World and Me*. New York: Spiegel & Grau.
Coates, T.N. 2017. 'The first white president'. Accessed 13 November 2017, https://www.theatlantic.com/magazine/archive/2017/10/the-first-white-president-ta-nehisi-coates/537909/?utm_source=fbb.
Coulthard, G. 2014. *Red Skin, White Masks: Rejecting the Colonial Politics of Recognition*. Minneapolis: University of Minnesota Press.
Davis, A.Y. 2016. *Freedom is a Constant Struggle: Ferguson, Palestine and the Foundations of a Movement*. Chicago: Haymarket Books.
Du Bois, W.E.B. [1903] 2007. *The Souls of Black Folk*. Oxford: Oxford University Press.
Ehrlich, A. 2002. 'Palestine, global politics and Israeli Judaism'. In *Fighting Identities: Race, Religion and Ethno-Nationalism*, Socialist Register 2003, edited by L. Panitch and C. Leys. London: Merlin Press, pp. 51–72.
Ehrlich, A. 2015. 'Israel's hegemonic right'. In *The Politics of the Right*, Socialist Register 2016, edited by L. Panitch and G. Albo. New York: NYU Press, pp. 250–271.
Gilmore, R.W. 2007. *Golden Gulag: Prisons, Surplus Crisis and Opposition in Globalising California*. Berkeley and Los Angeles: University of California Press.
Glaser, D. and Walker, D.M. (eds). 2007. *Twentieth-Century Marxism: A Global Introduction*. London and New York: Routledge.
Huntington, S.P. 1997. *The Clash of Civilizations and the Remaking of World Order*. New York: Touchstone.

James, C.L.R. 1989. *The Black Jacobins: Toussaint L'ouverture and the San Domingo Revolution*. New York: Vintage Books.
Lazarus N. and Varma R. 2009. 'Marxism and postcolonial studies'. In *Critical Companion to Contemporary Marxism*, edited by J. Bidet and S. Kouvelakis. Chicago: Haymarket Books, pp. 309–332.
Marx, K. [1867] 1976. *Capital*. London: Penguin Books.
Mayer, A. 2016. *Naija Marxisms: Revolutionary Thought in Nigeria*. London: Pluto Press.
McLaverty, P. 2005. 'Class'. In *Marx and Other Four Letter Words*, edited by G. Blakely and V. Bryson. London: Pluto Press.
Miles, R. and Brown, M. 2003. *Racism*. London and New York: Routledge.
Mpofu, W. 2016. '*Devil on the Cross*: Ngugi wa Thiong'o's politics of decolonisation'. In *Decolonising the University, Knowledge Systems and Disciplines in Africa*, edited by S.J. Ndlovu-Gatsheni and S. Zondi. Durham, NC: Carolina Academic Press, pp. 85–106.
Ndlovu-Gatsheni, S.J. and Zondi, S. (eds). 2016. *Decolonising the University, Knowledge Systems and Disciplines in Africa*. Durham, NC: Carolina Academic Press.
Odendal, A. and Forman, S. (eds). 1992. *A Trumpet from the Housetops: The Selected Writings of Lionel Forman*. UWC Mayibuye history series. London: Zed Books.
Panitch, L. and Albo, G. (eds). 2015. *The Politics of the Right*. Socialist Register 2016. New Delhi: Leftword.
Panitch, L. and Leys, C. (eds). 2002. *Fighting Identities: Race, Religion and Ethno-Nationalism*. Socialist Register 2003. London: Merlin Press.
Prashad, V. 2007. *The Darker Nations: A People's History of the Third World*. New York and London: The New Press.
Prashad, V. 2012. *The Poorer Nations: A Possible History of the Global South*. New York: Verso.
Reed, A. Jnr. 2016. 'Revolution as "national liberation"? The origins of neoliberal anti-racism'. In *Rethinking Revolution*, Socialist Register 2017, edited by L. Panitch and G. Albo. New York: NYU Press, pp. 299–322.
Robinson, C. 1983. *Black Marxism: The Making of the Black Radical Tradition*. Chapel Hill, NC: University of North Carolina Press.
Rodinson, M. 2015. *Marxism and the Muslim World*. London: Zed Books.
Roediger, D. 2017. *Class, Race and Marxism*. London and New York: Verso.
Said, E. 1979. *Orientalism* (second edition). New York: Vintage Books.
Satgar V. 2009. 'Global capitalism and the neoliberalisation of Africa'. In *A New Scramble for Africa? Imperialism, Investment and Development*, edited by R. Southall and H. Melber. Pietermaritzburg: University of KwaZulu-Natal Press, pp. 35–55.
Satgar, V. (ed.). 2018. *The Climate Crisis: South African and Global Democratic Eco-Socialist Alternatives*. Johannesburg: Wits University Press.
Scott, H. 2002. 'Was there a time before race? Capitalist modernity and the origins of racism'. In *Marxism, Modernity and Postcolonial Studies*, edited by C. Bartolovish and N. Lazarus. Cambridge: Cambridge University Press, pp. 167–182.
Taylor, K.Y. 2016. *From #BlackLivesMatter to Black Liberation*. Chicago: Haymarket Books.
Turner, B.S. [1978] 2014. *Marx and the End of Orientalism*. New York: Routledge.
Vitalis, R. 2015. *White World Order, Black Power Politics: The Birth of American International Relations*. Ithaca and London: Cornell University Press.

PART
ONE

AGAINST RACISM IN THE WORLD

CHAPTER

2

THE INTERNATIONAL INDIGENOUS PEOPLES' MOVEMENT: A SITE OF ANTI-RACIST STRUGGLE AGAINST CAPITALISM

Roxanne Dunbar-Ortiz

THE DOCTRINE OF DISCOVERY AND RACIALISED DISPOSSESSION

In 1982, the government of Spain and the Holy See (the Vatican, which is a non-voting state member of the United Nations) proposed to the Third Committee of the United Nations General Assembly that the year 1992 be commemorated in the UN as an 'encounter' between Europe and the indigenous peoples of the Americas, honouring Europeans for having brought the gifts of civilisation and Christianity. To the dismay and irritation of the North Atlantic states that supported Spain's resolution (including the US and Canada), the entire African delegation walked out of the meeting – the chairperson of the meeting, a European ambassador, querying into the still-live microphone, 'What does Columbus have to do with Africa?' The African delegation, the largest bloc of member states of the UN, returned with an impassioned statement explaining the relevance, condemning a proposal to celebrate the onset of European colonialism and the onset of the transatlantic slave trade in the UN, which was established, as they pointed out, for the purpose of ending colonialism.[1]

The Doctrine of Discovery had reared its head in the wrong place. According to the centuries-old Doctrine of Discovery, European nations acquired title to the lands they 'discovered', and indigenous inhabitants lost their natural right to that land after Europeans had arrived and claimed it (Robertson 2005; Watson 2012). Under this legalistic cover for theft, Euro-American wars of conquest and colonisation, especially settler colonialism, devastated indigenous nations and communities, ripping their territories away from them and transforming the land into private property, and in the US, real estate – the basis of accumulation of capital. Despite the cant of democracy and free land to settlers, most of that appropriated land ended up in the hands of land speculators and agribusiness operations (for example, slave-worked cotton plantations). Arcane as it may seem, the Doctrine of Discovery, articulated in Medieval European papal law, remains the basis for nation-states not recognising the territorial rights of indigenous peoples, while in the US, federal laws still in effect control indigenous peoples' lives and destinies. The era that Columbus's voyage symbolises remains a contemporary reality to indigenous peoples.

From the mid-fifteenth century to the mid-twentieth century, most of the non-European world was colonised under the Doctrine of Discovery, one of the first principles of international law that Christian European monarchies promulgated to legitimise investigating, mapping and claiming lands belonging to peoples outside of Europe. It originated in a papal bull issued in 1455 that permitted the Portuguese monarchy to seize West Africa for exploitation of resources, including enslaving human bodies. This marked the beginning of the transatlantic slave trade, initially between West Africa and Lisbon and other European slave markets. Following Columbus's infamous exploratory voyage in 1492, sponsored by the king and queen of the emerging Spanish state, another papal bull extended similar permission to Spain in the western hemisphere. Disputes between the Portuguese and Spanish monarchies led to the papal-initiated Treaty of Tordesillas (1494), which, besides dividing the globe equally between the two Iberian empires, clarified that only non-Christian lands fell under the Doctrine of Discovery (Miller 2011).[2]

This doctrine upon which all European states relied to justify land theft, genocide and chattel slavery thus originated with the arbitrary and unilateral establishment of the Iberian monarchies' exclusive rights, under Christian canon law, to colonise foreign peoples. This right was later adopted by other European monarchical colonising projects, including Protestant Christian ones. But, not only monarchies initiated colonisation of non-European peoples and territories, so did the nineteenth-century republics that rejected monarchical control. The French Republic used this legalistic instrument for its nineteenth- and twentieth-century settler colonialist projects in North Africa, South-East Asia and the South Pacific, as did the newly independent US when it continued the colonisation of North America that was started by the British. A few decades later, the colonies of Central and South America fought wars of liberation to free themselves from Spanish control, even outlawing slavery – unlike the US – but still proceeded to claim indigenous territories under the Doctrine of Discovery. Indeed, the populist settler colonialism of those republics proved to be the most insidious, including genocidal policies in the case of Anglo-colonised North America, Australia and New Zealand.

The fact that the US quickly grew to world economic dominance, followed by political and military dominance, the application of the Doctrine of Discovery in this 'nation of laws' and the anti-colonial resistance of the indigenous peoples in North America are particularly important to understanding the development of capitalism as it exists in the world today – what historian Cedric Robinson termed 'racial capitalism' (Kelley 2017).

Indicating the intentions of the newly independent US, in 1792, Secretary of State Thomas Jefferson asserted that the Doctrine of Discovery developed by European states was international law applicable to the new US government as well. The US Supreme Court issued the noteworthy decision in *Johnson v. McIntosh*, thus codifying the Doctrine of Discovery as domestic law in 1823. Writing for the majority, Chief Justice John Marshall held that the Doctrine of Discovery had been an established principle of European law and of English law in effect in Britain's North American colonies and was also the law of the US. The court defined the exclusive property rights that a European country acquired by dint of discovery: 'Discovery gave title to the government by whose subjects, or by whose authority, it was made, against all other European governments, which title might be consummated by possession.'[3]

Therefore, European and Euro-American 'discoverers' had gained property rights in the lands of indigenous peoples by merely planting a flag. Of course, they were met with resistance by the peoples they claimed to have conquered, which is a major theme of this book. Indigenous rights were, in the court's words, 'in no instance, entirely disregarded; but were necessarily, to a considerable extent, impaired'. The court further held that indigenous 'rights to complete sovereignty, as independent nations, were necessarily diminished'.[4] Indigenous people could continue to live on the land, but title resided with the discovering power, the US, which had total control to remove the indigenous inhabitants at will. The decision concluded that native nations were 'domestic, dependent nations'. Soon, it emerged that the indigenous nation in question, the Cherokee, were *not* allowed to remain in its territory. Cherokee citizens were deported, walking a thousand miles surrounded by armed troops in the harsh winter on the Trail of Tears, which killed half the population. Before the Cherokee were force-marched to Indian Territory (today, Oklahoma state), the large agricultural nations of the Muskogee peoples were removed, followed by other indigenous peoples east of the Mississippi. Any indigenous person or group that evaded deportation, and there where many, were stripped of all territorial rights and identity.[5]

The Doctrine of Discovery is so taken for granted that it is rarely mentioned in historical or legal texts used in US public schools or universities, including law schools, or in any of the other states where indigenous communities exist. Arguably, only in the US is it the codified legal basis upon which the government controls indigenous nations under a continuing colonial system. The doctrine was again invoked and validated unanimously as recently as the 2005 US Supreme Court case, *City of Sherrill v. Oneida Nation of Indians*, in which the 1820s' Supreme Court decisions were cited as precedent for denying the Oneida nation land claims. Significantly, despite a reactionary split among the nine Supreme Court justices, the most liberal of them, Ruth Bader Ginsburg, wrote the unanimous decision. The United Nations' 2007 Declaration on the Rights of Indigenous Peoples specifically repudiates the Doctrine of Discovery, and most of the liberal US Protestant churches, as well as the World Council of Churches, have called for its nullification.

THE INDIGENOUS PEOPLES' ALTERNATIVE

Since the 1982 Columbus incident at the UN, the indigenous peoples of the Americas non-governmental conference at the UN Geneva headquarters, five years later, proposed that 1992 be made the UN 'year of mourning' for the onset of colonialism, African slavery and genocide of the indigenous peoples of the Americas, and that 12 October be designated as the UN International Day of the World's Indigenous Peoples. As the time drew near to the Columbus quincentennial, Spain, although no longer proposing a UN celebration, took the lead, along with the Vatican, in lobbying against indigenous peoples' attempts to secure 12 October as a UN day. Spain and the Vatican also spent years and large sums of money preparing for their own celebrations of Columbus, successfully enlisting the support of all of the countries of the western hemisphere, except Cuba, which refused (and paid for this action in withdrawn Spanish financial investments). In the US, the George H.W. Bush administration cooperated with the project and produced its own series of events. In the end, compromise won at the UN: indigenous peoples garnered a Decade for the World's Indigenous Peoples, which officially began in 1993 but was inaugurated at UN headquarters in New York in December 1992. August 9, not 12 October, was designated as the annual UN International Day for the World's Indigenous Peoples. The Nobel Peace Prize went to Guatemalan Mayan leader Rigoberta Menchú, which was announced in Oslo on 12 October 1992, a decision that infuriated the Spanish government and the Vatican. The organised celebrations of Columbus flopped, thanks to multiple, highly visible protests by indigenous peoples and their allies. Particularly, support grew for the work of indigenous peoples at the UN to develop new international law standards.

On winter solstice in 2010, the UN General Assembly approved by consensus a resolution in which member states agreed to hold a special high-level meeting of the General Assembly,[6] to be known as the World Conference on Indigenous Peoples, on 22–23 September 2014.[7] The conference was scheduled to mark the end of the Second International Decade of the World's Indigenous Peoples (2005–2014), with the intention of exchanging criteria for the fulfilment of the objectives of the UN Declaration on the Rights of Indigenous Peoples, which the General Assembly passed in 2007.[8] Some indigenous representatives were concerned that the member states of the UN called for such a significant meeting without consulting them. But it was President Evo Morales of Bolivia who proposed the conference from the podium of the General Assembly when it opened that autumn. It was an odd moment, when, in fact, an indigenous person, brought to the presidency of a country by a mass indigenous movement that he led, was in the position of making such a dramatic proposal. For the first time, the issue of indigenous peoples was brought from the human rights arena into the political centre of the UN.

THE ROOTS OF STRUGGLE

This may all sound like top-down graciousness on the part of the UN, bestowed upon oppressed peoples without a voice. But, on the contrary, the project was born of fierce struggle and community organising. The indigenous peoples' UN project was inaugurated when more than a hundred indigenous representatives from all over the western hemisphere gathered in Geneva for the officially titled 'International NGO Conference on Discrimination Against Indigenous Populations in the Americas – 1977'. However, three decades of renewed indigenous peoples' struggles for land and self-determination preceded this event and made it possible and dynamic. In tandem with the African-American freedom movement post-Second World War, indigenous communities and nations rose up to resist the cold war US state security and congressional legislation that mandated the termination of all indigenous nations and their atrophied land bases. One argument for the 1953 Indian Termination Act was that the collective landholding of the indigenous nations that had fought long wars to maintain their existence and won much-reduced territories as reservations were socialistic and a threat to private property. But the proposal for privatising the land into allotments, which was government policy in the 1880s and continued into the 1930s, was no longer reducing the indigenous commons by three-fourths. Rather, the Termination Act would unilaterally dissolve the indigenous estates. Two decades of struggle were required to reverse termination, which gave birth to local, regional and national indigenous organisations, including the American Indian Movement, founded in 1968.[9]

With the Vietnam War still ongoing and the imminent re-election of Richard Nixon in November 1972, a coalition of eight indigenous organisations arranged the Trail of Broken Treaties (Smith and Warrior 1996). These included the American Indian Movement, the National Indian Brotherhood of Canada (later renamed Assembly of First Nations), the Native American Rights Fund, the National Indian Youth Council, the National American Indian Council, the National Council on Indian Work, National Indian Leadership Training, and the American Indian Committee on Alcohol and Drug Abuse. Armed with a '20-Point Position Paper' that focused on the federal government's responsibility to implement indigenous treaties and sovereignty, caravans set out in the autumn of 1972. The vehicles and numbers of participants multiplied at each stop, converging in Washington DC one week before the presidential election. Hanging a banner from the front of the Bureau of Indian Affairs (BIA) building that proclaimed it to be the 'Native American Embassy', hundreds of protesters from 75 indigenous nations entered the building to sit in. BIA personnel, at the time largely non-indigenous, fled, and the Capitol police chain-locked the doors, announcing that the indigenous protesters were illegally occupying the building. The protesters stayed for six days, enough time for them to read damning federal documents that revealed gross mismanagement of the federal trust responsibility, which they boxed up and took with them. The Trail of Broken Treaties solidified indigenous alliances, and the '20-Point Position Paper',[10] the work mainly of Hank Adams, provided a template for the affinity of hundreds of native organisations. Five years later, in 1977, the document would be presented to the UN, forming the basis for the 2007 UN Declaration on the Rights of Indigenous Peoples.

Three months after the BIA building takeover, Oglala Lakota traditional people at the Pine Ridge Sioux Reservation in South Dakota invited the American Indian Movement (AIM) to assist them in halting collusion between their tribal government, formed under the terms of the Indian Reorganization Act, and the federal government. The people opposed the increasingly authoritarian reign of the elected tribal chairperson, Richard Wilson. On 27 February 1973, long deliberations took place in the Pine Ridge Calico Hall between the local people and AIM leaders, led by Russell Means, a citizen of Pine Ridge. The AIM activists were well known following the Trail of Broken Treaties, and upon AIM's arrival, the FBI, tribal police, and the chairman's armed special unit, the Guardians of the Oglala Nation (they called themselves the 'GOON squad'), mobilised. The meeting ended with a decision to go to Wounded Knee in a caravan to protest the chairperson's misdeeds and the violence of his GOONs. The law enforcement contingent followed and circled the protesters. Over the following days, hundreds more armed men surrounded Wounded Knee, and so began a two-and-a-half-month siege of protesters at the 1890 massacre site. The late twentieth-century hamlet of Wounded Knee was made up of little more than a trading post, a Catholic church and the mass grave of the hundreds of Lakota people slaughtered in 1890. Now armed personnel carriers, Huey helicopters and military snipers surrounded the site, while supply teams of mostly Lakota women made their way through the military lines and back out again in the dark of night.

The ongoing siege at Wounded Knee in 1973 elicited some rare journalistic probing into the 1890 army massacre. In 1970, university librarian Dee Brown had written *Bury My Heart at Wounded Knee*, which documented and told the 1890 Wounded Knee story, among many other nineteenth-century anti-Indian crimes and tragedies. The book was a surprise best-seller, so the name Wounded Knee resonated with the broader public by 1973. During the siege, on the front page of one newspaper, editors placed two photographs side by side, each of a pile of bloody, mutilated bodies in a ditch. One was from My Lai in Vietnam in 1968, the other from the Wounded Knee army massacre of the Lakota in 1890. Had they not been captioned, it would have been impossible to tell the difference in time and place.

Wounded Knee galvanised indigenous peoples in North America as well as national and global attention and support. The chief demand of the hundreds of occupiers concerned the Sioux–US treaty of 1868, which guaranteed Sioux sovereignty over a large contiguous land base that had since been reduced to small, separate reservations by illegal federal annexations, along with an erosion of Sioux government sovereignty.

The leadership that was formed there, along with a number of international law specialists guided by Sioux attorney and best-selling author Vine Deloria Jnr,[11] formulated a set of demands that called on the international community to intervene and international law to be applied. The following year, 1974, 5 000 indigenous representatives from many parts of the world and representing more than 90 indigenous communities founded the International Indian Treaty Council (IITC) (Dunbar-Ortiz [1974] 2013). The Declaration of Continuing Independence of June 1974, by the First IITC at Standing Rock Indian Country, highlighted the historical injustices of the US, particularly its genocidal violence and unilateral undermining of treaty rights of indigenous people; sought recognition of treaty rights of indigenous peoples, through legal, diplomatic and political engagement, to affirm the right to land and sovereignty; confronted the exclusion of indigenous peoples from the UN system; and affirmed the importance of collective institutional indigenous leadership through the establishment of the IITC.[12]

The year 1974 marked the founding of both the IITC and the World Council of Indigenous Peoples (WCIP) (Crossen 2014), an initiative of the National Indian Brotherhood of Canada. The two organisations were mutually distrustful. AIM eschewed any governmental funding and the very existence of the tribal governments established under the 1934 Indian Reorganization Act. The WCIP, on the other hand, from its inception, was funded by the Canadian, Norwegian and US governments, the latter through the National Congress of American Indians, which is a federally funded federation of federally recognised tribal governments. The IITC identified and allied with the Non-Aligned Movement and African, Asian, Latin American and Caribbean national liberation movements, particularly Puerto Rico, while the WCIP looked to European governments for support. The 1977 Geneva conference was organised by the

IITC, the Haudenosaunee and the Indian Council of South America, based in La Paz. Although a few members of the WCIP attended as individuals, including the founder and head, George Manuel, the WCIP was not involved in organising the conference. The 1981 follow-up conference on global indigenous peoples was arranged by the same organisations four years later, but the WCIP was fully involved (Dunbar-Ortiz 1984, 2015; Willensem-Díaz 2009).

These two conferences were sponsored by human rights NGOs, led by the World Peace Council and the Women's International League for Peace and Freedom, with strong support from national liberation movements that held UN observer status – the African National Congress (ANC, South Africa), the South West Africa People's Organisation (Namibia) and the Palestine Liberation Organization. The conferences created a momentum that led to the establishment in 1981 of the Working Group on Indigenous Populations (WGIP), as a part of the Sub-Commission on Racism and Racial Discrimination, composed of a group of independent experts, and itself a subsidiary body of the UN Commission on Human Rights (reconstituted and renamed the UN Council on Human Rights in 2006) (Dunbar-Ortiz et al. 2015).

The first meeting of the WGIP took place in 1982, with only a handful of indigenous peoples' representatives, although one was notably Menchú, reporting on genocide by the Guatemalan military dictatorship against the Mayan communities. The WGIP grew every year to become the largest single body meeting regularly at the UN. In the late 1980s, the WGIP focused on drafting a declaration, and, in 1993, submitted a draft to the Sub-Commission, and that year was declared the UN International Year of Indigenous Peoples. The following year, it was approved by the Sub-Commission and sent on to the Commission on Human Rights, which rather than approving it, established a working group to negotiate the final text. Thirteen arduous years of indigenous peoples' insistence on maintaining the core elements of the declaration, notably self-determination, ensued before it was approved by the UN Council on Human Rights in 2006, and a year later by the UN General Assembly (Daes 2009; Eide 2009).[13]

Although global in scope, the Study of Treaties produced by the WGIP is especially important for the aspiration of indigenous peoples in North America and the Pacific. In 1987, Miguel Alfonso Martínez, international law professor at the University of Havana and later chair of the WGIP, was appointed as special rapporteur to investigate the status of treaties and agreements between indigenous nations and the original colonial powers and the national governments that now claim authority over indigenous nations by virtue of those treaties. The treaty study, approved in 1999, is an essential tool for indigenous peoples in their continuing struggles for land restoration and sovereignty. The investigation concluded that these treaties have contemporary effective status, and furthermore that even in situations where indigenous land was taken without a formal treaty, implied treaties exist and have status as such.[14]

By the early 1990s, when the WGIP completed the Draft Declaration on the Rights of Indigenous Peoples and the approval process finally reached the UN member states of the Commission on Human Rights in 1995 for approval, before it could be submitted to the General Assembly, it stalled, mired in proposals for revisions from a number of countries. For several years, the indigenous peoples' caucus had to struggle to simply keep the designation 'Peoples' in the Declaration, with many states insisting on people or populations, and with good reason. In international human rights and self-determination law that developed in the UN system, the term 'peoples' is interchangeable with 'nations', and triggers the right to self-determination, a collective right rather than an individual human right, as many governments, none more than the US, insisted on. At UN meetings in New York and Geneva, indigenous representatives and their allies demonstrated, carrying placards with simply 'S' written on them. And they won that designation, although the US government insisted on a footnote claiming that it did not indicate self-determination.

CHANGING GEOPOLITICS AND THE RIGHTS OF INDIGENOUS PEOPLES

World politics and alignments had changed vastly from 1990, and it is noteworthy that the indigenous peoples' international work survived this rapidly transformed geopolitical reality. As the Soviet Union devolved into its constituent republics, as did Yugoslavia soon after, those re-formed states became allies of the Atlantic states, whereas before they had either supported the indigenous peoples' work, as Yugoslavia actively did, or at least did not oppose it. These shifting alliances also negatively affected the leadership position in the work of the IITC and other indigenous groupings who had friendly relations with and support from the Non-Aligned Movement and particularly from several African states.

However, representatives of indigenous nations, communities and organisations persisted. In order to deal with suggested revisions in the Declaration, the Commission on Human Rights established an open-ended inter-sessional working group with full participation of indigenous representatives, and with a mandate to complete its work by 2004. This date had to be extended due to US insistence on 'reforming' the Commission on Human Rights, and its replacement with the Human Rights Council. With the demise of the Commission, the Sub-Commission on Racism, which the WGIP was a part of, was shut down. Some indigenous representatives from North America mused that the US was going to extremes to get rid of the WGIP, which had grown to be the largest working group in the history of the UN, and in the process kill the Draft Declaration. With persistence from the indigenous representatives, along with some supportive governments, and with several problematic revisions, the Draft Declaration was finalised and submitted to the General Assembly's Third Committee. It stalled again in December 2006, with objections from a number of African states, which produced further revisions.

Finally, on 13 September 2007, the Declaration on the Rights of Indigenous Peoples was adopted by a majority of 144 states in favour, four votes against (Australia, Canada, New Zealand and the US) and eleven abstentions.[15] In 2009, Australia, New Zealand, the US and Canada, apparently embarrassed by their isolation as the only negative votes, reversed their positions. In April of that year, 182 member states reached consensus on a resolution that included an endorsement of the Declaration.[16]

International law is inherent in the indigenous international project, which also includes instruments developed by the Organization of American States with its establishment of a WGIP, as well as the International Labour Organization and its treaty on indigenous and tribal peoples, and many other international bodies. The international indigenous work, community-based as it is, has enhanced the liberatory politics of indigenous peoples' struggles and made these visible to the world (Anaya 2009; Erakat 2014; Graham and Wiessner 2011).

MARXISM AND INDIGENOUS PEOPLES' RIGHTS

In the process of struggle, a number of those involved (and in conversations with non-European Marxists) have gained provisional trust in Marxist historical materialist analysis. This happened in a context in which European and Euro-American Marxist theory and practices were blind to racial oppression and completely ignorant of or had little interest in the existence of indigenous peoples' histories, movements and aspirations.

Since the demise of the institutionalisation of state socialism with the disintegration of the Soviet Union and the socialist bloc, accompanied by the triumphalism of capitalist ideologues claiming that 'there is no alternative (TINA)', Marxists the world over had to rethink while many abandoned the idea of a future socialism, opening a growing space for reviving the anarchist tradition, which at its root eschews the nation-state, all nationalisms and often Marxism itself. Since indigenous peoples' involvement in the UN and other state-based bodies is largely based on their insistence on the right to self-determination, up to and including independent nation status, a contradiction arises. Many of the new generation(s) of indigenous intellectuals and organisers have moved away from Marxism as they claim it is not relevant to indigenous peoples' futures.

In North America, half the indigenous population lives and works in cities, although they remain closely tied to their traditional lands, as well as moving back and forth. So, many native people are in fact also part of the working class, employed or unemployed, but cannot be reduced to that identity solely or even primarily, not even in the Andean region and in Central America, where the indigenous comprise the majority of the workforces of those settler states.

The engagement with Marxism among indigenous intellectuals and activists, in order to understand their communities and nations, has been happening since the 1960s and 1970s, influenced by the decolonisation movements in the peripheries of capitalism. During this period, Marxists concerned with indigenous peoples saw parallels with the concept of underdevelopment (that Europe had 'underdeveloped' the societies they colonised), embraced development theory (Frank 1967) and also adopted the concept of 'internal colonies' theorised by Mexican leftist sociologists and leading dependency theorists, Pablo González Cassanova and Rodolfo Stavenhagen.[17] In North America, Howard Adams was a native Marxist who adapted development theory to the study of the colonisation of indigenous peoples and mentored many native students. He obtained a doctorate from the University of California and became a professor and a leader in Métis politics in Saskatchewan. In his 1975 classic, *Prison of Grass*, Adams dissects the effects of colonialism on the individual psyche as well as the very existence of the people. In the US Southwest, non-indigenous Marxist development economist Philip Reno influenced a generation of young Navajo students and politicians. Reno had been blacklisted during the second Red Scare in the US in the 1950s. Fired from his tenured professorship in economics at the University of Colorado, he moved to Guyana where he worked with the future Marxist president, Cheddi Jagan, in developing the project of CARECOM, the Caribbean Economic Community. Reno returned to the US and took residence at Taos Indian Pueblo in New Mexico, later working for many years at the Navajo Community College in Shiprock. When Navajo nationalist firebrand Peter McDonald was elected chairperson of the Navajo Nation in 1970, he invited Reno to create a development plan to declare economic self-determination (Reno 1980). Although the Navajo Council endorsed the plan for integrated economic development based on traditional Navajo socio-economic pursuits, McDonald moved increasingly to mineral resource export, founding the Council of Indian Resource Tribes. Reno continued to work with Navajo youth, many of them part of the coalition that elected Peterson Zah to head the Navajo Nation in 1982. He also co-founded a training programme for reservation economic planners established by Native American Studies at the University of New Mexico in 1978.[18] For indigenous activists, the 1970s' development perspective has been largely discredited,[19] but the indigenous struggle against the continued, even accelerated, exploitation of their resources and wreckage of the land and ecology (for instance through fracking and oil pipelines), often in complicity with recognised tribal governments, remains a primary issue.

Some Red Power activists, most of whom remain committed to indigenous peoples' liberation, also adopted a Marxist perspective during the 1970s. In 1971, the Native Study Group was founded by Ray Bobb, Lee (Bobb) Maracle and other native youth in Vancouver, BC. In 1975, a sister study group was formed in San Francisco, of which this author was a member.[20] The Marxism of the two groups was Maoist in orientation in privileging rural movements, but mainly inspired by revolutionary national liberation movements taking place in Africa, particularly the ANC in South Africa and the African Party for the Independence of Guinea and Cape Verde (PAIGC), led by Amilcar Cabral, who was trained in agronomy and a Marxist. Cabral, unlike any other national liberation thinker, privileged culture as the source of liberation, calling on the people to 'return to the source', where autonomous history left off under European colonialism, and to find the threads upon which the newly liberated society could be built.[21]

At the same time in Latin America, Marxism was far more widespread. The roots of indigenous socialism in the Andes goes back to the days of communist parties' ascendency in the Americas.[22] In Bolivia, Aymara intellectual and activist, Ramiro Reinaga, son of Fausto Reinaga who founded the influential Bolivian Indian Party, wrote extensively on Marxism, criticising Latin American Marxists for what he deemed as distortions of Marx. Reinaga argued that despite the fact that the majority of workers in Latin America were Indians and blacks, the class struggle could not destroy national oppression. He pointed out that communist parties formed in the 1920s to 1940s in the Americas fell apart in the 1950s and 1960s because they failed to create Indian involvement and leadership. Reinaga called for 'nationalising' Marxism, meaning Indianising Marxism, abandoning the European vision and accepting the American reality. He envisaged the Marxist–Indian revolution as something new; new in the sense of authenticity that could transform all of Latin America (Batalla 1981).

Two other Marxist studies of primitive accumulation under colonialism in indigenous territories also need to be noted. One is my own study of the history of land tenure in New Mexico, first published in 1980 and in a new and revised edition in 2007 (Dunbar-Ortiz 2007). The Spanish New Mexico settler colony occupied several native nations that had specific relationships to the land, the 98 city-states (reduced to 19) that the Spanish called 'pueblos' being the most numerous, and also having long practised irrigation agriculture. The pueblos were surrounded by and sometimes in conflictual relationships with the Athabascan (Apaches, the Navajos and Diné) hunting and trading groups that had migrated from the north before Spanish colonisation. By focusing on land tenure, several primitive accumulations of capital were identified, culminating in mercantile and full-blown capitalisation under the US following its annexation of the northern half of Mexico in 1948. This historical materialist approach could be useful for the study of a number of peoples who were subjected to multiple colonialisms in North America and the Arctic (French, British, Dutch, Russian), as well as for studying the pre-colonial interrelationships of neighbouring peoples with diverse cultures and economies. Marx's concept of the mode of production is useful for analysis, but also relies on inaccurate historical information. Take the example of indigenous land tenure and mode of production of the city-states along the Río Grande River in New Mexico, in which irrigation was used for intensive hydraulic agriculture: Marx, having no knowledge of indigenous agriculturalists of the Americas, theorised that such a mode of production produced hierarchy, slave labour and patriarchal social orders ('Oriental Despotism'). However, this was not the case in New Mexico, where a radically egalitarian and matrilineal order, reliant on ritual and ceremony, prevailed for millennia and survived Spanish, Mexican and US colonialisms. Before making sweeping assumptions about indigenous social orders of the past, it is essential for each indigenous community and nation to research and study its own source. Marxism will be a useful tool in that endeavour, but also has its limitations.

The other study of capitalism and indigenous people is by Lawrence David Weiss (1984). Weiss employs the methodology developed by Lenin in his 1899 Marxian study of primitive accumulation in Russia, *The Development of Capitalism in Russia*. Weiss (1984: 13) uses Lenin's study as 'a theoretical guide and appropriate, suggestive methodology . . . Lenin's work provides a different historical case which is useful as a heuristic device to better understand the particular development in the Navajo case . . . as a Marxist historical analysis of the development of a home market, and more generally capitalism, in a state making the historical transition from a natural economy to a predominately capitalist economy.'

Weiss is concerned centrally with a specific form of expropriation, that is, a capitalist/colonialist state's use of mercantile capital to drain the resources of the country it has occupied or colonised. Since this was the case in most of North America, it provides a valuable model for better understanding how capitalism/colonialism worked. This itinerary and dialogue between a non-Eurocentric Marxism and indigenous radicalism is still relevant today, given the continued challenges facing indigenous sovereignty.

However, while there might be a generational difference about indigenous peoples' sovereignty, there is a consensus among the new generation of indigenous activists and scholars that capitalism and the capitalist state (including those states that claim the brand 'socialism') are not the solution. This also requires a critical engagement with a non-Eurocentric Marxism. As Dene scholar, Glen Coulthard, who himself identifies with the anarchist tradition, writes in his influential text, *Red Skin, White Masks: Rejecting the Colonial Politics of Recognition* (2014: 8):

> To my mind, then, for Indigenous peoples to reject or ignore the insights of Marx would be a mistake, especially if this amounts to a refusal on our part to critically engage his important critique of capitalist exploitation and his extensive writings on the entangled relationship between capitalism and colonialism . . . All of this is not to suggest, however,

that Marx's contributions are without flaw; nor is it meant to suggest that Marxism provides a ready-made tool for Indigenous peoples to uncritically appropriate in their struggles for land and freedom . . . Marx's theoretical frame relevant to a comprehensive understanding of settler-colonialism and Indigenous resistance requires that it be transformed in conversation with the critical thought and practices of Indigenous peoples themselves.

Coulthard (2014: 173) concludes, 'For Indigenous nations to live, capitalism must die. And for capitalism to die, we must actively participate in the construction of Indigenous alternatives to it.'

NOTES

1 The author was present at the meeting as an observer.
2 See also Deloria (1971) and Newcomb (2008).
3 *Johnson v. McIntosh*, 21 U.S. (8 Wheat) 543 (1823), p. 573.
4 *Johnson v. McIntosh*, p. 574.
5 In the wake of indigenous peoples' resurgence and demands during the US massive Civil Rights Movement of the 1950s and 1960s, the descendants of those indigenous communities, who remained in their homelands east of the Mississippi, have battled and won, in most cases, acknowledgement of their indigenous nation status along with some restored lands. They had never lost connection with those who were removed to Indian Territory. It is a movement and process that remains active in the twenty-first century.
6 UN Document A/RES/65.198.
7 See http://www.un.org/en/ga/69/meetings/indigenous/#&panel1-1 (accessed 23 August 2017).
8 See http://www.un.org/esa/socdev/unpfii/documents/DRIPS_en.pdf (accessed 23 August 2017).
9 See Cobb (2008) and Shreve (2011).
10 'Trail of Broken Treaties 20-Point Position Paper', *American Indian Movement*, http://www.aimovement.org/ggc/trailofbrokentreaties.html (accessed 23 August 2017).
11 At the time, Deloria had published two best-sellers during the indigenous occupation of Alcatraz Island, 1969–1971: *Custer Died for Your Sins: An Indian Manifesto* (Norman, OK: University of Oklahoma Press, 1969) and *We Talk, You Listen; New Tribes, New Turf* (Lincoln, NE, and London: University of Nebraska Press, 2007); he would go on to author or co-author 30 books on Indian sovereignty and cultures and US colonial law.
12 See http://www.iitc.org/about-iitc/the-declaration-of-continuing-independence-june-1974/ (accessed 23 August 2017).

13   The WGIP ceased to exist with the demise of the Commission on Human Rights, but an 'Expert Mechanism' on indigenous peoples was established within the new Council on Human Rights. The text of the Declaration is available at http://www.un.org/esa/socdev/unpfii/documents/DRIPS_en.pdf (accessed 23 August 2017).
14   UN Commission on Human Rights, Sub-Commission on Prevention of Discrimination and Protection of Minorities, 51st sess., *Human Rights of Indigenous Peoples: Study on Treaties, Agreements and Other Constructive Arrangements between States and Indigenous Populations: Final Report*, by Miguel Alfonso Martínez, special rapporteur, 22 June 1999, UN Document E/CN.4/Sub.2/1999/20. See also *Report of the Working Group on Indigenous Populations on its Seventeenth Session, 26–30 July 1999*, UN Document E/CN.4/Sub.2/1999/20, 12 August 1999. The text of the final report can be accessed at http://hrlibrary.umn.edu/demo/TreatiesStatesIndigenousPopulations_Martinez.pdf (accessed 23 August 2017). See also Schulte-Tenckhoff (2012).
15   For the voting record see http://www.un.org/press/en/2007/ga10612.doc.htm (accessed 23 August 2017).
16   Official UN historical overview of the drafting and approval of the Declaration on the Rights of Indigenous Peoples: https://www.un.org/development/desa/indigenouspeoples/declaration-on-the-rights-of-indigenous-peoples.html (accessed 23 August 2017).
17   Stavenhagen was appointed by the UN as the first special rapporteur on the Rights of Indigenous Peoples in 2001, when the position was established. His six-year term ended in 2008 and subsequent appointments have gone to indigenous persons.
18   I was director of the programme. The project resulted in the publishing of a book of research articles, with a case study of the Navajo Nation (see Dunbar-Ortiz 1978).
19   See Saldaña-Portillo (2003). Here she focuses on Central American nationalist revolutions and their development schemes for indigenous peoples.
20   See Dunbar-Ortiz (2005). See also R. Bobb, 2012, 'Red power and socialist study: 1967–1975', http://revolutionary-initiative.com/2012/04/26/overview-of-red-power-movement-in-vancouver-1967-1975/ (accessed 23 August 2018).
21   See Manji and Fletcher (2013) and Cabral (1973).
22   See Becker (2008) and Dunbar-Ortiz (2009). A number of native individuals were also active in communist parties in Canada and the US, although there is little documentation. See also Balthaser (2014).

REFERENCES

Adams, H. 1975. *Prison of Grass: Canada from a Native Point of View*. Saskatoon: Fifth House Publishers.

Anaya, S.J. 2009. 'The right of indigenous peoples to self-determination in the post-declaration era'. In *Making the Declaration Work: The United Nations Declaration on the Rights of Indigenous Peoples*, edited by C. Charters and R. Stavenhagen. Copenhagen: IWGIA, pp. 184–199.

Balthaser, B. 2014. '"Travels of an American Indian into the hinterlands of Soviet Russia": Rethinking indigenous modernity and the Popular Front in the work of Archie Phinney and D'Arcy McNickle', *American Quarterly*, 66 (2): 385–416.

Batalla, G.B. (ed.). 1981. *Utopía y Revolución: El Pensamiento Político Contemporáneo de los Indios en América Latina*. México City: Editorial Nueva Imagen.
Becker, M. 2008. *Indians and Leftists in the Making of Ecuador's Modern Indigenous Movements*. Durham, NC: Duke University Press.
Cabral, A. 1973. *Return to the Source: Selected Speeches by Amilcar Cabral*, edited by Africa Information Service. New York: Monthly Review Press.
Cobb, D.M. 2008. *Native Activism in Cold War America: The Struggle for Sovereignty*. Lawrence, KS: University of Kansas Press.
Coulthard, G.S. 2014. *Red Skin, White Masks: Rejecting the Colonial Politics of Recognition*. Minneapolis, MN: University of Minnesota Press.
Crossen, J. 2014. 'Decolonization, Indigenous internationalism, and the World Council of Indigenous Peoples', PhD thesis, University of Waterloo, Waterloo, Ontario.
Daes, E.A. 2009. 'The contribution of the Working Group on Indigenous Populations to the genesis and evolution of the UN Declaration on the Rights of Indigenous Peoples'. In *Making the Declaration Work: The United Nations Declaration on the Rights of Indigenous Peoples*, edited by C. Charters and R. Stavenhagen. Copenhagen: IWGIA, pp. 48–77.
Deloria, V. Jnr. 1971. *Of Utmost Good Faith*. San Francisco: Straight Arrow Books.
Dunbar-Ortiz, R. (ed.). 1978. *Economic Development in American Indian Reservations*. Albuquerque, NM: Native American Studies, University of New Mexico.
Dunbar-Ortiz, R. 1984. *Indians of the Americas: Human Rights and Self-Determination*. London: Zed Books.
Dunbar-Ortiz, R. 2005. *Blood on the Border: A Memoir of the Contra War*. Cambridge, MA: South End Press.
Dunbar-Ortiz, R. 2007. *Roots of Resistance: A History of Land Tenure in New Mexico*. Norman, OK: University of Oklahoma Press.
Dunbar-Ortiz, R. 2009. 'Indigenous resistance in the Americas and the legacy of Mariátegui', *Monthly Review*, 61: 4.
Dunbar-Ortiz, R. (ed.). [1974] 2013. *The Great Sioux Nation: An Oral History of the Sioux-US Treaty of 1868*. Lincoln, NE: University of Nebraska.
Dunbar-Ortiz, R. 2015. 'The first ten years, from study to Working Group, 1972–1982'. In *Indigenous Peoples' Rights in International Law: Emergence and Application*, edited by R. Dunbar-Ortiz, D.S. Dorough, G. Alfredsson, L. Swepston and P. Wille. Copenhagen: IWGIA, pp. 42–87.
Dunbar-Ortiz, R., Dorough, D.S., Alfredsson, G., Swepston, L. and Wille, P. (eds). 2015. *Indigenous Peoples' Rights in International Law: Emergence and Application*. Copenhagen: IWGIA.
Eide, A. 2009. 'The indigenous peoples, the Working Group on Indigenous Populations and the adoption of the UN Declaration on the Rights of Indigenous Peoples'. In *Making the Declaration Work: The United Nations Declaration on the Rights of Indigenous Peoples*, edited by C. Charters and R. Stavenhagen. Copenhagen: IWGIA, pp. 32–47.
Erakat, N. 2014. 'What role for law in the Palestinian struggle for liberation?' Accessed 23 August 2017, http://www.nouraerakat.com/blogi/what-role-for-law-in-the-palestinian-struggle-for-liberation.
Frank, A.G. 1967. *Capitalism and Underdevelopment in Latin America: Historical Studies of Chile and Brazil*. New York: Monthly Review Press.

Graham, L.M. and Wiessner, S. 2011. 'Indigenous sovereignty, culture, and International Human Rights Law', *South Atlantic Quarterly*, 110 (2): 403–428.

Kelley, R.D.G. 2017. 'What did Cedric Robinson mean by racial capitalism', *Boston Review*, 12 January. Accessed 23 August 2017, http://bostonreview.net/race/robin-d-g-kelley-what-did-cedric-robinson-mean-racial-capitalism.

Lenin, V.I. 1899. *The Development of Capitalism in Russia*. Accessed 23 August 2017, http://www.marx2mao.com/PDFs/Lenin%20CW-Vol.%203.pdf.

Manji, F. and Fletcher, B. Jnr. (eds). 2013. *Claim No Easy Victories: The Legacy of Amilcar Cabral*. Dakar: CODESRIA and Daraja Press.

Miller, R.J. 2011. 'The international law of colonialism: A comparative analysis', *Lewis and Clark Law Review*, 15 (4): 847–922.

Newcomb, S.T. 2008. *Pagans in the Promised Land: Decoding the Doctrine of Christian Discovery*. Golden, CO: Fulcrum.

Reno, P. 1980. *Mother Earth, Father Sky, and Economic Development: Navajo Resources and their Use*. Albuquerque, NM: University of New Mexico.

Robertson, L.G. 2005. *Conquest by Law: How the Discovery of America Dispossessed Indigenous Peoples of their Lands*. New York: Oxford University Press.

Saldaña-Portillo, M.J. 2003. *The Revolutionary Imagination in the Americas and the Age of Development*. Durham, NC: Duke University Press.

Schulte-Tenckhoff, I. 2012. 'Treaties, peoplehood, and self-determination: Understanding the language of indigenous rights'. In *Indigenous Rights in the Age of the UN Declaration*, edited by E. Pulitano. New York: Cambridge University Press, pp. 31–63.

Shreve, B.G. 2011. *Red Power Rising: The National Indian Youth Council and the Origins of Native Activism*. Norman, OK: University of Oklahoma Press.

Smith, P.C. and Warrior, R.A. 1996. *Like a Hurricane: The Indian Movement from Alcatraz to Wounded Knee*. New York: New Press.

Watson, B. 2012. *Buying America from the Indians: Johnson v. McIntosh and the History of Native Land Rights*. Norman, OK: University of Oklahoma Press.

Weiss, L.D. 1984. *The Development of Capitalism in the Navajo Nation: A Political-Economic History*. Minneapolis, MN: MEP Publications.

Willensem-Díaz, A. 2009. 'How indigenous peoples' rights reached the UN'. In *Making the Declaration Work: The United Nations Declaration on the Rights of Indigenous Peoples*, edited by C. Charters and R. Stavenhagen. Copenhagen: IWGIA, pp. 16–31.

CHAPTER

3

EMANCIPATION, FREEDOM OR TAXONOMY? WHAT DOES IT MEAN TO BE AFRICAN?

Firoze Manji

> In France, immediately after Thermidor, anyone who resisted the turn intended to re-establish if not slavery, then the regime of white supremacy in the colonies, was branded 'African'.
>
> – Florence Gauthier, *Triomphe et mort du droit naturel en Révolution*

> We talk a lot about Africa, but we in our Party must remember that before being Africans we are men, human beings, who belong to the whole world.
>
> – Amilcar Cabral, *Unity and Struggle*

What does it mean to be 'African'? The apartheid state, like colonialism, long used the term 'African' to classify those with particular skin colour, curly hair and certain facial features, based on assumptions about biological differences that supposedly separate the human species into 'races'. Others use the term to refer to those who live in, or whose origin is from, any part of the continental land mass referred to as 'Africa'. Still others use the term to refer to those in or from the continent but exclude the Arabic-speaking people of the northern parts of the continent. Some exclude even those who may have migrated to the continent centuries ago because their facial and hair features are not consistent with an essentialised idea of the African. Are all those who are citizens of African countries (and its associated islands) to be considered African? Just what is meant by the term? It is surprising how widely the term African is used despite there being so many interpretations on what it means to be African.

In this chapter, drawing in particular on the ideas of the Guinea-Bissau revolutionary, Amilcar Cabral, I discuss how the term African became a synonym for the non-human or lesser human being that justified enslavement, slavery, colonialism and exploitation, and how the meaning of the word evolved subsequently to consider the African as 'uncivilised' under colonialism, and then 'underdeveloped' in the post-independence period. I discuss how the term African was appropriated by those engaged in the struggles against enslavement, slavery, exploitation and colonialism and came to represent the assertion and affirmation by Africans of their humanity, and as human beings, both makers of history and contributors to the history of human emancipation. That proud assertion did not last long: in the neocolonial period, and especially in the neoliberal period post-1980, the term African became disarticulated from any connection with the struggle for emancipation, freedom, justice, dignity and a universal humanity. Being African thus became merely a taxonomic term that has become indistinguishable from the individualistic identity politics that is so prevalent today, to which the current fad for 'intersectionality' falls victim. I will argue that it is not possible to understand, or even recognise, African people's humanity without taking into account their long history of struggles for emancipation. That is only possible, I suggest, if the politics of African histories are understood and transcended to reveal their fundamental contributions to the universal human condition – experiences that, as Cabral (1979: 80) put it, 'belong to the whole world'.

Cabral was the founder and leader of the Guinea-Bissau and Cabo Verde liberation movement, Partido Africano da Independência da Guiné e Cabo Verde (PAIGC), and one of the founders of the Frente de Libertação de Moçambique (Frelimo) in Mozambique and the Movimento Popular de Libertação de Angola – Partido do Trabalho (MPLA) in Angola. He was a revolutionary, humanist, poet, military strategist and agronomist. The struggles that he led against Portuguese domination in Guinea-Bissau and Cabo Verde contributed to the collapse not only of Portugal's African empire, but also to the downfall of the dictatorship of the fascist regime in Portugal and to the development of the Portuguese revolution in 1974. Sadly, that victory was not witnessed by Cabral: he was assassinated on 20 January 1973 by some of his own comrades, with, it is said, the support of the Portuguese secret police. Cabral was not merely a guerrilla strategist. He was prolific in his writings on revolutionary theory, on culture and liberation; many texts of his writing, transcriptions and recordings of speeches that he made to the people, to party members, to Africans in the diaspora, and at international conferences, remain untranslated (Manji and Fletcher 2013). Along with Frantz Fanon, Cabral should be considered one of the leading African thinkers on emancipation and freedom.

My starting point here is the following excerpt from an important speech Cabral made to party members of the PAIGC:

> We talk a lot about Africa, but we in our Party must remember that before being Africans we are men, human beings, who belong to the whole world. We cannot therefore allow any interest of our people to be restricted or thwarted because of our condition as Africans. We must put the interests of our people higher, in the context of the interests of mankind in general, and then we can put them in the context of the interests of Africa in general. (Cabral 1979: 80)

There are three elements in this statement around which I will structure this chapter. First, how did a section of humanity come to be viewed as 'African'? Second, how might the 'condition as Africans' restrict or thwart the interests of the people? And finally, what is meant by putting 'the interests of our people higher' in the context of the interests of humankind in general, a people who 'belong to the whole world'?

HOW DID HUMANS BECOME AFRICANS?

It has long been established how the peoples who lived on the continent of Africa formed a diverse range of social formations that parallelled, and, in some instances, were in advance of those that emerged in other parts of the world (see, for example, Anta Diop 1987; Parris 2015; Pithouse 2016; Rodney 1972). While these societies occurred on the vast geographic landmass that today we refer to as Africa, the inhabitants of these societies would not have considered themselves at the time as being 'African', even if today we might refer to them as 'African' societies. The continent was home to many of the world's great civilisations, such as Kush, Aksum, Ghana, Mali and Great Zimbabwe. Peoples of the continent were the source of major scientific ideas well before they became adopted by Europe, including the concept of the Earth being spherical and the adoption of Arabic numerals and the concept of zero (adapted from India and the Middle East) to simplify mathematical calculations. The southern regions of Europe were conquered by North African (so-called 'Moorish') civilisations in the eighth century that lasted some 700 years. The establishment of the state of Cordoba brought to Europe many of the developments in medicine, chemistry, astronomy, mathematics and philosophy that originated from Africa and were translated from Arabic scripts. Societies from Africa sent ships across the Atlantic as early as 500 BCE, and indeed the first European sailings to Africa were guided by pilots and navigators from Africa (Adi 2008; Robinson 1983; Rodney 1972).

There are many hypotheses about the etymology of the term African: the Latin term *Afri* refers to the people in the region south of the Mediterranean, which, it is believed, refers to a society around Carthage. There are hypotheses that the term has a Phoenician origin from the word 'Afar', meaning dust; still others claim that its origins come from the word *Ifriqya*, the Arabic name for the region that is roughly Tunisia today. There are, in fact, many theories about the origin of the term. Whatever its origin, it is clear that prior to the fifteenth century the term referred only to limited areas of the continental land mass. The term African was not a self-proclaimed identity of the people inhabiting that part of the world. Rather, it was a term used by *others* to refer to those that lived in a limited part of a region south of the Mediterranean Sea (Mazrui 2005; Mudimbe 1994).

It was not until the fifteenth century that the concept African came to be applied as the nomenclature of all the peoples who lived on the continent, a derogatory word that was even subsequently applied to those people in France who opposed white supremacy (Gauthier 1992). It was a term conceived by Europe that came to prominence in the period of the establishment of enslavement, the Atlantic slave trade and the condemnation of large sections of humanity to chattel slavery. While Europe was aware that there was a great diversity of societies and cultures of the people across the continent (which were exploited to facilitate the capture and enslavement of Africans), they assigned the category 'African' to all those who in their minds belonged to the 'dark continent'.

To be able to subject millions of humans to the barbarism of enslavement and slavery required defining them as non-humans, and to do so required their *dehumanisation*. The process required a systematic and institutionalised attempt at the destruction of existing cultures, languages, histories and capacities to produce, organise, tell stories, invent, love, make music, sing songs, make poetry, produce art, philosophise, and to formulate in their minds that which they imagine before giving it concrete form – all things that make a people human. This attempt to destroy the culture of Africans turned out to be a signal failure. For while they destroyed the institutions on the continent, the memories of their culture, institutions, art forms, music and all that which is associated with being human remained both on the continent and in the diaspora where the enslaved Africans found themselves. The enslavers, the slave owners, and all those who profited from these horrors, including the emerging capitalist classes of Europe, engaged in a systematic re-casting of human beings as non-humans or lesser beings, a process in which the Christian church and the European intelligentsia were deeply involved (see Losurdo 2014; Parris 2015; wa Thiong'o 1986).

In essence, if we were to search for a word that, in the period of the emergence of enslavement, the Atlantic slave trade and chattel slavery, encapsulated the outcome of this dehumanisation process, it is the word 'African', a word that represented the transformation of humans from a particular geography into non-humans or subhumans. Africans were to be considered as a people without a history, without culture, without any contribution to make to human history, a view perpetuated by philosophers of the Enlightenment (see Losurdo 2014). To be defined as African was to be considered non-human, to have all aspects of being human eliminated, denied and suppressed. As slaves, they were mere chattel, that is, property or 'things' that can be owned, disposed of and treated in any way that the 'owner' thought fit. Anthropologists, scientists, philosophers and a whole industry developed to 'prove' that these people were not human, that they constituted a different, subhuman, biological 'race'.

Enslavement and chattel slavery played a critical role for the accumulation of capital that gave birth to capitalism in Europe (Du Bois 1962; James 1963; Williams 1966). These were the cornerstones of capital accumulation, as were the concurrent genocides of the indigenous populations of the Americas and beyond (Dunbar-Ortiz 2015; see also Dunbar-Ortiz in this volume). The systematic dehumanisation of sections of humanity by virtue of their supposed race or origin as enslaved or as colonial subjects – that is *racism* – was intimately intertwined with the birth and growth of capitalism, and continues to play a role in the survival of capital today.

Racism was a fundamental feature of nascent capitalism and later a fundamental feature of the emergence of capitalism and the subsequent period of colonisation that subjugated vast sections of humanity across the globe to its voracious need for increasing the rate of accumulation of capital. As such we cannot talk of capitalism, and its evolution as a colonising power, as imperialism, and in the form of modern-day 'globalisation', as something independent of racism – the process by which vast sections of humanity are defined as being less than human. As Domenico Losurdo points out, liberalism and racial slavery had a twin birth and have remained forever intertwined since. The history of liberalism has been one of contestation between the cultures of what Losurdo refers to as the sacred and profane spaces. The democracy of the sacred space the Enlightenment gave birth to in the New World was a '*Herrenvolk* democracy', a democracy of the white master race, a democracy that refused to allow blacks, let alone indigenous peoples, or indeed even white women, to be considered citizens (Losurdo 2014: 181). They were considered part of the profane space occupied by the less-than-human. The ideology of a master-race democracy was reproduced as capital colonised vast sections of the globe.

It is important here to make a distinction between the term *racism* as a systemic feature of capital, and *racialism*, which refers to subjective views or prejudices with which it is often associated. As Kwame Ture (Stokely Carmichael) is said to have stated: 'If a white man wants to lynch me, that's his problem. If he's got the power to lynch me, that's my problem. Racism is not a question of attitude; it's a question of power. Racism gets its power from capitalism.'

Olúfémi Táíwò (2013: 356) states: 'When colonialism and its operators and ideologists denied that Africans are human, they were proceeding from a metaphysical standpoint defined by radical Otherness. Africans are radically different from human beings, and if they may be considered human, their humanity was of such a different temper that they may be treated as inferior beings.' Cabral knew, Táíwò (359) continues, 'that separating Africa and Africans from the general flow of common human experience could only lead to the retardation of social processes on the continent'.

This process of dehumanisation was to continue from its origins in the European enslavement of people from Africa to the expansion of Europe's colonial ventures into the continent. The representation of Africans as inferior and subhuman justified – or perhaps required – the slaughter, genocides, imprisonments, torture, forcible removal from their lands, widespread land-grabbing, forced labour, destruction of societies and culture, violent suppression of expressions of discontent, restrictions on movement, and establishment of 'tribal' reserves or 'bantustans'. But central to that process was the attempt to destroy – or remould – the culture of the peoples of the continent since culture, at its heart, is a form of resistance (Manji 2017a). It justified the dividing up of the land mass and its peoples into territories at the Berlin Conference in 1884–1885 by competing imperial powers, reflecting the relative power of each.

> When imperialism arrived in Guinea it made us leave our history – our history . . . the moment imperialism and colonialism arrived, it made us leave our history and enter another history . . . After the slave trade, armed conquest and colonial wars, there came the complete destruction of the economic and social structure of African society. The next phase was European occupation and ever-increasing European immigration into these territories. The lands and possessions of the Africans were looted. The Portuguese 'sovereignty tax' was imposed, and so were compulsory crops for agricultural produce, forced labour, the export of African workers, and the total control of the collective and individual life of Africans, either by persuasion or violence. (Cabral 1979: 17–18)

While originally the term African was employed by empire to refer to all the peoples of the continent, there have been shifts over time in what the west believes constitutes 'African'. A distinction has subsequently been made between 'black Africa' and the people of the northern part of the continent, a reflection of a long-held belief that Ancient Egypt was not part of the civilisations of Africa, a perspective that was thoroughly countered by Cheikh Anta Diop's groundbreaking work, which has shown that the Egyptian Empire was one of the greatest empires of Africa, a civilisation that contributed to the emergence of European civilisation and science (Anta Diop 1987). But the Egyptian Empire, at its apogee, stretched as far north to what today is Syria on one side, and as far west to what today is Libya – which, incidentally, would make Palestinians African. Today, imperialism and its institutions (aid agencies, the International Monetary Fund, the World Bank, international NGOs, as well as the mainstream media) divide, somewhat arbitrarily, the continent into North Africa and sub-Saharan Africa, seeking to drive a wedge into the emancipatory histories of the peoples of what are described as 'Arab' and those who are 'black Africans'. 'It divides Africa according to white ideas of race, making North Africans white enough to be considered for their glories, but not really white enough . . . [It] is a way of saying "Black Africa" and talking about black Africans without sounding overtly racist' (Mashanda 2016). A greater part of those countries that are west and south of the Sahara are arbitrarily defined as 'sub-Saharan'. Of course the problematic essentialisation involved in the definition of 'African' as an ontological concept (Brown 2004) is not confined to the institutions of capitalist development or to the media: it is also manifested in the growing school of Afro-pessimism (Bassil 2011; Louw and De B'beri 2011), which has been influential in the #RhodesMustFall and #FeesMustFall mobilisations in South Africa. And it also formed the basis for the development of the politics of Negritude (on which I will comment later).

Whatever these debates today about who ought to be considered African, the term was an invention of Europe, a shorthand for describing those it considered to be non-human or lesser beings.

RECLAIMING HUMANITY: REDEFINING AFRICAN IN EMANCIPATORY TERMS

If being cast as African was to be defined as being dehumanised, the resounding claim of every movement in opposition to enslavement, every slave revolt, every opposition to European colonisation, every challenge to the institutions of white supremacy, every resistance to racism constituted an assertion of their identity as humans. Where the European considered Africans subhuman, the response was to claim the identity of 'African' as a positive, liberating definition of a people, a people who are part of humanity (Manji 2017a). As in the struggles of the oppressed throughout history, a transition occurs over time in which derogatory terms used by the oppressors to 'other' people are eventually appropriated by the oppressed and turned into terms of dignity and assertions of humanity. 'A reconversion of minds – of mental set – is thus indispensable to the true integration of people into the liberation movement,' wrote Cabral. 'Such reconversion – re-Africanization, in our case – may take place before the struggle, but it is complete only during the course of the struggle, through daily contact with the popular masses in the communion of sacrifice required by the struggle' (Cabral 1973: 45).

The most important breakthrough in asserting the universalist humanity of Africans occurred on an island in the Caribbean. The San Domingue revolution, which began with the uprising of slaves in 1791, ended with the establishment of the independent state of Haiti in 1804, the first successful revolution led by African slaves (most of whom were originally enslaved from what is today the northern regions of Angola and the southern regions of the Congo). This was to shake the western world because of its truly emancipatory nature. 'Few transformations in world history have been more momentous, few required more sacrifice or promised more hope' (Hallward 2004: 2). It resulted not merely in the freeing of African slaves, as Toussaint Louverture put it: 'It is not a circumstantial freedom given as a concession to us alone which we require, but the adoption of the absolute principle that any man born red, black or white cannot be the property of his fellow man' (Louverture cited and translated by Neocosmos 2016: 69). 'Toussaint Louverture, the first leader of the rebellion, drew on an explicit commitment to a universal humanism to denounce slavery. Colonialism defined race as permanent biological destiny. The revolutionaries in Haiti defined it politically. Polish and German mercenaries who had gone over to the side of the slave armies were granted citizenship, as black subjects, in a free and independent Haiti' (Pithouse 2016). Being Haitian was defined, thus, not by colour, but *politically* in terms of the role played in the struggle for emancipation.

It was this same cry to assert that Africans are humans that informed the movements for national liberation in the post-Second World War period, and indeed informed the emerging revolution in South Africa from the mid-1980s until 1994. It was the mass mobilisations of those seeking to overthrow the oppressive yoke of colonialism that formed the basis upon which the nationalist movements were thrown into power. The struggle for independence in Africa was informed, at the base, by the experience of struggles against oppression and brutal exploitation experienced in everyday life. '[N]ational liberation is the phenomenon in which a socio-economic whole rejects the denial of its historical process. In other words, the national liberation of a people is the regaining of the historical personality of that people, it is their return to history through the destruction of the imperialist domination to which they were subject' (Cabral 1966: 130).

In the struggles for national liberation, the term African had become intimately associated with the concept of freedom and emancipation. The very definition of African came to be viewed in *political*, not racial or ethnic, terms. Cabral went so far as to draw a distinction between those whom he defined as 'the people' and those whom he classed as 'the population', based on their political stance against colonialism: the definition of people depends, he insisted, on the historical moment that the land is experiencing:

> Population means everyone, but the people have to be seen in the light of their own history. It must be clearly defined who are the people at every moment of the life of a population. In Guiné and Cape Verde today the people of Guiné or the people of Cape Verde mean for us those who want to chase the Portuguese colonialists out of our land. They are the people, the rest are not of our land even if they were born there. They are not the people of our land; they are the population but not the people. This is what defines the people today. The people of our land are all those born in the land, in Guiné or Cape Verde, who want what corresponds to the fundamental necessity of the history of our land. It is the following: to put an end to foreign domination in our land. (Cabral 1979: 89)

In other words, the people or the nation comprise those who fight consistently against colonialism and the domination of colonialism – a political definition.

'RICE ONLY COOKS INSIDE THE POT': DELINKING AFRICAN FROM EMANCIPATORY FREEDOMS

> We cannot therefore allow any interest of our people to be restricted or thwarted because of our condition as Africans.
>
> – Amilcar Cabral, *Unity and Struggle*

What happens when the concept of 'African' becomes delinked from the idea of the struggle for emancipation, freedom or sovereignty? What then is left of the meaning of the term African? As I have argued, the concept of African had been appropriated from the original definition imposed by Europe as being a synonym for the dehumanised subject, to being politically defined as representing those who sought to fight for freedom, emancipation, justice and dignity.

But the outcome of the national liberation struggles did not always result in the achievement of emancipation. The rise of neocolonial regimes in the post-independence period, many of which arose out of the defeat or grinding down of the mass movements, gradually resulted in the demise of the struggles for emancipatory freedoms in Africa, and consequently had the result of delinking the concept of African from an emancipatory goal.

The blame for what happened after independence cannot be placed entirely at imperialism's door. As Cabral points out: 'True, imperialism is cruel and unscrupulous, but we must not lay all the blame on its broad back. For, as the African people say: "Rice only cooks inside the pot"' (1979: 160).

Despite coming to power on the tide of the anti-colonial mass upsurges, once in power, the nationalist leadership (composed usually of representatives of the newly emerging middle class) saw its task as one of preventing 'centrifugal forces' from competing for political power or seeking greater autonomy from the newly formed 'nation'. Having grasped political self-determination from colonial authority, it was reluctant to accord the same rights to its own citizens. The new controllers of the state machinery saw their role as the 'sole developer' and 'sole unifier' of society. The state defined for itself an interventionist role in 'modernisation' and a centralising and controlling role in the political realm (Manji 1998: 15). The idea of modernising was reduced to developing only the infrastructure of capitalism in the peripheries that would allow more efficient integration of the former colonies into the world capitalist economy. The term 'development' provided an implicit allusion to progress of some kind, and acted as a counterweight to the attraction of socialism that the US saw as a threat to its growing hegemony. Whereas the movements for independence were characterised by mass actions in which the people *presented* themselves on their own terms and defined their ambitions and aspirations on their own terms, the nationalists assumed that they could *represent* the masses in terms defined by the elites, not by the people (for discussions on the politics of presentation and representation, see Neocosmos 2017).

Born out of a struggle for the legitimacy of pluralism against a hegemonic colonial state, social pluralism began to be frowned upon. The popular associations that had projected the nationalist leadership into power gradually began to be seen as an obstacle to the new god of 'development'. No longer was there a need, it was argued, for popular participation in determining the future. The new government would bring development to the people. The new government, they claimed, represented the nation and everyone in it. Now that political independence had been achieved, the priority was 'development' because, implicitly, the new rulers concurred with evolving imperialism that its people were 'underdeveloped'. Social and economic improvements would come, the nationalist leaders said, with patience and as a result of combined national efforts involving everyone. In this early period after independence, civil and political rights soon came to be seen as a 'luxury', to be enjoyed at some unspecified time in the future when 'development' had been achieved. For the present, said many African presidents, 'our people are not ready' – echoing, ironically, the arguments used by the former colonial rulers against the nationalists' cries for independence a few years earlier (Manji 1998: 15).

The post-independence period was an era of 'developmentalism'. Camouflaged in the rhetoric of independence, the prevailing narrative treated the problems faced by the majority – deprivation and impoverishment and its associated dehumanisation – not as consequences of colonial domination and an imperialist system that continued to extract super-profits, but rather as the supposedly 'natural' conditions of Africa. The solution to poverty was seen as a technical one, with the provision of 'aid' from the very colonial powers who had enriched themselves at the expense of the mass of African people whom they had systematically dehumanised to maintain their control over the continent. Developmentalism was characterised by a growing commonality of the interests of the African elites with those of imperial powers.

Despite some of the shortcomings of the nature of many of the neocolonial regimes that emerged after independence, it is nevertheless important to recognise here that in a very short period of time, essentially from the mid-1950s to the beginning of the 1990s, there were remarkable social achievements. This was the case across the decolonised world. The gains made in the post-independence period internationally have been well documented by Surendra Patel (1995) for a UN/WIDER report. He recorded the achievements of the Third World in sustaining average annual growth of over five per cent over a period of 40 years from 1950–1990 by a population 10 times larger than that of the developed world. Significant economic transformation included increasing urbanisation and a declining share of agriculture in GDP, increasing industrialisation and share of manufacturing in exports, an increase in the rates of savings and investment and an unprecedented expansion of capital formation, including health and education, both public and private:

> While the development gap in terms of GDP per capita was large and continued to increase, the social gap was significantly reduced: life expectancy increased from around 35 to 60–70 years; infant mortality rates declined from about 250 to 70 per thousand; literacy rates rose to

50 per cent in Africa and 80 per cent in Latin America; and while there were 10 times more students enrolled in higher education in the North than in the South at the start of the post-war era, 40 years later the numbers were approximately equal.[1]

Such achievements notwithstanding, there were few examples of fundamental transformations of the economic system of production or in the relationship with imperialism (save that the US became increasingly dominant in the economic, political, military and cultural fields). The former colonial state, which had been established, together with its armed forces, military and police, to serve the interests of colonialism and international capital, was in most cases not transformed but, rather, occupied by the newly emerging elites. In exceptional cases, such as in Burkina Faso, where attempts were made to transform the colonial state machinery from within, assassination and coups were used to ensure the continuity of a state that protected the interests of capital. Indeed, the repressive arms of the state remained largely unchanged. Freedom fighters of the liberation movements were, if not entirely marginalised in the post-independence period, incorporated, integrated and placed under the command of the existing colonial military structures.

It was against this tendency that Cabral was adamantly opposed. He did not think that independence movements could take over the colonial state apparatus and use it for their own purposes. It was not the colour of the administrator that was the issue, he argued, but the fact that there was an administrator (Cabral 1979: 60). 'We don't accept any institution of the Portuguese colonialists. We are not interested in the preservation of any of the structures of the colonial state. It is our opinion that it is necessary to totally destroy, to break, to reduce to ash all aspects of the colonial state in our country in order to make everything possible for our people' (Cabral 1973: 83).

Cabral (1969: 65) argues further: 'We are fighting so that insults may no longer rule our countries, martyred and scorned for centuries, so that our peoples may never more be exploited by imperialists, not only by people with white skin, because we do not confuse exploitation or exploiters with the colour of men's skins; we do not want any exploitation in our countries, not even by Black people.'

He argues that the failure of the national liberation movements in Africa was their dismissal of theory and of ideology: 'The ideological deficiency, not to say the total lack of ideology, on the part of the national liberation movements – which is basically explained by the ignorance of the historical reality which these movements aspire to transform – constitutes one of the greatest weaknesses, if not the greatest weakness, of our struggle against imperialism' (Cabral 1979: xii).

For Cabral, theory is an essential weapon in the struggle against imperialism and for the emancipation of humankind. 'It is true that a revolution can fail,' he argued, 'even though it be nurtured on perfectly conceived theories, [but] nobody has yet successfully practiced revolution without a revolutionary theory' (Cabral 1966).

As I have argued elsewhere (Manji 2017b), emancipatory freedoms require and express the collective power of peoples to determine their own destiny. They are an expression of what Lewis Gordon (2008: 51) characterises as a historical aspiration, one that continues to exist and transcends the constraints that might have been wrung in any given historical period. Emancipatory freedom implies, therefore, an assertion of dignity, of self-worth, a commitment to a project that transcends frequently even the threat or possibility of death, a proclamation and assertion of, and an insistence upon, a claim to be part of humanity. By definition, emancipatory freedoms require a conception of the 'long arc of history', an ability to think and act in terms of historical eras. But that very understanding of the need to continue the struggle for emancipatory freedoms gradually became lost in the growing hegemony of the idea of 'development', 'modernisation' and 'globalisation'.

Whereas the mass movements for liberation were informed by the need for emancipatory freedoms, the neocolonial states that emerged substituted the struggle for emancipation with aspirations only for concessionary freedoms, that is, freedoms whose parameters are set by constraints imposed by others than those who seek their own freedom. Those seeking concessionary freedoms accept the authority of those who set its limits. The focus of the newly independent governments was on seeking concessions from imperialism and its institutions. In the early period, there were concessions that permitted some degree of 'modernisation' that would improve the ability of capital to extract profits from the former colonies while permitting some degree of social improvement for the population, such as health care, education and access to water.

THE DEPOLITICISATION OF IDENTITY

Once the struggles for independence became delinked from the historical emancipatory struggles for reclaiming humanity that were embodied in the movements for African liberation, then all that was left in the meaning of being 'African' was a taxonomic identity and seemingly apolitical definition of a people. The delinking of the concept of African from its connection with the search for freedom results, in effect, in a depoliticisation that renders people merely objects rather than determinants of history. The concept becomes associated with the delinking of Africans as humans who, being human, seek constantly to emancipate themselves, to becoming instead at best mere 'citizens' of African countries, at worst the 'beneficiaries' of development.

The meaning of being 'black' has not been immune from a similar phenomenon. W.E.B. Du Bois, C.L.R. James, Angela Davis, the Black Power Movement, Malcolm X and even Martin Luther King Jnr all connected the identity of being black as a liberating identity intimately bound up with the reaching for emancipatory freedoms. With the defeat of the black liberation movement in the US (and indeed in Europe as well), following the rise of Ronald Reagan and Margaret Thatcher, came the emptying of political identity into a form of taxonomy – African American, black, brown, Asian, Latino, in the US; and Asian, African, Caribbean, Indian, etc. The recent rise of the Black Lives Matter movement has perhaps begun to shift the identity of black back towards an association with freedom as a political, not a 'racial', identity.

In mainstream media today and, sadly, even among sections of the left, it is not uncommon to hear people write about different 'races' in Africa. The concept has been widely used as the basis for explaining, for example, the Darfur conflict, where, we are told, 'Arabs' have been terrorising 'black Africans'. In doing so, they perpetuate the colonial mythology of the existence of 'races' among human beings, which has its origins in Europe, and ironically, adopt the spurious racial categorisation of people of the Sudan developed by the British (Mamdani 2009). There is, in fact, no biological basis for claims for the existence of race in humans. For the human species, race is a social, not a biological category (Lewontin, Rose and Kamin 1984).

'And it is all too true that the major responsibility for this racialization of thought, or at least the way it is applied, lies with the Europeans who have never stopped placing white culture in opposition to the other noncultures' (Fanon 1961: 151). Nevertheless, it is surprising that even among post-apartheid South African intellectuals there appears to be a resurgence of the idea of race, especially ironic given how clearly the concept of race was a political construct under apartheid. The official categorisation of people according to race, as established by apartheid, has hardly changed. Race is a term that needs to be avoided. It sidesteps or masks the real issue – *racism* – which is an instrument of capitalism and of white supremacy. And struggles *against racism* reassert a meaning to being black or African as something that is connected with an emancipatory goal, a reclamation, if not an invention, of humanity.

If being human (or for that matter, being African) is devoid or emptied of an association with the aspiration for freedom, then, in effect, the resultant identity as taxonomy remains a form of dehumanisation, no better an identity than the one perpetuated by white supremacy in dividing humanity into so-called races, a social construct with no biological basis. As Táíwò (2013: 299) puts it:

> As bad as this racism-infected denial of our humanity is, it is worse that, in negating it, we have, in the main, adopted its dubious starting point and made it our own. That is, many African scholars have embraced the metaphysics of difference, and it now informs a large part of scholarship by both African and Africanist scholars. There is a high degree of essentialisation that characterises discussions of African phenomena from the criteria of what it is to be African – in its many forms and manifestations – to how one ought to conduct oneself, one's social relations, or with whom one may have relations and in what depth. From reacting to the ravages of difference-denominated denial of our humanity, we have become earnest apostles of the metaphysics of difference and censorious guardians against its transgressors. In our earnestness to affirm African difference, we have forgotten or chosen to ignore the racist provenance of this ahistorical, false metric.

Cabral's assertion in the excerpt referred to earlier that the interest of his people could potentially be restricted or thwarted because of 'our condition as Africans' holds true, I have argued, so long as that identity remains unlinked with aspirations for emancipatory freedoms. The taxonomic concept of 'African' renders the definition essentially a racial one, locking people out of having a commonality with humanity or an ability to determine their own future.

The ideology of Negritude that emerged in the 1930s and 1940s in Paris was to become associated with the writings of Léopold Sédar Senghor and Aimé Césaire. Its philosophy was based on essentialising Africa and Africans, claiming that Africans have a core quality that is inherent, eternal and unalterable, and which is distinct from the rest of humanity.

However, as Michael Neocosmos (2016: 530) points out, if Africa 'historically was a creation of liberalism's sacred space which claimed a monopoly over history, culture and civilisation, then as a way of resisting, Africans have understandably tended to emphasize and idealize their own distinctive identity, history, culture and civilization'. And as Fanon (1989: 47) puts it: 'It is the white man who creates the Negro. But it is the Negro who creates negritude.' Furthermore, 'Colonialism did not think it worth its while denying one national culture after the other. Consequently the colonised's response was immediately continental in scope . . . Following the unconditional affirmation of European culture came the unconditional affirmation of African culture' (Fanon 1961: 151).

While the ideas of Negritude had positive impacts on the way in which the colonised viewed themselves, and helped to inspire the flourishing of poetry, art and literature and of research about the pre-colonial civilisations in Africa – such as the exceptional work of Anta Diop – it also contributed to depoliticising the meaning of African and of culture that was once powerfully associated with freedom.

This resulted in eschewing the idea of human universality, preventing African people's 'return to history through the destruction of the imperialist domination to which they were subject' (Cabral 1966).

Depoliticising the nature of African identity through delinking it with an emancipatory agenda meant that what constituted being African increasingly resorted to colonial tropes of tribe. Those considered by colonial powers to be 'indigenous' to the colony were described as tribal and rendered under the command of the 'native authority' of chiefs backed by the state, a status that was in many cases a continuity of colonial methods of rule, while those considered non-indigenous were considered to be races (Mamdani 1996), people whose legitimacy as citizens were frequently contested. And from considering tribes as cultural, not political, identities, there was an almost inevitable transition to essentialise the idea of the tribe, assigning to each its supposed unique characteristic. The nation, forged in the cauldron of the liberation struggle, lost its meaning, and became defined as a collection of tribes, whose definition in many cases were forged or adapted by colonialism. And those who still held on to the 'old-fashioned' notions of liberation, emancipation and freedom, were denounced as trouble-makers, standing against the national interests, and more recently simply as 'terrorists'. As Robert Sweeny (2009: 36) puts it, 'Ethnically determined history is almost always racialized history', based on certain characteristics being considered as part of the essential character of the so-called tribe. He continues, '... essentialism always dehumanizes, because it denies that people are making choices.' Such tendencies became accelerated in the 1980s with the establishment of the hegemony of neoliberalism.

THE NEOLIBERAL ERA

By the 1980s, with the rise of structural adjustment policies, the agenda became that of creating extreme privatisation aimed at opening up new avenues for capital expansion. The state was declared 'inefficient' (despite its considerable achievements in the short period since independence), and public services were first run down before being sold off to the oligopolies for a song. The state was prohibited from investing in social infrastructure, from subsidising agricultural production, with prohibitions on capital investment in health, education, transport and telecommunications, until eventually public goods were taken over by the 'private' (read oligopoly) sector. Tariff barriers to goods from the advanced capitalist countries were removed, access to natural resources opened up for pillaging, tax regimes relaxed, and 'export processing zones' established to enable raw exploitation of labour without any regulations from the state or trade unions. Over time, privatisation was extended to agriculture, land and food production. Repression was increasingly used against any opposition to the effect of these policies. Governments became increasingly more accountable to the transnational corporations, international financial institutions and to the so-called aid agencies who set the parameters for all social and economic policies.

Whereas in the colonial period it was the missionaries who played a central role in depoliticising the processes that led to the impoverishment of millions, today a similar role is played by development NGOs (Manji 1998; Manji and O'Coill 2002) as well as by human rights organisations (Mutua 2001). While in the colonial period, Africans were cast as primitive and in need of being civilised, in the post-colonial period African people are defined as 'underdeveloped'. Today, African people are considered chaotic not ordered, traditional not modern, tribal not democratic, corrupt not honest, underdeveloped not developed, irrational not rational, lacking in all of those things the west presumes itself to be. White westerners are still today represented as the bearers of 'civilisation', the brokers and arbiters of development, while black, post-colonial 'others' are still seen as uncivilised and unenlightened, destined to be development's exclusive objects (Manji and O'Coill 2002). As a consequence, a vast industry of 'development' evolved to satisfy the white saviour complex, a complex that needs victims to survive and propagate itself. And the process of othering people in order to present them as victims – that is, a process of victimisation – was one that continued, albeit in new forms, the process of dehumanisation of Africans, rendering them apparently incapable of agency (Manji 2015).

It was hardly surprising that Africa increasingly became presented as the 'basket case', in Tony Blair's infamous characterisation of the continent. The New Partnership for Africa's Development, (NEPAD) developed and promoted by President Thabo Mbeki, was a response to this characterisation, seeking to assert, on the basis of a proclaimed 'African Renaissance', that the continent could develop economically. But in essence, the set of policies amounted to little more than a self-managed implementation of liberalisation, remaining essentially in the realms of concessionary freedoms.

It is true that in the beginning of the second decade of the twenty-first century, the phenomenon of 'Africa Rising' was to become the new slogan for Africa's development. As the *Economist* (3 December 2011) put it in an editorial describing Africa as the hopeful continent and with the headline 'Africa Rising': 'After decades of slow growth, Africa has a real chance to follow in the footsteps of Asia.' For the *Economist*, however, this meant: 'Africa still needs deep reform. Governments should make it easier to start businesses and cut some taxes and collect honestly the ones they impose. Land needs to be taken out of communal ownership and title handed over to individual farmers so that they can get credit and expand. And, most of all, politicians need to keep their noses out of the trough and to leave power when their voters tell them to.'

But despite the propaganda, there was little actual evidence that Africa was indeed entering a new period that would benefit its citizens. As I have argued elsewhere (Manji 2014), the claim of Africa Rising was based on claims of GDP growth rates of five to six per cent. But much of this is due to soaring primary commodity prices, especially in the extractive industries. Oil for example, rose from US$20 a barrel in 1999 to US$145 in 2008. Although the price has fallen since, it remains way above the levels prevailing in the 1990s. There have been significant increases in prices of other minerals and grains. Africa is one of the richest continents: it has 10 per cent of the world's reserves of oil, 40 per cent of its gold, and 80 to 90 per cent of its chromium and platinum. Natural resource extraction and associated state expenditure account for more than 30 per cent of Africa's GDP growth since 2000. The primary contributors to the growth in GDP have been a small number of oil and gas exporters (Algeria, Angola, Chad, the Congo, Equatorial Guinea, Gabon, Libya [at least, before the NATO invasion] and Nigeria), which had the highest GDP on the continent but are also the least diversified economies. It is hardly surprising that, according to a McKinsey report, 'the annual flow of foreign direct investment into Africa increased from US$9 billion in 2000 to US$62 billion in 2008 – relative to GDP, almost as large as the flow into China', most of it into the extractive industries (Leke et al., 2010). As Carlos Lopes (2013), then executive secretary of the United Nations Economic Commission for Africa puts it: 'Average net profits for the top 40 mining companies grew by 156% in 2010 whereas the take for governments grew by only 60%, most of which was accounted for by Australia and Canada.' He points out that the profit made by the same set of mining companies in 2010 was US$110 billion, which was equivalent to the merchandise exports of all African least developed countries in the same year.

So, while profiteering from Africa was apparently rising, it was rising principally for the extractive transnational corporations. In reality, the most significant rise has been the growing unemployment or never-employment, landlessness, dispossessions, environmental destruction and growing contributions to climate change.

It is important also to bear in mind, however:

> The reality is that Africa is being drained of resources by the rest of the world. It is losing far more each year than it is receiving. While $134 billion flows into the continent each year, predominantly in the form of loans, foreign investment and aid; $192 billion is taken out, mainly in profits made by foreign companies, tax dodging and the costs of adapting to climate change. The result is that Africa suffers a net loss of $58 billion a year. As such, the idea that we are aiding Africa is flawed; it is Africa that is aiding the rest of the world. (Health Poverty Action et al. 2014: 5)

The supposed growth rates have also been challenged as 'dubious' by Roger Southall and Henning Melber (2009), who argue that there are parallels to be drawn between the nineteenth-century scramble for Africa and the current pillage of the continent's resources by transnational corporations.

While there are doubts as to the extent to which Africa Rising constituted a reflection of real economic developments, the opening decades of the twenty-first century did represent a rise in protests, uprisings and the opening of a new phase in the history of the African revolution. In Tunisia and Egypt, millions rose up to redefine what it meant to be Tunisian or Egyptian as a people seeking their own emancipation. These were followed by protests, strikes and other actions in Western Sahara, Zimbabwe, Senegal, Gabon, Sudan, Mauritania, Morocco, Madagascar, Mozambique, Algeria, Benin, Cameroon, Djibouti, Côte d'Ivoire, Botswana, Namibia, Kenya, Swaziland, South Africa and Uganda (Manji and Ekine 2012). In Burkina Faso, the uprising led to the removal of Blaise Campaoré, the assassin of revolutionary leader, Thomas Sankara, while in Senegal, attempts to change the constitution to enable Abdoulaye Wade to establish his dynasty were prevented through mass mobilisations. Each of these uprisings and protests have been a challenge to neoliberalism in which governments had become more accountable to the transnational corporations, banks and financial institutions than to the citizens that elected them.

TOWARDS A UNIVERSAL HUMANISM

Cabral's (1979: 80) statement that 'We must put the interests of our people higher, in the context of the interests of mankind in general, and then we can put them in the context of the interests of Africa in general' reminds us that the struggles to reinvent ourselves as humans is relevant not just for those in the location in which such processes take place. They are of universal importance and have value for the struggles to claim and express humanity everywhere. His statement is also a challenge to the Eurocentrism of the many who assume that only the western experience and its associated revolutions in France and America are of universal significance. The silence about the importance of the San Domingue revolution in much of left literature is shameful. It is a failure to recognise that the experiences and struggles of African people to assert and invent their humanity belong to the whole of humankind.

Those who have, for centuries, experienced dehumanisation inevitably and constantly struggle to reclaim their humanity, to assert that they are human beings. The process of reclamation is not, however, a harking back to some supposed glorious past when everyone was human, but rather a present and continuing process of constant invention, constant re-invention, and redefinition of what it means to be human.

For example, those who have suffered over millennia from the dehumanisation processes that are associated with patriarchy have an experience that helps define what being human really means: the gains of the women's and lesbian, gay, bisexual and transgender movements over recent years have provided glimpses into the potential being that humans could become, countering the narrow-minded, tradition-focused and often violent constructs that patriarchy portrays. In the perpetuation of patriarchy, men have themselves become dehumanised, unable to map out what being human is about, and it is only through the emancipatory struggles of those oppressed and exploited by patriarchy that insights into the possibility and potentials of what it means to be human can be found.

Similarly, those who have experienced and struggled against the horrors of enslavement, chattel slavery, colonisation and imperial domination have insights that emerge from their struggles into what it means to be human and what the potentials and possibilities are that can be released in becoming human. One can see in the struggles against oppression and exploitation the release of invention, creativity, different ways of organising and of making decisions, in each struggle that takes place, as in the revolutionary uprisings in Egypt and Tunisia. The anti-colonial struggles that Cabral led in Guinea-Bissau, for example, released a torrent of creativity in the way in which society could be organised, how education could be transformed, how health services could be provided, and how people could exercise democratic control. In every revolution or uprising that is informed by desires for emancipation, there are examples of such creativity and drive to invent what humans, as social beings, are and can become.

One final point has important implications for those in Africa seeking their own emancipation. The process of dehumanising others has an effect not only on the victims but also on the perpetrators. As Chinua Achebe (2010) puts it: 'We cannot trample upon the humanity of others without devaluing our own. The Igbo, always practical, put it concretely in their proverb *Onye ji onye n'ani ji onwe ya*: "He who will hold another down in the mud must stay in the mud to keep him down". The 500 or so years of dehumanising Africans (and indeed of peoples of the global South) has resulted in the profound dehumanisation of large sections of the populations of the North over whom capital has exercised its hegemony. The historical task that is faced by those engaged in the struggle for freedom and the universality of humanity is therefore not only the achievement of their own emancipation and freedom but also providing the way forward for the reclamation of the humanity of the peoples of the North. For it is the 'post-apocalyptic' societies that survived genocide, mass killings, enslavement, colonisation and dispossession who can point the way forward for humankind as to what it really means to be human.

CONCLUSIONS

The condition of being 'African' was a creation of the European, a synonym for the non-human or lesser human being, that justified enslavement, slavery, colonialism and exploitation. The specific terminology evolved subsequently to consider the African as 'uncivilised' under colonialism, and then 'underdeveloped' in the post-independence period. The struggles against enslavement, slavery, exploitation and national liberation represented the reassertion by Africans of their humanity, and as human beings, as makers of history, as contributors to the history of human emancipation. When the term 'African' becomes devoid of, or disarticulated from any connection with the struggle for emancipation and freedom, as it did in the aftermath of independence, it becomes indistinguishable from the taxonomy of race and of identity politics created by the European that identifies 'Africa', rather than its continued exploitation of its people and resources, as the 'problem'. So long as the experiences arising from emancipatory struggles are perceived as merely 'African', it is not possible to understand their contribution to universal humanity. That is only possible if the politics of African experiences are transcended and considered as part of the human condition that 'belong to the whole world'.

NOTE

1   K. Polanyi Levitt, Personal communication, from incomplete manuscript on development economics, 2016.

REFERENCES

Achebe, C. 2010. *The Education of a British Protected Child: Essays* (Kindle edition). London: Allan Lane.

Adi, H. 2008: 'Africa before slavery'. Accessed 20 May 2018, http://www.africanholocaust.net/news_ah/africa%20before%20slavery.htm.
Anta Diop, C. 1978. *The Cultural Unity of Negro Africa* (English edition). Paris: Présence Africaine.
Anta Diop, C. 1987. *Precolonial Black Africa: A Comparative Study of the Political and Social Systems of Europe and Black Africa, from Antiquity to the Formation of Modern States*. Translated by Harold J. Salemson. Westport, CT: Lawrence Hill.
Bassil, N.R. 2011. 'The roots of Afropessimism: The British invention of the "Dark Continent"', *Critical Arts*, 25: 377–396.
Brown, L.M. 2004. 'Understanding and ontology in traditional African thought'. In *African Philosophy: New and Traditional Perspectives*, edited by L. M. Brown. Oxford: Oxford University Press, pp. 158–178.
Cabral, A. 1966. 'The weapon of theory'. Address delivered to the first Tricontinental Conference of the Peoples of Asia, Africa and Latin America, Havana, January.
Cabral, A. 1969. *Selected Texts by Amilcar Cabral: Revolution in Guinea: The African People's Struggle*. London: Stage 1.
Cabral, A. 1973. *Return to the Source: Selected Speeches of Amilcar Cabral*. New York: Monthly Review Press.
Cabral, A. 1979. *Unity and Struggle: Speeches and Writings*. Translated by M. Wolfers. New York: Monthly Review Press.
Du Bois, W.E.B. 1962. *Black Reconstruction in America 1860–1880*. New York: Atheneum.
Dunbar-Ortiz, R. 2015. *An Indigenous Peoples' History of the United States: Revisioning American History*. Boston: Beacon Press.
Fanon, F. 1961. *The Wretched of the Earth*. Translation by R. Philcox. New York: Grove Press.
Fanon, F. 1989. *Studies in a Dying Colonialism*. London: Earthscan.
Gauthier, F. 1992. *Triomphe et mort du droit naturel en Révolution*. Paris: Presses Universitaires de France.
Gordon, L. 2008. *An Introduction to Africana Philosophy*. Cambridge: Cambridge University Press.
Hallward, P. 2004. 'Haitian inspiration: On the bicentenary of Haiti's independence', *Radical Philosophy*, 123: 2–7.
Health Poverty Action, Jubilee Debt Campaign, World Development Movement, African Forum and Network on Debt and Development (AFRODAD), Friends of the Earth Africa, Tax Justice Network, People's Health Movement Kenya, Zimbabwe and UK, War on Want, Community Working Group on Health Zimbabwe, Medact, Healthworkers4All Coalition, groundWork, Friends of the Earth South Africa, JA! Justica Ambiental/Friends of the Earth Mozambique. 2014. 'Honest accounts? The true story of Africa's billion dollar losses'. Accessed 20 May 2018, https://www.francophonie.org/IMG/pdf/honest-accounts_final-version.pdf.
James, C.L.R. 1963. *The Black Jacobins: Toussaint Louverture and the San Domingo Revolution*. New York: Random House.
Leke, A., Lund, S., Roxburgh, C. and Van Wamelen, A. 2010. 'What's driving Africa's growth?' Accessed 20 May 2018, https://www.mckinsey.com/featured-insights/middle-east-and-africa/whats-driving-africas-growth.
Lewontin, R.C., Rose S. and Kamin, L.J. 1984. *Not in Our Genes*. New York: Pantheon Books.

Lopes, C. 2013. 'Africa must benefit from its mineral resources'. Accessed 2 July 2017, http://www.uneca.org/es-blog/africa-must-benefit-its-mineral-resources.

Losurdo, D. 2014. *Liberalism: A Counter-History*. Translated by Gregory Elliot. London: Verso.

Louw, P.E. and De B'beri, B.E. (eds). 2011. 'Special issue: The Afropessimism phenomenon', *Critical Arts*, 5 (3): 335–466.

Mamdani, M. 1996. *Citizen and Subject: Contemporary Africa and the Legacy of Late Colonialism*. Princeton: Princeton University Press.

Mamdani, M. 2009. *Saviors and Survivors: Darfur, Politics, and the War on Terror*. New York: Pantheon Books.

Manji, F. 1998. 'The depoliticisation of poverty'. In *Development in Practice: Development and Rights*, edited by D. Eade. Oxford: Oxfam, pp. 12–33.

Manji, F. 2014. 'Rising dispossessions, rising impoverishment and rising discontent', *Amandla* 37/8 (December): 28–29.

Manji, F. 2015. 'Solidarity not saviours', *New African*, January: 14–15.

Manji, F. 2017a. 'Culture, power and resistance: Reflections on the ideas of Amilcar Cabral'. *State of Power 2017*. Accessed 20 May 2018, http://longreads.tni.org/state-of-power/culture-power-and-resistance/.

Manji, F. 2017b. 'Can NGOs play an emancipatory role in contemporary Africa?' In *NGOs and Social Justice in South Africa and Beyond*, edited by S. Matthews. Pietermaritzburg: University of KwaZulu-Natal Press, pp. 19–31.

Manji, F. and Ekine, S. (eds). 2012. *African Awakening: The Emerging Revolutions*. Oxford: Pambazuka Press.

Manji, F. and Fletcher, B. Jnr. (eds). 2013. *Claim No Easy Victories: The Legacy of Amilcar Cabral*. Dakar: CODESRIA and Daraja Press.

Manji, F. and O'Coill, C. 2002. 'The missionary position: NGOs and development in Africa', *International Affairs*, 78 (3): 567–583.

Mashanda, T.C. 2016. 'Rethinking the term "Sub-Saharan Africa"'. Accessed 16 January 2017, https://www.africanexponent.com/blogs/realistechoes/rethinking-the-term-sub-saharan-africa-36.

Mazrui, A.A. 2005. 'The re-invention of Africa: Edward Said, V.Y. Mudimbe, and beyond', *Research in African Literatures*, 36 (3): 68–82.

Mudimbe, V.Y. 1994. *The Idea of Africa*. Bloomington: Indiana University Press.

Mutua, M. 2001. 'Savages, victims, and saviours: The metaphor of human rights', *Harvard International Law Journal*, 41 (1): 201–245.

Neocosmos, M. 2016. *Thinking Freedom in Africa*. Johannesburg: Wits University Press.

Neocosmos, M. 2017. 'Navigating the pitfalls of state democracy: Thinking NGOs from an emancipatory perspective'. In *NGOs and Social Justice in South Africa and Beyond*, edited by S. Matthews. Pietermaritzburg: University of KwaZulu-Natal Press, pp. 32–53.

Parris, L.T. 2015. *Being Apart: Theoretical and Existential Resistance in Africana Literature*. Charlottesville, VA: University of Virginia Press.

Patel, S. 1995. *Technological Transformation in the Third World: Volume 5: The Historic Process*. Brookfield, WI: Avebury Ashgate.

Pithouse, R. 2016. 'Being human after 1492', *The Con*, 16 November. Accessed 16 January 2017, http://www.theconmag.co.za/2016/11/16/being-human-after-1492/.

Robinson, C.J. 1983: *Black Marxism: The Making of the Black Radical Tradition*. London: Zed Books.

Rodney, W. 1972. *How Europe Underdeveloped Africa*. London: Bogle-L'Ouverture Publications.

Southall, R. and Melber, H. 2009. *A New Scramble for Africa? Imperialism, Investment and Development*. Pietermaritzburg: University of KwaZulu-Natal Press.

Sweeny, R.C.H. 2009. *Why Did We Choose to Industrialise: Montreal, 1819–1849*. Montreal: Montréal l'avenir du passé.

Táíwò, O. 2013. 'Cabral, culture, progress and the metaphysics of difference'. In *Claim No Easy Victories: The Legacy of Amilcar Cabral*, edited by F. Manji and B. Fletcher Jnr. Dakar: CODESRIA and Daraja Press, pp. 297–305.

wa Thiong'o, N. 1986. *Decolonising the Mind: The Politics of Language in African Literature*. London: James Curry.

Williams, E. 1966. *Capitalism and Slavery*. New York: Capricorn Books.

CHAPTER

4

COLONIALISM, APARTHEID AND THE NATIVE QUESTION: THE CASE OF ISRAEL/PALESTINE

Ran Greenstein

SETTLER COLONIALISM

In the last decade settler colonialism has gained currency as a new field of study. It identifies a cluster of societies in which colonial rule was combined with large-scale immigration of European settlers. Politically, it allows us to focus on resilient forms of domination that serve the interests of settlers who made a new home for themselves in overseas territories. Facing resistance from indigenous people, settler societies were shaped by ongoing political conflict. This provided them with common features and a sense of shared destiny, based on the similar challenges they faced. Solidarity between those at the losing end – indigenous groups, slaves and other people marginalised through this form of colonial rule – is the counterpart of the process (Davis 2016). At the same time, the extent to which the concept serves a useful purpose in historical and theoretical analysis is less obvious. I argue here that its utility in these respects is limited (Bhandar and Ziadah 2016; Greenstein 2016).

What is the problem with settler colonialism as a historical concept? Its strongest point is also its weakest: it is applicable to cases that exhibit a great diversity of conditions. It is applied to societies that saw settlers overwhelm the indigenous population to the point that it became demographically and economically marginal: two to three per cent of the population in the US, Canada and Australia. In other places – Kenya, Rhodesia, Algeria, Mozambique and South Africa – indigenous people remained the bulk of the population and the main source of labour. Slavery featured in some cases, such as the US and early colonial South Africa, but not in others. European settlers retained legal and political links to the mother country in Algeria, Kenya, Rhodesia and Portugal's African colonies but became independent in the US, South Africa and other British territories, often as a result of a violent intra-colonial conflict.

In some countries, most settlers left the territory after independence – Algeria, Mozambique, Angola and Rhodesia – but substantial numbers stayed in other places such as Namibia and South Africa. And, of course, where they became numerically dominant, settlers used their political independence to consolidate their rule and marginalise 'natives' further, but also to incorporate them into the new polity once they ceased posing a demographic threat to settler domination. This contrasts with the retention of legal-racial divisions in places where indigenous people remained a majority of the population.

Resistance strategies differed as well: attempts by natives to integrate as individuals on an equal basis in some societies, maintenance of pre-colonial identities and modes of organisation in others, formation of nationalist movements on the new ground created by colonial settlement, a focus on race, all with varying degrees of recognising settlers as legitimate members of the envisaged liberated society.

It is not only the broad contours of history that vary greatly in settler colonial societies but also patterns of social change over time. Constant geographical expansion while driving out indigenous people in some places such as the US and Australia, constant expansion while incorporating indigenous people as labour power in others, South Africa most notably, initial takeover of the entire territory with more or less fixed relations of subordination throughout the period (Algeria, Kenya, Rhodesia, Namibia). The diverse dynamics coexisted with different degrees of incorporation of 'urban natives' in a relatively privileged position compared to rural populations, and different combinations of direct and indirect rule. These continued to affect the evolution of societies in the post-colonial period (Mamdani 1996).

The concept of settler colonialism, then, is compatible with different demographic ratios, different trajectories of indigenous-settler relations, different relations between settlers and metropolitan centres, different destinies of settlers in the post-colonial period, and different social structures, ranging from reliance on free white labour, indentured immigrant labour – from Europe, India, China – to African slavery, indigenous labour subordination, and many combinations of the above. In short, settler-colonial societies do not move in a similar direction, be it the consolidation of settler rule or its demise through indigenous resistance.

In the absence of a unique historical trajectory, does settler colonialism display perhaps specific conceptual features? That is to say, does it work as a theoretical model? Does it outline distinct ways in which theoretical forces, such as class, race, ethnicity, state, power, ideology, space and time, are manifested concretely or intersect with one another? If we pose the question in this way, the conclusion seems unavoidable: settler colonialism as a model does not establish any *specific social-theoretical dynamics* unique to it, which may serve to distinguish it analytically, not just descriptively, from other types of societies, be they colonial or not.

Since settler colonialism has no specific historical or theoretical dynamics, how do we deal with societies that fall within its definition? As an alternative method of investigation, I suggest a strategy of addressing the multiplicity of colonial and post-colonial societies with a three-track approach:

- Studying them in their full historical specificity without imposing artificial boundaries between classes;
- Deploying general analytical concepts instead of developing idiosyncratic models (such as 'colonialism of a special type', 'ethnic democracy combined with protracted military occupation', 'exclusionary colonialism', or 'regimes of separation'), which may serve as useful political labels but are theoretically without predictive value; and
- Engaging in selected comparisons in order to highlight general and unique features by examining them against each other.

To illustrate this approach, I apply it here to the case of Israel/Palestine. In what ways does it offer a useful prospect for historical analysis? Is the concept of apartheid, increasingly applied to this case, a good conceptual substitute for settler colonialism?

THE 1948 NAKBA AND ITS IMPLICATIONS

Israeli state officials and their supporters overseas invoke the notion of 'singling out' as a problem in analyses and campaigns aimed to address oppressive Israeli practices, frequently seen as colonial in nature. They do not necessarily reject all criticism of government policies, but they explain these away as results of a difficult security situation that calls for restrictive measures of a limited and temporary nature. Such measures, the argument goes, are not unique to Israel. They can be found in many places throughout the world. Why regard Israel, then, as a unique state deserving of special treatment?

To answer that, let us start with 1948. On the face of it, that year saw a war between two communities, each trying to gain control of as much land and power as possible from the departing British forces. The Jewish side managed to acquire a larger territory and to evict many of the Palestinians who resided there, sending them to areas under the control of Arab forces. It was a messy outcome but no different in essence from that of other conflicts unfolding under similar circumstances: Turkey and Greece in the aftermath of the First World War, Czechoslovakia and Germany in the aftermath of the Second World War, India and Pakistan in the aftermath of the 1947 Partition that ended colonial rule on the subcontinent.

The similarities between all these situations as pointed out by this mainstream version of history are real enough, but three crucial differences make the case of the Nakba (the 1948 ethnic cleansing of Palestinians) distinctive:

- The Nakba involved the displacement of indigenous people by recently arrived settler immigrants. In the other cases above, those involved were equally indigenous: they had coexisted in the same territory for centuries.
- The Nakba affected almost exclusively one side: for every Jew in Palestine displaced in the war there were hundreds of Palestinians. In other cases, displacement of populations was usually mutual. Jews were indeed displaced from other Arab countries, but not by Palestinians, not at their behest or on their behalf.
- The Nakba saw the displacement of 80 per cent of the Arab population residing in what became Israel (60 per cent of the overall Palestinian population), and their replacement by Jewish immigrants from East Europe and the Middle East. In other cases, only a small segment on either side

of the divide was involved, perhaps two to three per cent of the total. The bulk of the population was not affected directly.

Putting all this together makes it clear that the partition of Palestine and subsequent war resulted in the destruction of indigenous society and the rise of a settler-dominated society in its place (Khalidi 2006; Morris 2004; Pappé 2006).

This was not a coincidence, a series of unfortunate events, or an outcome of chaotic war conditions. Since the beginning of the twentieth century, the Jewish settlement project in Palestine, led by the Zionist movement, embarked on building an ever-expanding zone of exclusion from which all local Arabs were barred. Tenants were not allowed to stay on land bought by settlement agencies, nor were Palestinians accepted as residents in new rural Jewish communities or urban neighbourhoods. The campaigns for Conquest of Land and Conquest of Labour were not always or completely successful, but they did set in motion exclusionary dynamics aimed to remove Arab workers from Jewish-owned enterprises, and eliminate (or at least reduce) dependence on Palestinian agricultural produce. The British imperial authorities facilitated this process.

The motivation behind that had nothing to do with 'security'. Rather, the goal of the project was to build up a society in which Jews would be in control of their own affairs, overcoming their status elsewhere as a minority. Importantly, it was not an inevitable outcome of Jewish settlement as such. In the first Jewish immigration wave from 1882 to 1904, known as the First Aliyah, settlers made extensive use of local Arab labour, in the fields and at homes, in a pattern familiar from cases of European overseas expansion, such as Algeria, Kenya and South Africa. But, with a difference: the small scale of the project and its unfolding under the framework of an indigenous political order – the Ottoman Empire – meant that it had limited impact on local society. From the perspective of the Zionist movement, that pattern had a basic flaw. It limited employment opportunities for potential Jewish workers and therefore was not conducive for large-scale immigration and settlement.

By the second decade of the twentieth century, under the impact of the Zionist labour movement and against resistance from private Jewish farming interests, a new pattern of settlement had begun to dominate the process. It was based on job reservation for Jewish immigrants, which resulted in the eviction of cheaper and more productive Arab workers. It was followed by experimentation with collective forms of economic production, especially in agriculture, to allow more efficient use of resources in competition with local Arab producers (Shafir 1989; Sternhell 1999).

This shift was driven ideologically by socialist-oriented activists, who called for the 'normalisation' of Jewish existence, grounding it in productive labour – agriculture and industry. Strong political commitment and financial subsidies were required to sustain this effort, made possible by mobilising resources from numerous overseas-based individual supporters. Still a marginal perspective during the Ottoman period, the drive to base the Zionist project on the recruitment, training and deployment of large numbers of workers was given a boost with the transition to British rule and the launch of a 'Jewish national home' policy in the aftermath of the First World War.

The notion advanced by the Communist International, that the big Jewish bourgeoisie was driving the Zionist project, was devoid of substance. Such a class did not exist as a coherent entity and Jewish capitalists usually found more profitable avenues elsewhere for their investments. Diplomatic and military support by global powers, the British Empire first and the US later on, ensured the survival and success of the project against substantial odds. These factors allowed settlers to overcome constraints imposed by the need to maintain economic profitability. Thus it could override local class imperatives by relying on external resources made available due to ideological and strategic reasons.

The core elements of the emerging society had been put in place by 1948, and the war that year served to consolidate them further. Before then, land transfers and the eviction of Arab tenants and workers were limited by British administrative regulations and the lack of settler coercive capacity. But once the British departed from the scene, Israeli political independence and access to superior military force allowed the new state the freedom to pursue policies of ethnic cleansing and land dispossession on a massive scale. The Nakba took place three years after the end of the Second World War and the Holocaust, giving the Israeli side a sense of moral justification, bordering on impunity, to do whatever it took to ensure national survival.

The ethnic cleansing of 1948 shaped Israeli society in several ways that remain of crucial importance today, and account for its particular ethnic stratification patterns:

- By removing the bulk of the indigenous population it ensured that Jews became the undisputed majority and occupied a dominant position in society. From that point on, the new demographic status quo became a shared platform for all mainstream forces, from the hard right and religious orthodox parties to liberal and left-wing Zionists. It mandated unwavering support for the Law of Return for Jews, and resolute opposition to the Right of Return of Palestinian refugees. The notion of Israel as a 'Jewish democratic state' rests on this foundation, which became part of the global diplomatic consensus on the issue.

- By reducing the proportion of internal Palestinians to 15–20 per cent of all Israelis (and a similar percentage of all Palestinians), it entrenched their status as a minority, but also facilitated their incorporation as citizens. This would not have been possible had they remained a larger part of the population. From a truncated community, left defeated, without leadership and socially marginalised, they managed to consolidate themselves over the years into a self-conscious and unified minority, powerfully asserting their rights.
- By creating a large population of refugees across the borders (and even within them – the 'present absentees', internally displaced citizens), it ensured a state of permanent tension, requiring constant vigilance, militarisation and enhanced security consciousness, all of which became essential features of public life in Israel. On the Palestinian side, it created a political adversary located primarily outside the territory it sought to liberate, an unprecedented situation in the history of anti-colonial movements.
- Finally, by emptying parts of the country of their Arab population, it created both the space needed to settle new immigrants and the necessity for large numbers of people to fill in the resulting gaps, both geographical and social. Mizrahim ('Oriental' Jews from the Middle East and North Africa) were one group the state could access and manipulate with relative ease to play the roles of demographic barrier, cheap labour force and cannon fodder. Growing xenophobic sentiments among Arab nationalist movements and states contributed to the dislocation of Jewish communities into Israel in the post-1948 period. A new ethnic hierarchy thus emerged, affecting internal relations and the broader conflict.

In all these respects, the legacy of the 1948 war is alive. Of crucial importance is the excluded presence of the refugees, a spectre that permanently haunts Israeli society, not by directly shaping people's consciousness – many are not even aware of its existence – but by nurturing an ever-present siege mentality, expectations of doom and fears of imminent destruction. Not only must all precedents for the return of refugees be denied (even if they are Israeli citizens, as in those from the destroyed Galilee villages of Bir'im and Iqrit), but the impulse that led to the Nakba in the first place continues to be at work. House demolitions, land confiscations, forced removals of Bedouin communities on both sides of the Green Line, no recognition of informal Palestinian settlements and planning restrictions in formal settlements, denial of residence rights to Palestinian spouses of Israeli citizens – these policies are not as dramatic as those of 1948 but share the same imperative: to restrict and reduce the size, spread and capacity of the Palestinian population.

Bearing the brunt of such policies most intensely, however, are neither Palestinian citizens of Israel nor refugees living outside its boundaries. Rather it is another population segment that was added to the picture in 1967: residents of the territories occupied in that year – the West Bank and the Gaza Strip.

1967 AND ITS AFTERMATH

The 1967 war reaffirmed but also reversed some of the trends set in motion in 1948. The overall policy thrust was kept in place: incorporation of land, exclusion of people. But, this time it was with a difference. People beyond the Green Line, who fell under Israeli control in 1967, for the most part stayed put in their homes, villages and towns. With the exception of refugees from 1948, many of whom were subjected to another forced removal into Jordan, residents were spared the ethnic cleansing widely experienced in 1948. However, they were not granted citizenship rights. Some of them were incorporated into the Israeli labour market but in a limited and temporary manner as commuting workers in marginal industries. This mode of exclusionary inclusion brought about changes in the nature of the Israeli regime and its relations with its Palestinian subjects, with implications for democracy, demography, diplomacy and social divisions (Azoulay and Ophir 2012; Gordon 2008).

Let us start with *democracy*. Even if we ignore the physically excluded refugees, who obviously had no say in the way Israel was governed and were denied any political rights within its boundaries, before 1967 Israeli democracy was seriously deficient. Despite being granted voting rights, the majority of Palestinian citizens were subjected to military rule, which placed restrictions on their ability to move, have access to land and jobs, and organise freely. Arab nationalist associations were banned, teachers had to be vetted by the security forces, a network of informers kept watch on subversive activists (basically, anyone engaged in any form of protest), and political dissent was punished (Jiryis 1976).

With all these limitations, avenues of oppositional political expression remained open, above all in the shape of the Israeli Communist Party (known as Maki, and from 1965 as Rakah), which combined parliamentary and popular mobilisation. It grew to become the dominant force among Palestinian citizens in the decade following 1967, while remaining a marginal player on the broader political scene.

In comparison, residents of the 1967 territories were treated with far less concern with regard to nominal democratic notions and practices: thousands of activists who engaged in resistance were arrested or deported, political publications and associations were banned and, above all, no prospect of being granted citizenship ever existed. Over a million people (initially), 25–30 per cent of the total Palestinian population, were left with no access to basic human, civil and political rights. Their numbers grew over the years to reach four million, but their prospects of freedom from Israel or freedom within Israel, indeed any rights within the system of Israeli control, remain today as remote as ever.

For the last half a century, then, the Israeli regime has combined formal democracy within part of its territory and repressive rule backed by military force – making any participation by the local population impossible – in another part. Under these conditions, its democratic pretensions cannot be taken seriously. The only claim to international legality made by this regime is that it is temporary in nature, but after more than 50 years of rule this is not tenable any longer, if it ever was. Willing neither to terminate its control by withdrawing from the occupied territories, nor to grant their residents equal rights or contemplate any route towards that, Israel has entrenched a system of domination without parallel elsewhere in the world today.

Changing *demography* is both a cause and effect of this regime. The number of Palestinians under Israeli control tripled with the 1967 occupation. There was no way to incorporate them as equals without undermining the state as a mechanism in the service of Jewish exclusivity, a problem that became known as the demographic threat. The attempted 'solution' combined three elements: denial of citizenship rights to residents of the occupied territories; steps to reduce their numbers; and increased Jewish immigration into the country. The latter two were not sufficiently successful. A repeat of the ethnic cleansing of

1948 was not possible: the 1967 war was much shorter and more visible to the media. Further, having learnt the lesson of the Nakba, people realised that any departure from their homes would prove irreversible.

Most of those who fled or were expelled to Jordan in 1967 were second-time refugees from the 1948 period (Raz 2012). Constant bureaucratic harassment made it difficult for many others to retain residence if they left the country at any point, but the bulk of them remained in place. Large-scale Jewish immigration has taken place over the years, especially from the Soviet Union, but it only alleviated the demographic problem, not solved it. The proportions of Israeli Jews and Palestinian Arabs in the entire area under Israeli control hovered around 50 per cent for years.

The remaining option was to intensify the exclusion of Palestinians in the occupied territories and at the same time enhance the Jewish nature of the state. Many Palestinian workers from the territories were employed in sectors such as construction and agriculture, but their labour was never crucial to the leading industrial and high-tech sectors of the economy. The growing globalisation of labour supply in recent decades allowed Israel to replace locals with foreign workers, primarily from East Europe and South-East Asia. Since the first Gulf War in 1991, processes of labour displacement/replacement continued apace, facilitated by changing international conditions: the re-emergence of ethno-nationalism in Europe, the attacks of 11 September 2001 and growing anti-Islamic sentiments in the west, and the collapse of the traditional state order in the Middle East due to external interventions and internal revolts.

The main demographic project of the Israeli state thus involves accelerated inclusion of land coupled with growing exclusion of (non-Jewish) people. Palestinians cannot be removed en masse from the country, but their position can be diminished conceptually and legally through administrative means. The ongoing settlement project, land confiscation and fragmentation of the West Bank, and the siege on Gaza are well known, but the efforts go beyond that: admission committees in new settlements within the Green Line, ensuring they remain open in practice to Jews only; the nation-state bill, aimed to entrench exclusive Jewish claim to the country, its symbols and public spaces; forced resettlement of Bedouins in Israel and the West Bank; allocation of funds to enhance exclusionary Jewish identity at schools and forge links with the Jewish diaspora – sending young Israelis to Holocaust-themed sites in Europe, bringing young western Jews on trips to discover their 'birthright' in Israel – the list goes on.

Diplomacy is essential to sustain the legitimacy of these efforts. Based on the deliberately misleading notion that there is a genuine 'peace process' aimed at reaching agreement on a two-state solution, it allows no alternative approach to disrupt it. That the two powers most insistent on this idea are Israel and the US, after decades of resolute opposition to the mere mention of Palestinian statehood, is telling. Even the European Union, which has followed US diplomacy loyally for years, is beginning to explore other diplomatic and legal means to end the occupation. This also applies to the Palestinian Authority, though in a more hesitant manner due to its dependence on the very same powers intent on its continued subordination.

But the process is doomed. Nothing can possibly come out of another round of negotiations. This is plain for all to see – Israeli mainstream political debate has relegated the issue to the back burner, and the current government, or any other in sight, makes no effort to revive the process, beyond occasional token statements. The sole function of the two-state discourse today is to entrench the status quo and prevent a search for alternatives. Are there any serious forces willing and able to pick up the challenge of formulating a different way forward?

Divisions of a socio-political nature are crucial to the answer to this question, with a focus on two groups that stand at the intersection of the Jewish-Arab divide. The role of one of them is straightforward. Palestinian citizens of Israel are the only segment of the population of the entire country that is fully bilingual and immersed in cultural and social realities on all sides. They suffer from enough socio-economic and legal disadvantages – relative to other Israelis – to position them against the regime, but also enjoy enough privileges – relative to other Palestinians in the West Bank and Gaza – to enable them to organise effectively within the system and on its margins. They can act as a powerful catalyst for regime change. The formation of a unified electoral front – the Joint List – in 2015, and its possible move beyond parliamentary politics to engage in mass action and social mobilisation, is a promising sign of what is yet to come.

Social inequality, including class exploitation, is an important dimension of the position of Palestinians in Israel. As the 2007 Haifa Declaration, one of the Vision Documents guiding their collective struggle, says: 'The state has exercised against us institutional discrimination in various fields of life such as housing, employment, education, development, and allocation of resources' (Mada al-Carmel 2007: 18). Labour issues have not been central to the Palestinian struggle inside the Green Line, however, with its focus on legal and political rights. Land, on the other hand, has been crucial as a national asset, and a major point of political contention, in addition to its obvious relevance for material production and economic prosperity. Holding on to what was left after wars and occupation became a central principle of the strategy of Sumud, steadfastness or perseverance by staying put, physically and symbolically, on both sides of the Green Line.

The other segment of the population to consider here presents a complex picture (Greenstein 2015a). As noted earlier, Mizrahim were brought to Israel to fill the gaps left by the Nakba. To gain admission as legitimate members of the dominant European-oriented Jewish group, they had to leave their Arab cultural heritage behind. With the exception of small groups of intellectuals in Iraq and Egypt, identification with Arab nationalism and active opposition to Zionism were rare among Middle Eastern Jews in the pre-1948 period, and unknown in North African communities. The Jewish masses spoke local dialects of Arabic and other regional languages. They were similar in their daily practices to their Muslim and Christian neighbours, all of whom identified largely in traditional religious terms. Referring to them anachronistically as 'Arab Jews' is misleading. They rarely joined the political revival that formed the basis for the Arab national movement, which began to flourish after the First World War, and they continued to adhere to the pre-war mode of communal organisation prevalent in the Ottoman Empire.

Post-Ottoman realities saw Middle Eastern Jews positioned uncomfortably between two competing modes of nationalist identification – Zionism and Arabism – both of which were at odds with their pre-existing identities, and neither of which allowed for ambiguity or dual loyalties. The dilemma was resolved in the decade after Israel's establishment through the mass migration, under duress, of hundreds of thousands of Jews from all over the Middle East and North Africa to Israel. Most of them were forced to abandon their property and arrived at their destination with limited assets. Cultural disadvantage – they were regarded by Ashkenazi (East and central European) Jews in charge of the state as primitive, lacking in culture and education – together with material deprivation and social discrimination made them easy to manipulate and control. Many were sent to remote areas along the borders, with access to inferior education and fewer opportunities to find decent jobs. Others found themselves in 'development towns' created as new industrial zones relying on cheap labour, and in poor city neighbourhoods whose former Arab residents had become refugees.

Although living conditions placed them next to Palestinian citizens in the bottom rungs of Israeli society, Mizrahim had one precious asset – Jewish identity. Focusing on what they shared with other Jews, and distancing themselves from what set them apart and brought them closer to the enemy – Arab cultural background – made strategic sense. Mizrahi identity developed in Israel as a coping mechanism to deal with social marginalisation that had clear intra-ethnic undertones. The humiliating process of absorption in Israel created deep resentment against the establishment, which was led by the Labour Party. It took a generation for this attitude to consolidate into a full-fledged rejection of Labour and transfer of political allegiance to the ultra-nationalist, right-wing alternative, led by Menahem Begin. Having put greater emphasis on traditional Jewish components of identity, at the expense of the secular Israeli component associated with liberal elites, the right wing managed to increase its support among Mizrahim after 1967. This culminated with the 1977 upheaval that brought Begin's Likud Bloc to power.

It is important to realise that right-wing views, including hostility to Palestinians and other Arabs, based on xenophobia or desire for historical revenge, were *not* the primary reason for the support the Mizrahim granted Likud. Rather, it was the sense that Likud regarded them as equal Jewish citizens, free of the condescending attitudes they had experienced from the Labour-affiliated establishment that moved them to adopt Likud's right-wing agenda.

Initially, issues of historical redress, ethnic pride and access to social services were at the forefront of the political realignment. But the Likud and its new partners – the post-1967 religious-nationalist messianic settlers – had other priorities. Once Egypt signed a peace agreement with Israel in 1978, and the rejectionist Arab Steadfastness and Confrontation Front collapsed with the Iraq-Iran war, the road was clear for the Israeli nationalist-religious alliance to pursue its agenda in an accelerated manner: the massive project of Jewish settlement of the West Bank rapidly gained ground, the first Lebanon war erupted in 1982, followed by prolonged resistance, and the first Palestinian Intifada (uprising) broke out in the occupied territories in the late 1980s. All these contributed to retaining a focus on 'security' issues, with the social redress agenda taking a back seat.

By that time, the Mizrahi support for the right wing had become consolidated. The historical resentment towards the Labour establishment translated into hostility towards policies and discourses associated with Ashkenazi elites, who continued to treat Mizrahim with arrogance. These elites were accused of caring more for outsiders (Palestinians, refugees) than for their 'own' people. They lost political power in 1977, but retained control over media, academia and culture. Transforming these spheres and demoting the old elites became a goal common for Mizrahi activists, the right wing and the settler movement, though they came at the issue from different directions. Reinforcing the Jewish nature of the state against liberal notions of universal human rights, civil equality and western-style democracy, which threaten to transform Israel into a 'normal' state, has become the ideological unifying battle cry in this campaign.

This background explains why class relations on their own have not led to alliances between social groups that stand in different positions within the Israeli legal-political hierarchy. The principal Jewish-Arab divide in society presents a serious obstacle for mobilisation on grounds that might call for joint action under normal circumstances, let alone mobilisation with an explicit political content. The largest mass movement in recent years, the 2011 tent protests, which focused on housing and cost of living issues, inspired by the Arab Spring, saw hundreds of thousands of Israeli citizens marching in the streets to demand social justice, but shying away from addressing the occupation, or welcoming Palestinian citizens. Socially and culturally marginalised Jews – of Mizrahi, Ethiopian, Russian origins – felt out of place in what was seen as a protest led by the educated, mostly Ashkenazi middle classes.

THE REGIME AND RESISTANCE: MODELS AND ALTERNATIVES

How can we characterise the socio-political system that emerged from these processes? It has been referred to as settler-colonial but, as discussed earlier, this term covers many different situations and is too vague to be of use in historically grounded analysis. It fails to capture specific features that are essential both for understanding the dynamics of the system as well as the ways in which it could be changed. The ongoing centrality of the land issue, though, does attest to the legacy of colonialism and resistance to it.

Apartheid is a concept of greater relevance, capturing the power relations and conflict over resources between different groups that inhabit the same space and state structures. The definition of apartheid in the 2002 Rome Statute of the International Criminal Court – 'an institutionalised regime of systematic oppression and domination' of one group over another – applies to

Israel (UNGA 1998: 5). Two key features, however, set Israel apart from South African apartheid:

- The Israeli system is based on the exclusion of indigenous people as the main providers of labour, while South African apartheid was based on the exploitation of black labour power as the mainstay of a white-dominated economy and society. This difference has implications not only for our understanding of the regime but also for resistance. The key role played by the internal mass movement, led by black trade unions, which resulted in the demise of apartheid in South Africa, cannot be replicated in Israel/Palestine. An alternative configuration of internal and external forces must be found instead.
- The unique position of the Mizrahim – a settler group indigenous to the broader region, which shares cultural background with Palestinians but has no common political consciousness with them – is without equivalence in South Africa. Mizrahim have gone through decades of cultural and political assimilation into Israeli society, and expectations that they could have retained an Arab identity, even if in a dormant form, are delusional. At the same time, no political change would be possible without them. How to shatter their alliance with the right wing is the crucial political challenge in Israel today.

This system may be called 'apartheid of a special type' to capture both the similarities and the differences between it and historical apartheid in South Africa (Greenstein 2015b).[1] The real challenge though, is not to find elegant terminology but to fill it with concrete content for analysis and action. The political implications of the analysis are of particular concern.

What are some of the characteristics of this system?

- It is based on an ethno-national distinction between Jewish insiders and Palestinian Arab outsiders. This distinction has a religious dimension – the only way to join the Jewish group is through conversion – but is not affected by degree of religious adherence.
- It uses this distinction to expand citizenship beyond its territory, potentially to all Jews, and to restrict citizenship within it: Palestinian residents of the 1967 occupied territories, and the 1948 refugees beyond them, are not and cannot become citizens. Thus, the state is open to all non-resident

members of one group, wherever they are and regardless of their personal history and links to the territory. It is closed to all non-resident members of the other group wherever they are and regardless of personal history and links to the territory.
- It is based on the blurring of physical boundaries. At no point in its 70 years of existence have its boundaries been fixed by law. They are permanently temporary. And, they are asymmetrical: porous in one direction, expanding military forces and settlers into adjacent territories, and impermeable in another direction: severe restrictions or prohibition on entry of Palestinians – from the occupied territories and the diaspora – into its territories.
- It combines different modes of rule: civilian authority with formal democratic institutions within the Green Line, and military authority beyond it. In times of crisis, a military mode spills over to apply to Palestinian citizens. At all times, a civilian mode spills over to apply to Jews residing beyond the Green Line. The distinction between the two sides of the Line is eroding as a result; norms and practices of the occupation filter back into Israel: the Jewish democratic state is 'democratic' for Jews and 'Jewish' for Arabs.
- It is in fact a Jewish *demographic* state. Demography – the fear that Jews may become a minority – is the prime concern behind the policies of mainstream forces. State structures, policies and proposed solutions to the Israeli-Palestinian conflict are geared as a result to meet the need for a permanent Jewish majority exercising political domination.

How do these features compare with historical South African apartheid?

- The foundation of apartheid was a racial distinction between white and black people (further classified into sub-groups), not an ethno-national distinction. Racial groups were a product of the colonial division of labour, were divided internally on the basis of language, religion and location, and externally linked on these dimensions across the colour-line, creating an intricate picture (Winant 2001). In Israel/Palestine, lines of division usually overlapped. Potential cross-cutting affiliations that existed early on – anti-Zionist orthodox Jews, Arabic-speaking indigenous Jewish communities – were undermined by the simultaneous rise of the Zionist and Arab nationalist movements to a dominant position. This allowed no space for those straddling multiple identities.

- In South Africa then, there was a contradiction between the organisation of the state around the single axis of race, and social reality that allowed more diversity in practice and multiple lines of division as well as cooperation. This opened up opportunities for change. The apartheid state endeavoured to eliminate this contradiction by entrenching residential, educational, religious and cultural segregation, seeking to shift its basis of legitimacy from race to culture. But, its capacity was eroded over time and cracks opened up in the structure of domination. In Israel/Palestine the fit between state organisation and social reality is tighter, with a crucial exception: Palestinian citizens are positioned in between Jewish citizens and Palestinian non-citizens. Their role therefore is crucial.
- Under South African apartheid the central goal of the state was to ensure that black people performed their role as providers of cheap labour, without pursuing subversive social and political demands. The strategy focused on externalising them: they were physically present at white-owned homes, farms, mines, factories and service industries, but absent, legally and politically, as rights-bearing citizens. They were supposed to commute – daily, monthly or even annually, depending on the distance – between the places where they had jobs but no political rights and the places where they had political rights but no jobs ('homelands'). This system of migrant labour created tensions between political and economic imperatives. To fulfil the ideology of separation between working and living spaces, it broke down families and the social order, hampered efforts to create a skilled labour force, reduced productivity, and gave rise to crime and social protest. To control people, it created a bloated repressive apparatus that put a huge burden on state resources and capacities. Domestic and industrial employers faced increasing difficulties in meeting their labour needs. From an economic asset (for whites), it became a liability. While some forms of racialised labour remain useful for South African capitalism, the rigid forms of separation practised under apartheid increasingly became counterproductive and were eventually discarded.
- The imperative of the Israeli system, in contrast, has been to create employment for actual and potential Jewish immigrants. Arab labour power was used by some groups of employers in certain periods as it was available and convenient, but it never became central to Jewish prosperity in the country. The strategic sectors of the economy – energy, security-related industries, high-tech enterprises – have been largely reserved for

Jews. Following the first Intifada of the late 1980s, Palestinian workers from the occupied territories were increasingly replaced by 'safe' foreign labourers. The externalisation of Palestinians, through ethnic cleansing, blockade, and denial of work and residence permits, has not presented serious economic problems for Israel in recent decades.

In summary then, apartheid of a special type in Israel/Palestine is different from the South African system in three major respects:

- At its foundation there are consolidated and relatively impermeable ethno-national identities, with few cross-cutting affiliations across the principal divide in society.
- It is relatively free of economic imperatives that run counter to its overall exclusionary thrust, because it is not dependent on the exploitation of indigenous labour even though it is based on land expansion.
- Its quest is for demographic majority as the basis for military and political domination.

In all these respects it is less prone to integrative solutions along the lines of post-apartheid South Africa. At the same time, it is subject to contradictions of its own, which are crucial to its dynamics and present potential opportunities for political action:

- Its foundational act of ethnic cleansing in 1948 left behind a defeated and dislocated Arab minority group. No longer considered a major threat, this group used its limited but real legal and political incorporation to reorganise and build a foundation for resistance politics, combining parliamentary and protest activities that have challenged Israel's exclusionary structures from within. It is the only serious opposition in parliament, filling the gap between dissident Jewish activists and Palestinians in the occupied territories. Some of the issues it raises – land, housing, social services – may fit in a new agenda shared with allies within Israeli-Jewish society, while its rights-oriented programme is aligned with the broader Palestinian struggle. Its minority status makes it an unlikely leader of anti-systemic mobilisation but it could play a critical bridging role between groups.

- The Palestinian struggle against occupation and land dispossession in the 1967 territories has suffered from factionalism (especially between nationalist and Islamic forces) as well as the inability to forge alliances with activists inside the Green Line, Jews and Arabs. Internal unity and cooperation across the Line are essential for building an anti-colonial movement. The diplomatic route pursued by the Palestinian Authority and the military route pursued by Hamas have failed. A strategy of popular mass struggle by civil society, communities and political forces is the only way forward, though it is still in its infancy.
- The international scene is beginning to show signs of eroding support for some aspects of the Israeli regime. It is not facing serious external military or political challenges yet but some expressions of weaknesses are evident. Among them, solidarity with the Palestinian struggle plays a role. The rise of civil society and alternative media counteracts, to some extent, the unconditional support given by western governments and media to Israel and its policies. There may be room for cautious optimism that the tide is beginning to turn.

What role do the concepts of settler colonialism and apartheid play in all that? They have contributed to solidarity politics and symbolic mobilisation on issues of land and race (such as Black Lives Matter, the Dakota access pipeline protests in the US and boycott campaigns in South Africa). They may serve to encourage thinking about colonialism and resistance, liberation movements and mass participation, alliances and campaigns. But, the direct impact on the ground has been limited and the potential for action is contradictory due to the built-in tension between the settler-colonial and apartheid paradigms.

The apartheid paradigm focuses on the historical formation of a unified, albeit highly unequal, society, which gives rise to internal conflict over rights and resources. The settler-colonial paradigm retains a core distinction between indigenous people and settlers, focusing on the need to redress historical dispossession. These two are not mutually exclusive, as shown by post-apartheid South Africa, but they move in different directions: on the one hand, seeking to overcome racial barriers imposed under apartheid by building political alliances; on the other hand, mobilising to reverse settler expansion. Labour, social equality and political inclusion are central to the anti-apartheid thrust. Land and indigenous consolidation are central to the anti-colonial thrust. By definition, reversing apartheid means a challenge to its group categories and boundaries, while reversing colonialism frequently means reinforcing them to enhance resistance.

Paradigms deal with ideal types, of course, rather than messy historical cases. South African apartheid was a product of racial industrialisation superimposed on colonial settlement and indigenous dispossession, whereas race realities in the US are a product of genocide, racial slavery, and cross-border expansion and migration. Race in the United Kingdom is a product of immigration against the background of the rise and demise of empire. The balance between land, labour, legal and cultural concerns is based on the concrete conditions of emergence and evolution of each case.

The challenge with Israel/Palestine is to come up with a new synthesis that builds on the core strengths of each approach but goes beyond them. With an all but dead peace process, Arab states that show ever-decreasing interest in the conflict, international solidarity movements that have little impact on the ground, and a sterile 'anti-normalisation' campaign that isolates and incapacitates Palestinian activists even further, what is the alternative?

Combining the two paradigms means a focus on forging internal Palestinian unity on each side of the Green Line as well as across it. The move to consolidate a united indigenous anti-colonial front would work best if it were based on common core demands combined with a recognition of the specific issues and conditions of struggle that face the different segments of the Palestinian people in their own terrains. An anti-apartheid campaign to build social and political alliances across the Jewish-Arab divide would complement this focus in order to overcome the regime's strategy of entrenching segregation (Hafrada). Its aim would be to pursue struggles together with progressive and socially marginalised Jewish constituencies, based on shared concerns.

Without doubt, getting Israeli Jews involved in a joint struggle with Palestinians (even on relatively 'apolitical' issues) is the most difficult part of this approach. The Israeli version of apartheid has been founded on the deployment of Jewish ethno-religious identity as a mechanism of exclusion. Social class-based concerns have been relegated to a secondary position to be pursued only within Jewish boundaries, not across them. There is no ready-made formula available to detach marginalised Jewish communities from their alliance with the nationalist-religious trend dominant in Israeli politics, but recognising the challenge is the first step towards a solution.

NOTE

1 See also http://jwtc.org.za/volume_3/ran_greenstein.htm (accessed 23 August 2018).

REFERENCES

Azoulay, A. and Ophir, A. 2012. *The One-State Condition: Occupation and Democracy in Israel/Palestine*. Stanford: Stanford University Press.
Davis, A. 2016. *Freedom Is a Constant Struggle: Ferguson, Palestine, and the Foundations of a Movement*. Chicago: Haymarket Books.
Bhandar, B. and Ziadah, R. 2016. 'Acts and omissions: Framing settler colonialism in Palestine Studies'. *Jadaliyya*, 14 January. Accessed 1 August 2017, http://www.jadaliyya.com/pages/index/23569/acts-and-omissions_framing-settler-colonialism-in-palestine-studies.
Gordon, N. 2008. *Israel's Occupation*. Berkeley: University of California Press.
Greenstein, R. 2015a. 'Where do the Mizrahim fit in?'. *Jadaliyya*, 25 August. Accessed 1 August 2017, http://www.jadaliyya.com/pages/index/22469/israel_where-do-the-mizrahim-fit-in-(part-1) and http://www.jadaliyya.com/pages/index/22470/israel_where-do-the-mizrahim-fit-in-(part-2).
Greenstein, R. 2015b. 'Israel–Palestine and the apartheid analogy: Critics, apologists and strategic lessons'. In *Israel and South Africa: The Many Faces of Apartheid*, edited by I. Pappé. London: Zed Books, pp. 335–362.
Greenstein, R. 2016. 'Settler colonialism: A useful category of historical analysis?' *Jadaliyya*, 6 June. Accessed 1 August 2017, http://www.jadaliyya.com/pages/index/24603/settler-colonialism_a-useful-category-of-historica.
Jiryis, S. 1976. *The Arabs in Israel*. New York: Monthly Review Press.
Khalidi, R. 2006. *The Iron Cage: The Story of the Palestinian Struggle for Statehood*. New York: Beacon Press.
Mada al-Carmel. 2007. The Haifa Declaration. Accessed 31 October 2018, http://mada-research.org/en/files/2007/09/haifaenglish.pdf.
Mamdani, M. 1996. *Citizen and Subject: Contemporary Africa and the Legacy of Late Colonialism*. Princeton: Princeton University Press.
Morris, B. 2004. *The Birth of the Palestinian Refugee Problem Revisited*. Cambridge: Cambridge University Press.
Pappé, I. 2006. *The Ethnic Cleansing of Palestine*. Oxford: Oneworld Publications.
Raz, A. 2012. *The Bride and the Dowry: Israel, Jordan and the Palestinians in the Aftermath of the June 1967 War*. New Haven: Yale University Press.
Shafir, G. 1989. *Land, Labor and the Origins of the Israeli-Palestinian Conflict, 1882–1914*. Berkeley: University of California Press.
Sternhell, Z. 1999. *The Founding Myths of Israel: Nationalism, Socialism, and the Making of the Jewish State*. Princeton: Princeton University Press.
UNGA (United Nations General Assembly). 1998. 'Rome Statute of the International Criminal Court' (Last amended 2010). Accessed 1 August 2017, https://www.icc-cpi.int/NR/rdonlyres/EA9AEFF7-5752-4F84-BE94-0A655EB30E16/0/Rome_Statute_English.pdf.
Winant, H. 2001. *The World is a Ghetto: Race and Democracy since World War II*. New York: Basic Books.

CHAPTER

5

THE ROLE OF RACISM IN THE EUROPEAN 'MIGRATION CRISIS': A HISTORICAL MATERIALIST PERSPECTIVE

Fabian Georgi

In the 2010s, racism in Europe is becoming more open, militant and aggressive, resulting in stark political polarisation. It is most visibly expressed by the protests and electoral successes of right-wing forces, which combine fierce nationalism with welfare chauvinism and a thinly veiled racism, directed primarily against refugees and migrant workers of colour, especially Muslims. In Germany, the weekly protests of the PEGIDA-movement (Patriotic Europeans Against the Islamisation of the Occident) and the rise of the new right-wing party Alternative for Germany (AfD), which gained 12.6 per cent in the federal election of September 2017, thereby becoming the third-strongest party in the Bundestag, has incited violence against migrants and people of colour, contributing to more than 1 000 attacks on refugee homes in 2015 (Deutsche Welle 2016; Friedrich and Kuhn 2017a). In the Austrian presidential election of December 2016, the far-right candidate Norbert Hofer was defeated only narrowly, gaining 46.2 per cent of the vote. In Britain, right-wing campaigners used vitriolic language to mobilise against 'foreigners' in order to win the Brexit referendum in June 2016.[1] In Poland and Hungary, governments are using anti-Muslim racism to legitimise an increasingly authoritarian rule (Edwards 2016). Although, in 2017, the Dutch anti-Muslim populist Geert Wilders and the French Front

National were defeated in the general elections in the Netherlands and in the presidential elections in France, their vitriolic mix of anti-European Union (EU) chauvinism and racism remains a potent, dynamic factor in the European balance of forces.[2] 'A spectre is haunting Europe. Not for the first time, right-wing racist movements are on the march across that continent' (Vieten and Poynting 2016: 533). This chapter focuses on one key aspect of these dynamics. Its central question is how the current dynamics of racism in Europe are interwoven with the struggles within and over the European migration and border regime.[3] It seems clear that the so-called European refugee or migration crisis of 2015/2016 – when, within one year, more than one million people claimed asylum in the EU – was exploited by right-wing populists to successfully push for a more repressive EU refugee policy. But how does the current conjuncture of racism shape the form and direction of the border regime? And conversely, how do the complex struggles of the European border regime influence the dynamics of racism? The chapter's main argument is that Europe's so-called migration crisis can be understood as a fierce and multi-sided transnational social conflict of which racism and racist forces are one part. In order to understand racism in Europe today, then, it is productive to analyse the social struggles and structural contradictions associated with migration and border regimes, which are shaped by racism and in turn shape racism's dynamic.

THE CRISIS OF THE EUROPEAN MIGRATION AND BORDER REGIME

Between summer 2015 and spring 2016, the European migration regime experienced an extraordinary dynamic. While between 2004 and 2011 the number of asylum claims in the EU had dropped to between 200 000 and 300 000 a year, more than 1.3 million people claimed asylum in 2015 and almost 1.2 million in 2016 (Eurostat 2017a, 2017b). Within the media and academia, this dynamic is commonly referred to as the European 'refugee crisis' or 'migration crisis', thereby declaring the refugees and migrants to be the problem. In rejection of this narrative, critical scholars in Germany speak more optimistically about the 'Long Summer of Migration' (see Hess et al. 2016),[4] a time when the ability of national and EU institutions to control and prevent the movements of people seeking safety, work and better lives, at long last, partially broke down. The Long Summer began with the maritime disaster of 19 April 2015 when about 800 people drowned near the Italian island of Lampedusa, creating shock and media attention throughout Europe. In the following months, the flight routes shifted east, from Italy to the Aegean Sea between Turkey and Greece. From about 18 000 in May and 31 000 in June, their number rose to 54 000 in July and nearly 108 000 in August (IOM 2017: 9). Partly, this shift resulted from the change of government in Greece in January 2015, where the left-wing Syriza government had reduced the illegal push-back of refugee boats, which the Greek coast guard had previously conducted (see Chick 2015). In late August, this dynamic came to a head. On 28 August, the bodies of 71 refugees were found in Austria. They had suffocated in a truck. In the following days, refugee protests in Budapest escalated. Thousands set off on the so-called March of Hope to reach Austria on foot, walking on Hungarian motorways (Santer and Wried 2017: 141). Then, on 3 September, images of the three-year-old Syrian refugee Aylan Kurdi were broadcast around the world. His dead body had washed up on a beach near the Turkish town of Bodrum.

In Germany, these events made a significant impact. On 31 August, pressured by left-wing forces, liberal media and the agency of migrant mobility, Chancellor Angela Merkel declared Germany ready to help hundreds of thousands of refugees: 'We can do it, and where something is in our way, it has to be overcome' (Merkel 2016; my translation). On 5 September, the Merkel government decided to partially open Germany's borders for refugees on the Balkan route.[5] Citizens in Germany and Austria welcomed refugees at train stations with applause, gifts and an outpouring of practical help (Blume et al. 2016; Karakayali and Kleist 2016). On 15 September, Merkel defended her policy in humanitarian terms: 'If we now have to start apologizing for showing a friendly face in response to emergency situations, then that's not my country' (cited in *Spiegel Online* 2015a). In the following weeks, even more people made their way to Greece: 147 000 did so in September and 211 000 in October (IOM 2017: 9). Leftist observers, who for years had criticised the inhumanity of EU asylum policy, were rubbing their eyes in disbelief. With Germany taking refugees in, other countries (with the notable exception of Hungary), from Greece over the West Balkans to Austria, decided to let refugees pass their territory. For a few weeks in the late summer and autumn of 2015, Europe's borders were open like never before since the fall of the Iron Curtain in 1989/1990. This period of almost euphoric solidarity with refugees was short-lived. After being blind-sided for a few weeks, conservative forces of the political centre and chauvinist actors from the right started an aggressive counter-offensive and demanded restrictive border controls and mass deportations (Friedrich and Kuhn 2017a; *Spiegel Online* 2015b).[6] Based on street protest, (social) media discourses and opinion polls, their strength in the relationship of forces increased and had institutional effects. As a result, the Long Summer of Migration can be seen to have ended in mid-November 2015 when terrorist attacks in Paris enabled right-wing forces to associate refugees with 'Islamic terrorism'. Shortly thereafter, Macedonia decided to let only people from Syria, Iraq and Afghanistan cross the border from Greece and continue to western Europe. In a probably too broad understanding, the Long Summer could be said to have ended only in March 2016 when the Aegean and Balkan route was effectively blocked by a deal between the EU and Turkey (Santer and Wriedt 2017: 145). Even though the number of arrivals dropped significantly, racist rhetoric among many Europeans did not disappear. Moreover, the number of border deaths in the Mediterranean in 2016 was even higher than in the previous years: 5 143, compared to 3 784 in 2015 and 3 283 in 2014. In 2017, 3 116 perished and from January to early June 2018 a further 785 people died (IOM 2018). The crisis of death and inhumanity in the European border regime is set to retain its normal mode of operation.

Despite this continuity, the Long Summer shifted the relationship of forces, resulting in an even more restrictive EU migration policy than was previously the case. In May 2015, shortly after the deadly shipwreck near Lampedusa, the European Commission (2015) published yet another policy initiative – the so-called European Agenda on Migration, under which it continued to push hard for repressive reforms of EU refugee policy. From May to July 2016, it released a whole set of (legislative) proposals, aiming to further tighten the EU border regime and externalise it to North Africa and beyond (European Commission 2017). By 2017, as noted by an Amnesty International report, these policies had turned the central Mediterranean route, through Libya towards Italy, into a ghastly death trap: 'This reckless European strategy is not just failing to deliver the desired outcome of stopping departures and preventing further loss of life, but is in fact exposing refugees and migrants to even greater risks at sea and, when intercepted, to disembarkation back in Libya, where they face horrific conditions in detention, torture and rape' (Amnesty International 2017: 5).

A RELATIONAL UNDERSTANDING OF BORDER REGIMES AND RACISM

What was the role of racism in shaping these dynamics? And how have the recent turbulences in the border regime influenced racism in Europe? My attempt to answer these questions starts from an approach I have developed elsewhere and termed historical materialist border regime analysis (Buckel et al. 2014; Georgi 2016). Its main contention is that the policies, institutions and state apparatuses of border regimes result from social and political struggles that are fundamentally shaped by a set of migration-related structural contradictions within a capitalist and racist world system. Migration policies and border regimes are, to speak through Nicos Poulantzas ([1978] 2000: 128), 'material condensations of relationships of forces' between manifold actors and social forces. The strength of this approach is that the categories, policies and institutions of these regimes (for example, illegality or residence categories) are de-naturalised and historicised.

This approach corresponds to a relational understanding of racism as presented by David Camfield, who interprets racism as distinct and historically shifting social relations of oppression, '*oppression of a multi-gender social collectivity on the basis of differences (not limited to those surrounding sexuality or impairment) that are treated as inherited and unchangeable*' (Camfield 2016: 47; emphasis in original). On this basis, several points can be made. First, the term 'oppression' stresses that the harm done as well as the benefits and privileges accrued by racism do not operate only on an individual level or in micro-situations. They affect social groups and are material and systemic, that is, they are connected to the way society as a whole reproduces itself. Second, by stressing that the social groups oppressed by racism are 'multi-gender' and are targeted *not* on the basis of sexuality or impairment, Camfield distinguishes racism from other relations of oppression, namely sexism, heteronormativity and ableism.

Third, to assert that 'racism is a social relation, not the mere ravings of racist subjects' (Balibar 1991b: 41) highlights that the racist essentialisation and hierarchisation of socially constructed differences is not always or primarily the result of explicit discourses, thought-out ideologies or conscious intentions. Instead, the essentialisation is (also) produced by *effectively treating* certain differences as inherited, unchangeable and inferior in order to reap the associated advantages of doing so. It is a product of *praxis*. Historically, 'racial ideology did not precede racist practices' (Camfield 2016: 43). Rather, racist ideologies emerge and reproduce to justify practices of oppression that have psychological, social and/or economic benefits for the privileged groups.[7] Or, as explained by Adam Kotsko (2017): '[B]eing a member of a certain race is not something inherent, it is something that is *done* to you. And it is done to you in order to mark you out as something that needs to be tamed, controlled, and subdued. It is a way of naturalizing an order of domination.' By giving praxis and action ontological precedence over ideas and language, it becomes understandable how racism reproduces in a historical situation where the notion of races is widely discredited – 'racism without races' (Balibar 1991a: 21) – and virtually nobody wants to be a racist – 'racism without racists' (Bonilla-Silva 2017). Still, even if 'a materialist method should prioritise human activity' (Camfield 2016: 43), it should not do so in a one-dimensional way. The challenge is to analyse the interplay between praxis and discourse. Racist essentialisation 'happens both in practice and in how racially-oppressed groups are presented ideologically; we should not limit ourselves to the latter' (Camfield 2016: 47).

Fourth, to interpret racism as a distinct social relation of oppression means that, although it is often highly functional for the regulation of capitalist contradictions, it is not reducible to class or capitalist relations of production. 'Although processes of racialization are always embedded in other forms of hierarchy, they acquire autonomy and have independent social effects' (Bonilla-Silva 2001: 37). To see racism as a constantly contested social relation also follows Stuart Hall's (1980: 336) argument that there are only ever 'historically-specific racisms' shaped and shifted by social struggles and numerous facets of historical context. One might say, then, that there is never 'pure racism'. There is only ever an intersectional racism, intertwined with and formed by the dynamic interdependence with other relations of oppression. 'Racism is no fixed ideological pattern, instead it changes its character, its arguments, its objects, its appearance, its aims, its forms of organisation. In this sense, we can only analyse conjunctures of racism in history' (Bojadžijev 2006; my translation). Despite this fluidity, there are of course historical continuities. In Germany and Austria, for example, the social imagery of current racist discourses is infused with the old ontology of the German *Volk*, understood not only as a cultural and linguistic group, but, ultimately, as a biological 'community of blood' (*Blutsgemeinschaft*) to which 'outsiders' can never truly belong (see Mense 2017). Thus, historical racisms are characterised by both discontinuities and the persistence of key aspects.

One challenge in analysing the current conjuncture of racism with regard to the European border regime, then, is to understand how racist power relationships intersect with other relations of oppression. Another is how to explain the dynamics of racism as the result of specific social conflicts (see Bonilla-Silva 2001: 45). This means, for example, that the struggles of refugees or communities of colour have to be understood as key actors because they force racism to adapt: '[I]n order to interpret the way racism fluctuate[s] . . . one must take account of the groups against whom it is aimed and their actions and reactions' (Balibar 1991b: 41). Still, neither border regimes nor the conjunctures of racism are driven alone or primarily by the groups oppressed by them – nor should they be portrayed in this way. Instead, in my view, they have to be reconstructed as the complex conflicts they are.[8] These conflicts are structurally conditioned and fought out by a whole range of different social forces, including the movements of refugees and migrant workers, communities of colour, the protests of liberal institutions and left-wing activists, the ambivalent position of trade unions and welfare organisations, the pressure of different capital factions, and the chauvinist reactions of nationalist and racist forces. Thus, if we want to understand the current crisis of the European border regime and the role of racism within it, we have to analyse the struggles between these and other forces and reconstruct their shifting alliances, political offensives and defensive manoeuvres.

DYNAMICS OF RACISM IN THE EUROPEAN BORDER REGIME

On the defensive I: Counter-reaction to post-migrant societies

Starting out on such an analysis, the current resurgence of racism in Europe can be interpreted as a counter-reaction to a series of political defeats inflicted on chauvinist forces in Europe. Racism and racist forces are on the defensive in at least two respects. First, in the previous decades, anti-racist forces, migrant communities and communities of colour have made substantial political, social and cultural gains, thereby creating what has been termed 'post-migrant societies' (Foroutan 2015). Compared to the 1990s, European societies have become more ethnically and culturally diverse as a result of movements and struggles of migration. The share of people of colour and persons whose families have often complex migration histories has increased in almost all European countries, especially within cities (see IOM 2015). Furthermore, as a result of anti-racist struggles, the acceptance of these processes has unequally spread to larger sections of European societies, being affirmed not only by the political left, but, at least in some countries, by the centre-right. Together with a higher visibility and recognition of people of colour in business, politics, media, culture and sports, has gone a stronger rejection of the old-style, open racism still prevalent in the 1980s and early 1990s. 'More frequent and more successful than ever before, (former) immigrants and their descendants demand equal participation and force new opportunities to reject and legally challenge discrimination and racist exclusions' (Espahangizi et al. 2016: 11; my translation). Thus, despite constant political push-back, one example being assimilationist discourses in Germany that demand immigrants and their descendants should follow an allegedly existing German *Leitkultur* or 'leading culture' (cf. Pautz 2005), anti-racist struggles did make actual strides forward.

On a theoretical level, these dynamics can be interpreted as results of a relational autonomy of migration (Bojadžijev and Karakayali 2010). A key contention of this concept is that, as a tendency, human beings do not passively accept situations, living conditions or social relations they perceive as negative. Instead, they struggle, either at their present localities, or by using escape options: they move, leave, abscond, desert, flee or emigrate to achieve a better life elsewhere (see Papadopoulos, Stephenson and Tsianos 2008). Within the European border regime, the practices of refugee and migrant communities constitute a powerful force to which racist actors and migration controls are constantly forced to react. The Long Summer of Migration is a case in point. After a quarter century in which the EU attempted to integrate and perfect its border controls, the movements of migration pushed this regime into its gravest crisis so far. Despite massive EU attempts to prevent this and despite the fierce resistance of nationalist and racist forces, the number of asylum claims in the EU rose to record highs, many of them made by people of colour and Muslims, who are especially targeted by European racism.[9]

From a materialist perspective, these movements of refugees, (illegalised) migrant workers and their families can be understood as strategies with which people from the European periphery and the global South tend to react to the creative destruction inflicted on their countries of origin by processes of 'accumulation by dispossession' and the multi-dimensional crises of contemporary capitalism, among them a severe overaccumulation of capital on a world scale, crises of (wage) labour, of food sovereignty and climate change. These social, economic and ecological problems often escalate into political crises that turn violent and erupt into uprisings and civil wars, which then frequently have their own ethnicised and religious dynamics. The Arab Spring and its consequences are obvious examples (see Heydarian 2014; Parenti 2012).

These processes point to two crucial insights: first, the bitter sense of defeat articulated by the European far-right, who lament the emergence and increasing acceptance of culturally diverse post-migrant societies in Europe, is, *from their perspective*, actually justified. The gains made by the relational autonomy of migration and anti-racist struggles, since the 1990s, have weakened racist forces. Their current resurgence is a backlash to these successes. Second, given the multiple crisis tendencies of global capitalism and the inability of the EU to effectively control the escape practices with which people react to such crises, it becomes clear that right-wing 'racial projects' (Winant 2001) are unlikely to succeed because they have strong structural tendencies against them.

On the defensive II: A shifting migration management compromise

Besides suffering defeats as a result of the struggles of migration, right-wing racist forces are on the defensive in a second respect. According to my analysis, the implicit coalition between right-wing conservative and neoliberal forces that has underpinned the hegemonic compromise of an EU 'migration management', since the late 1990s, has increasingly frayed and partially broken down. Instead, since around 2010, neoliberal actors have aligned their rhetoric closer with the migration policy of liberal and centre-left forces, pushing a positive and rights-based discourse on migration and thereby putting right-wing racist forces on the defensive.

In the 2000s, the migration management concept dominated much of international and European migration policy (Georgi 2010: 55). From a historical materialist perspective, migration management can be understood as a political project with which neoliberal actors tried to subordinate migration and refugee policy – like virtually all other policy fields – under the imperatives of competitiveness, profits and economic growth. Representatives of European industry and service capital, and their ideological allies in civil society and (international) state apparatuses, have relentlessly tried to 'se[t] societies on a course to reap the positive economic and social benefits that migration can continue to offer' (IOM 1993: 2). From their perspective, migration is positive as long as it is economically beneficial to the dominant forces of the immigration countries. Led by the European Commission (2000), EU migration policy became increasingly seen as a strategy to solve specific labour problems, be it farming labour from Morocco in Spain or Brazilian IT workers in the United Kingdom.

Since the 1990s, the main resistance against such neoliberal strategies has come from those large segments of the European population who – motivated by a mix of nationalism, welfare chauvinism and racism – oppose immigration, especially of people of colour. Neoliberal experts time and again have expressed their frustrations with this 'irrational' resistance. For example, in 2011 a representative of the International Organization for Migration (IOM) complained: 'Human capital had the potential to be one of the key resources of exchange for global economic growth and prosperity. However, in reality, attitudes remained largely ambivalent towards migration' (IOM 2012: 14). The migration management concept was a strategic attempt by neoliberal actors to incorporate these chauvinist forces into a compromise. The migration of refugees and migrant workers who were deemed not to be economically beneficial, or to be a security risk, were to be so restrictively and effectively controlled that Europe's anti-immigration electorates could be convinced to accept a 'regulated openness' (Ghosh 2000: 25) for the select groups who were 'truly needed' in the labour market.

This strategy had mixed results. While EU border and refugee policy became in fact evermore restrictive, neoliberal forces never fully succeeded in achieving the liberal labour immigration policy they desired. The failure of the EU Blue Card directive, passed in 2009, to attract a substantial number of 'highly qualified migrants' into the EU, illustrates this (Bellini 2016). This failure of neoliberal forces to overcome the resistance of anti-immigration electorates, in my analysis, led some neoliberal actors to change their approach and follow a strategy that Nancy Fraser (2017) has described as 'progressive neoliberalism'. Instead of primarily pushing for evermore restrictive controls, they now attempted to convince hostile electorates with a new, meritocratic rhetoric of diversity and multiculturalism, stressing economic gains and other positive effects of migration. For example, in 2012, the director general of the IOM, William Lacy Swing (2012: 26), expressed this strategy: '[I]t would be important to actively support . . . intensive public information and public education efforts on the part of all industrialized countries to prepare their populations for the substantial implications that a growing mobile population holds for destination countries.'

The new liberal elements of German migration policy in 2015 can be interpreted as an expression of this same reorientation, evidenced by the significant support some factions of German capital gave to the partial opening of Germany's borders. In September 2015, more than 60 per cent of German managers believed their companies could profit from a fast integration of the refugees.[10] The president of the Federation of German Industries, Ulrich Grillo, defended Merkel's policy: 'We have a demographic problem in the future. That is, we have a shortage of labour. This shortage can be reduced' (Grillo 2015; my translation). In January 2016, the president of the Confederation of German Employers' Associations, Ingo Kramer, made it clear that German capital was opposed to right-wing demands for border closures because it threatened the free circulation of goods, services and labour in the EU internal market, a key condition for profits: 'The closing of borders is the opposite of what has made this nation great. What is accepted here as collateral damage in order to appease the *Stammtisch* is ludicrous.'[11] The strategy to circumvent the conservative blockade against increased immigration by a legally dubious opening of the border outraged racist forces. It was perceived by them as a bitter political defeat. The current resurgence of racism in Europe started, therefore, as a backlash first to the successes of anti-racist struggles and communities of colour that gave rise to post-migrant societies in Europe, and, second, to an at least temporary and partial reorientation of neoliberal capital factions.

On the offensive: Opportunities for racist mobilisations

To argue that racist forces in Europe are actually on the defensive begs the question of why there is currently a clear resurgence of racism in Europe. Why did so many Europeans react in chauvinist ways to the increased arrivals of refugees and migrants? And in what sense is this chauvinism driven by racism? In my view, the persistence of racism and its current conjuncture in Europe can be explained if we ask what 'problems' racism 'solves' for individuals and societies and why people, therefore, continue to reproduce it through their actions. A first hint is given by Eduardo Bonilla-Silva: 'Racial structures remain in place for the same reasons that other structures do. Since actors racialised as 'white' – or as members of the dominant race – receive material benefits from the racial order, they struggle (or passively receive the manifold wages of whiteness) to maintain their privileges' (cited in Camfield 2016: 57).

Thus, the task is to ask which benefits, if indeed any, racism has for *white* Europeans in the current context. The main argument of the following section is that the counter-mobilisations of right-wing racist actors occurs in a historical situation in which large segments of the *white* European working and middle classes experience the negative effects of a multi-dimensional crisis of neoliberal capitalism. Not since the global financial crisis of 2008/2009 and its aftermath (the Eurozone crisis, secular stagnation) have large parts of the European populations faced unemployment or underemployment with precarious, low-wage jobs, experienced justified fears, or have actual experience of social descent and poverty, especially in old age, and are excluded from adequate housing, health and child care and other social services. While those who have no work, or not enough of it, suffer from social stigmatisation and workfare regimes, many who do have jobs are subjected to high-pressure competition, unpaid overtime and stress. Even in countries where official unemployment statistics are relatively low (Germany, Denmark, the Netherlands), widespread precarity produces feelings of frustration and powerlessness, resulting in a rise of mental illness, including anxiety and depression. My hypothesis is, then, that in this situation, racist and nationalist mechanisms intersect to fulfil psychological, political and economic functions for large parts of the European populations. The analytical challenge is to dissect these mechanisms.

First, the persistence of racism and its current resurgence is partially based on the psychological functions it fulfils for many individuals and groups whose lives are dominated by the frustrations experienced as the result of capitalist dynamics and other relations of oppression. The argument was first made by Theodor W. Adorno et al. ([1950] 1993) in their classic study *The Authoritarian Personality*. Under capitalist conditions, many individuals, inevitably, suffer from an 'ego weakness', resulting from the denial of basic needs and emotional desires – and the inability to change these conditions. Confronted with the degradations of capitalist life, many people compensate these frustrations through an aggressive collective narcissism, directed against minority groups. Racism enables them to feel superior while looking down on groups racialised in an inferior position. Moreover, racism can offer psychological benefits of world explanation and of scapegoating: if the real reasons for narcissistic insults, frustrated hopes and damaged lives are beyond comprehension or power to change, it makes psychological sense to project the resulting resentments to inferior groups (see Hall 2012). The upsurge of anti-Muslim racism and its conspiracy theories, eerily similar to late nineteenth-century anti-Semitism, are a case in point (Schiffer and Wagner 2011). Crucially, not all people subjected to the heteronomy of capitalist and other relations of oppression react in this pathological way. Instead, different authoritarian personality types – who are themselves a product of historical conditions – are more likely to use racism to fulfil their psychological needs. Today, numerous studies use updated versions of Adorno's approach to explain the upsurge of racism in Europe and beyond (Cornelis and Van Hiel 2015; Gordon 2016).

A second reason why racism persists and currently surges in Europe is that *white* Europeans enjoy real material privileges from their superior position in the racist hierarchy and therefore tend either to actively defend these privileges or resist political measures that would undermine them. The advantages of racism are not illusions. 'Preferential access to information about job openings, treatment in competition for employment, jobs with better pay and conditions, and promotion are not imaginary. Nor is preferential treatment by landlords, service providers, business owners and the police' (Camfield 2016: 55; see also Bonilla-Silva 2001: 37). In the current social and economic crisis in Europe, many *white* Europeans perceive refugees and migrants as increased competition and threat to their social privileges. Thus, the defence of privileges incurred from a superior position in racist and nationalist hierarchies does have a certain rationality. The key contribution of a materialist perspective, however, is to contextualise these racist privileges in the economic and social order. Such an analysis can start with Étienne Balibar's (1991c: 92) concept of the 'national-social state'. Balibar argues that the European welfare states established in the post-war decades combined nationalism with social policy in order to regulate, that is, to temporarily pacify and contain the class struggles and economic crises that had destabilised Europe in the first half of the twentieth century. The welfare state became the central condition for capitalist hegemony in Europe. However, the social rights granted by these welfare states were limited by citizenship, thereby 'nationalising' the European working classes and tying them to the success of 'their' nation-state in the global competition. Crucially, these national-social states depend for their political and economic stability on the hierarchised exclusion of non-citizens. If borders were open and all newcomers were to receive full social rights, at least under neoliberal conditions, the viability of the European welfare models, a key mechanism of hegemony, would be threatened. Thus, the social chauvinism directed by European populations against mass immigration has a rational core. In the current situation of a multiplicity of European crises, this latent chauvinism intensifies. European populations try to defend their precarious social rights by struggling for new 'racial projects' and a nationalist re-regulation of capitalism.

This drive towards exclusion, facilitated by the national-social state, however, does not remain on the level of formal civic statutes, that is nationality or citizenship. Almost inevitably, it takes on a racist character that is connected to imperialism. From the start, European colonialism and imperialism were interwoven with racism. People of colour (and certain *white* populations) became associated with imperialised territories – and thereby located in inferior positions on racist hierarchies that were used to justify and defend imperialist exploitation. Importantly, these old hierarchies still strongly resemble the imperialist hierarchies of the present. Imperialism today creates 'a worldwide pattern of employment discrimination, violence, morbidity, impoverishment, pollution, and unequal exchange' and functions as 'a global system of social stratification' that 'correlates very well with racial criteria' (Winant, cited in Camfield 2016: 58). Among other factors, the exacerbation of these hierarchies in the last decades results from cold war interventions, the neoliberal regulation of transnational capitalism and climate change. 'None of these recent processes are explicitly racialised. Yet they build on and entrench an already racialised structural distribution of property and economic power, locally and globally, which is the product of the long history of global racialised dispossession' (Jones 2008: 924; see also Camfield 2016: 59). Even as the exclusionary practices of the European border regime are no longer openly justified by racist ideologies (and instead are officially based on citizenship), this exclusion is still partially driven by, relies on and reproduces racism. Thus, when EU citizens today implicitly support or openly demand a restrictive expansion of the European border regime to defend their national-social privileges, they inevitably do so in a strongly racialised context, which they then reproduce. *This* is the structural racism of the European border regime.

The current conjuncture: A national-social and neoliberal racism

Based on the analysis so far, it is now possible to summarise some key elements of the current conjuncture of racism in Europe. The European 'refugee crisis' or 'migration crisis' of 2015/2016 provided a crucial opportunity structure for a resurgence of right-wing racist forces and for the spread of racist discourses to large sections of European populations, which normally occupy the political centre ground (see Decker, Kiess and Brähler 2016). Partially, this resurgence was a counter-reaction to a series of political defeats that chauvinist forces suffered through the emergence of post-migrant societies and the more liberal rhetoric of capital factions on EU migration policy. Coming out of a defensive position, right-wing populists and large segments of the European populations used racist mechanisms to incur psychological benefits and defend their material privileges in a situation of social and economic crisis.

Still, the growing strength of racist actors in the European relationship of forces is not the only reason why the European border regime has become more restrictive since 2015. As argued above, it is not a 'pure racism' but one that specifically intersects with the dynamics of other relations of oppression. Thus, racism is almost indistinguishably intertwined with fierce (anti-EU) nationalism and a social welfare chauvinism that rejects immigration because it is seen as a danger to already precarious welfare states. Moreover, racist hierarchies in Europe are modified by the neoliberal profit rationality. The attempts of capital to utilise and exploit migrant labour result in a form of 'neoliberal racism' that modifies racist hierarchies along perceived economic utility, while at the same time resisting effective anti-racist reforms. As Camfield (2016: 61) points out, there is 'widespread opposition of capitalists and their political advocates to measures that would substantially improve the bargaining power of racially oppressed workers in labour markets, such as granting citizenship or permanent-resident status to non-status migrants and those with temporary residency rights and instituting effective anti-racist reforms to employment law'. A key reason for this ambivalence of European capital towards racism and a restrictive border regime is that capitalists continue to reap the 'profits of racism' (Camfield 2016: 59). Workers who are racially discriminated against can be forced to work harder for less. Racism still often functions as a 'magic formula' (Wallerstein 1991: 33), allowing capitalists to mobilise new (immigrant) workers while forestalling resistance of the existing labour force through the disenfranchisement of the newcomers.

Thus, only on a superficial level can the resurgence of racism in Europe be understood as a reaction to increased immigration. Instead, it needs to be interpreted as one element of a much broader dynamic. Right-wing factions from the French Front National to the Alternative for Germany have created an authoritarian, ultra-conservative and deeply chauvinistic challenge to the multi-dimensional crisis of European neoliberalism whose mantra of 'austerity forever' has lost almost all of its hegemonic appeal. Not unlike in the 1930s, the European Left is faced with the double challenge to overcome a crisis-ridden liberal capitalist formation while at the same time stopping a reactionary, even fascist, solution to the crisis.

CONCLUSION

What is to be done? How can anti-racist movements and the European left meet this double challenge, push racist forces back and, if abolishing racism seems like a far-fetched goal under present conditions, at least stop its current offensive? In this concluding section, I point to three anti-racist strategies that target today's national-social and neoliberal racism.

The first attack needs to be on racism directly. Because racism is a social relation that encompasses whole societies and a racist world system, this attack has to be directed at proximate targets. These are racist discourses, ideologies, everyday practices and right-wing groups and parties but also the exponents of racism from the political centre. A critical self-reflection of *white* Europeans on their racist knowledge and privileges is one key part of this, practical anti-fascism is another. The Long Summer of Migration in Europe, especially in Germany, has shown that such efforts are not in vain. Despite its profound ambivalences, the organic 'Welcome Culture' created by countless citizens in, often paternalistic, support of refugees can be seen as a dialectical step in the right direction. A more radical push-back against racism could be based on the egalitarian principles inherent in radical interpretation of human rights, visions of a post-Eurocentric world and in the rich history of internationalism.

The second attack, in my view, should be inspired by this internationalist tradition. It has to be directed against racism's close and sometimes almost indistinguishable ally, *nationalism*. While at least on a rhetorical level, racism is almost universally rejected, this is not true for the basic tenets of nationalism. The idea of national communities where one owes more solidarity to one's compatriots than to foreigners, the idea that certain people are not part of 'our society' and are seen as 'refugees' and 'migrants' and, therefore, can be excluded, hierarchised and deported, is very much alive. This nationalist common sense has been questioned by the No Border movement and an internationalist left in Europe that has become, in part, explicitly *anti-national*. It does not take much today to proclaim oneself in opposition to racism. To directly attack nationalism is more difficult but may be politically more productive. Anti-racism has to be internationalist. Common interests and strategies have to be created among 'old' and 'new' Europeans in order to overcome nationalist and imperialist divisions and struggle together.

Finally, from a Marxist perspective, it is clear that in order to push racism back or even to abolish it, it is necessary to overcome the social and economic conditions to which racism is not reducible but which make its recurrent resurgences all too likely. Today, the zombie-like continuity of neoliberalism in Europe, despite all its failures and lack of hegemonic support, creates widespread stress, anxiety, social exclusion and bitter competition over jobs and public resources. It is an ideal breeding ground for racism. To challenge the conflagration of neoliberalism, imperialism and racism, a 'new class politics' is necessary, a politics that clarifies 'where and how the specific experiences of workers based on gender, race, citizenship, and other factors converge. It must reveal the overlapping interests of workers as members of the class. This makes common struggles possible' (Friedrich and Kuhn 2017b). Still, to overcome neoliberalism, even to abolish the capitalist mode of reproduction and distribution, would be no guarantee that racism would disappear. Its continuing persistence would depend, among other factors, on which mode of production would replace capitalism and the concrete dynamics of such a postcapitalist formation. Racism is a historical phenomenon. Therefore, there could be historical conditions under which it might be abolished. However, as long as capitalism persists it seems highly unlikely that these conditions will ever be met.

NOTES

1. 'Nigel Farage's anti-migrant poster reported to police', *The Guardian*, 16 June 2016, http://www.theguardian.com/politics/2016/jun/16/nigel-farage-defends-ukip-breaking-point-poster-queue-of-migrants (accessed 9 August 2017).
2. R. Ramesh, 'Geert Wilders was beaten, but at the cost of fuelling racism in the Netherlands', *The Guardian*, 17 March 2017, https://www.theguardian.com/commentisfree/2017/mar/17/geert-wilders-racism-netherlands-far-right (accessed 9 August 2017).
3. I am aware that as a person (read as a *white* male) I am not able to as fully or equally understand racism as people negatively affected by it. For helpful comments and criticism on this chapter, I thank Lars Bretthauer, Sebastian Friedrich, John Kannankulam, Manjiri Palicha, Vishwas Satgar, Matti Traußneck and all participants of the Democratic Marxism workshop in Johannesburg in November 2016.
4. The 'Long Summer of Migration' is a word-play on 'The Short Summer of Anarchy', based on the 1972 novel on the Spanish Civil War by the German author Hans Magnus Enzensberger.

5   The opening was only partial because the visa regime and 'carrier sanctions' still prevented refugees from entering the EU safely and legally by plane or ferry. For a detailed reconstruction, see Blume et al. (2016).
6   See also 'Migrant influx may give Europe's far right a lift', *New York Times*, 7 September 2015, https://www.nytimes.com/2015/09/08/world/europe/right-wing-european-parties-may-benefit-from-migrant-crisis.html?_r=0 (accessed 9 August 2017).
7   Moreover, to perceive discourses or ideologies as racism's ontological centres runs the risk of analysing it in isolation from context or, even implicitly, as a functional aspect of the super-structure that will dissolve once the capitalist base has been historically superseded (see Camfield 2016: 49).
8   This argument refers to a controversy within German-language critical migration studies where some authors argue, from a post-operaist perspective, that 'it should be the task of critical migration and border regime research to stress those moments in which the movements of migration, together with solidarity, transnational, social and political movements, elude attempts to control and regulate them' (Hess et al. 2016: 18; my translation). While this is surely important, I am concerned that a critical research strategy that narrows its focus in this way is simplifying the societal struggles and structural dynamics associated with migration and border regimes, and, *therefore*, does not realise its full potential to contribute to the kind of complex and fundamental analysis of society that is necessary for its emancipatory transformation.
9   In 2015, most of them came from the war-torn states of Syria (363 000), Afghanistan (178 000) and Iraq (122 000), but significant numbers arrived from crisis-ridden countries in Africa and West and South Asia, among them Pakistan (46 000), Eritrea (33 000), Nigeria (30 000) and Iran (25 000) (Eurostat 2016: 3).
10 See 'Flüchtlinge: Sie arbeiten am nächsten Wirtschaftswunder', *Süddeutsche Zeitung*, 24 September 2015, http://www.sueddeutsche.de/wirtschaft/fluechtlinge-sie-arbeiten-am-naechsten-wunder-1.2661310 (accessed 9 August 2017).
11 *Stammtisch*: literally, the regulars' table at a pub; figuratively, populist, racist, small-minded people. Cited in 'Was Grenzkontrollen für die Wirtschaft bedeuten', *Süddeutsche Zeitung*, 22 January 2016, http://www.sueddeutsche.de/wirtschaft/fluechtlinge-und-die-eu-ein-rueckfall-in-die-er-jahre-1.2827966 (accessed 9 August 2017, my translation). On the support of German capital for a liberal refugee policy, see also their campaign website at http://www.wir-zusammen.de/.

REFERENCES

Adorno, T.W., Frenkel-Brunswik, E., Levinson, D. and Sanford, N. [1950] 1993. *The Authoritarian Personality*. New York: W.W. Norton & Company.
Amnesty International. 2017. 'A perfect storm: The failure of European policies in the central Mediterranean'. Accessed 9 August 2017, https://www.amnesty.org/download/Documents/EUR0366552017ENGLISH.PDF.
Balibar, E. 1991a. 'Is there a "neo-racism"?' In *Race, Nation, Class: Ambiguous Identities*, edited by E. Balibar and I. Wallerstein. London and New York: Verso, pp. 17–28.
Balibar, E. 1991b. 'Racism and nationalism'. In *Race, Nation, Class: Ambiguous Identities*, edited by E. Balibar and I. Wallerstein. London and New York: Verso, pp. 37–68.

Balibar, E. 1991c. 'The nation-form: History and ideology'. In *Race, Nation, Class: Ambiguous Identities*, edited by E. Balibar and I. Wallerstein. London and New York: Verso, pp. 86–106.

Bellini, S. 2016. *EU Blue Card: A promising tool among labour migration policies? A comparative analysis of selected countries*. Working Paper No. 76/2016. Berlin: Institute for International Political Economy. Accessed 9 August 2017, https://www.econstor.eu/bitstream/10419/148414/1/873980875.pdf.

Blume, G., Brost, M., Hildebrandt, T., Hock, A., Klormann, S., Köckritz, A., Krupa, M., Lau, M., Von Randow, G., Theile, M., Thumann, M. and Wefing, H. 2016. 'The night Germany lost control', *Zeit.de*, 30 September 2016. Accessed 9 August 2017, http://www.zeit.de/gesellschaft/2016-08/refugees-open-border-policy-september-2015-angela-merkel/komplettansicht.

Bojadžijev, M. 2006. 'Migration und Kämpfe'. *Jungle World*, 22 November. Accessed 9 August 2017, https://jungle.world/artikel/2006/47/migration-und-kaempfe.

Bojadžijev, M. and Karakayali, S. 2010. 'Recuperating the sideshows of capitalism: The autonomy of migration today', *e-flux journal* 17, June. Accessed 9 August 2017, http://www.e-flux.com/journal/recuperating-the-sideshows-of-capitalism-the-autonomy-of-migration-today/.

Bonilla-Silva, E. 2001. *White Supremacy and Racism in the Post-Civil Rights Era*. Boulder, CO and London: Lynne Rienner Publishers.

Bonilla-Silva, E. 2017. *Racism Without Racists: Color-blind Racism and the Persistence of Racial Inequality in America* (fifth edition). London: Rowman & Littlefield.

Buckel, S., Georgi, F., Kannankulam, J. and Wissel, J. 2014. 'Theorie, Methoden und Analysen kritischer Europaforschung'. In *Kämpfe um Migrationspolitik*, edited by Forschungsgruppe Staatsprojekt Europa. Bielefeld: Transcript.

Camfield, D. 2016. 'Elements of a historical-materialist theory of racism', *Historical Materialism*, 24 (1): 31–70.

Chick, K. 2015. 'Seeking refuge: Greece, long hostile to migrants, turns hospitable under Syriza', *Christian Science Monitor*, 24 June 2015. Accessed 9 August 2017, https://www.csmonitor.com/World/Europe/2015/0624/Seeking-Refuge-Greece-long-hostile-to-migrants-turns-hospitable-under-Syriza.

Cornelis, I. and Van Hiel, A. 2015. 'Extreme-right voting in western Europe: The role of social-cultural and antiegalitarian attitudes', *Political Psychology*, 36 (6): 749–760.

Decker, O., Kiess, J. and Brähler, E. (eds). 2016. *Die enthemmte Mitte: Autoritäre und rechtsextreme Einstellung in Deutschland*. Gießen: Psychosozial Verlag.

Deutsche Welle. 2016. 'Report: Five times more attacks on refugee homes in Germany in 2015', 29 January 2016. Accessed 9 August 2017, http://www.dw.com/en/report-five-times-more-attacks-on-refugee-homes-in-germany-in-2015/a-19011109.

Edwards, M. 2016. 'Rethinking eastern European racism'. *OpenDemocracy.net*, 2 March 2016. Accessed 9 August 2017, https://www.opendemocracy.net/can-europe-make-it/maxim-edwards/rethinking-eastern-european-racism.

Espahangizi, K., Hess, S., Karakayali, J., Kasparek, B., Pagano, S., Rodatz, M. and Tsianos, V. 2016. 'Rassismus in der postmigrantischen Gesellschaft: Zur Einleitung', *Movements: Journal for Critical Migration and Border Regime Studies*, 2 (1): 9–23.

European Commission. 2000. 'On a community immigration policy', 22 November 2000. Accessed 9 August 2017, http://eur-lex.europa.eu/LexUriServ/LexUriServ.do?uri=COM:2000:0757:FIN:EN:PDF.
European Commission. 2015. 'A European agenda on migration'. 13 May 2015. Accessed 9 August 2017, https://ec.europa.eu/home-affairs/sites/homeaffairs/files/what-we-do/policies/european-agenda-migration/background-information/docs/communication_on_the_european_agenda_on_migration_en.pdf.
European Commission. 2017. 'European agenda on migration: Legislative documents'. Accessed 9 August 2017, https://ec.europa.eu/home-affairs/what-we-do/policies/european-agenda-migration/proposal-implementation-package_en.
Eurostat. 2016. 'Asylum in the EU member states', Eurostat news release 44/2016, 4 March 2016. Accessed 9 August 2017, http://ec.europa.eu/eurostat/documents/2995521/7203832/3-04032016-AP-EN.pdf/790eba01-381c-4163-bcd2-a54959b99ed6.
Eurostat. 2017a. 'Asylum applicants by citizenship till 2007 annual data'. Accessed 9 August 2017, http://ec.europa.eu/eurostat/web/products-datasets/-/migr_asyctz.
Eurostat. 2017b. 'Asylum and first time asylum applicants by citizenship, age and sex annual aggregated data (rounded)'. Accessed 9 August 2017, http://ec.europa.eu/eurostat/en/web/products-datasets/-/MIGR_ASYAPPCTZA.
Foroutan, N. 2015. 'Unity in diversity: Integration in a post-migrant society'. Accessed 9 August 2017, http://www.bpb.de/gesellschaft/migration/kurzdossiers/205290/integration-in-a-post-migrant-society.
Fraser, N. 2017. 'The end of progressive neoliberalism'. *Dissent*, 2 January. Accessed 9 August 2017, https://www.dissentmagazine.org/online_articles/progressive-neoliberalism-reactionary-populism-nancy-fraser.
Friedrich, S. and Kuhn, G. 2017a. 'Between capital and Volk'. *Jacobin*, 29 June 2017. Accessed 10 August 2017, https://www.jacobinmag.com/2017/06/germany-afd-cdu-immigrants-merkel-xenophobia-neoliberalism.
Friedrich, S. and Kuhn, G. 2017b. 'A new class politics'. *Counter-Punch*, 20 July. Accessed 10 August 2017, https://www.counterpunch.org/2017/07/20/94236/#_ftnref2.
Georgi, F. 2010. 'For the benefit of some: The International Organization for Migration and its global migration management'. In *The Politics of International Migration Management*, edited by M. Geiger and A. Pécoud. Basingstoke: Palgrave Macmillan, pp. 45–72.
Georgi, F. 2016. 'Widersprüche im langen Sommer der Migration: Ansätze einer materialistischen Grenzregimeanalyse', *Prokla* 46 (2): 183–203.
Ghosh, B. 2000. 'Towards a new international regime for the orderly movement of people'. In *Managing Migration: Time for a New International Regime?* edited by B. Ghosh. New York: Oxford University Press, pp. 6–26.
Gordon, P.E. 2016. 'The authoritarian personality revisited: Reading Adorno in the age of Trump'. *boundary2*. Accessed 9 August 2017, http://boundary2.dukejournals.org/content/44/2/31.full.pdf+html?sid=c1c3109c-1dd1-4efc-9611-2f41986494eb.
Grillo, U. 2015. 'Es gibt Chancen, es gibt Risiken'. *Deutschlandfunk*, 3 November. Accessed 9 August 2017, http://www.deutschlandfunk.de/bdi-chef-grillo-zur-fluechtlingssituation-es-gibt-chancen.694.de.html?dram:article_id=335763.
Hall, R.E. 2012. 'Racism in the twenty-first century: An authoritarian political analysis', *International Review of Sociology*, 22 (3): 575–583.

Hall, S. 1980. 'Race, articulation and societies structured in dominance'. In UNESCO, *Sociological Theories: Race and Colonialism*. Paris: UNESCO, pp. 305–345.

Hess, S., Kasparek, B., Kron, S., Rodatz, M., Schwertl, M. and Sontowski, S. 2016. 'Der lange Sommer der Migration: Krise, Rekonstitution und ungewisse Zukunft des Europäischen Grenzregimes'. In *Der lange Sommer der Migratio: Grenzregime III*, edited by S. Hess, B. Kasparek, S. Kron, M. Rodatz, M. Schwertl and S. Sontowski. Berlin and Hamburg: Assoziation A, pp. 6–24.

Heydarian, R.J. 2014. *How Capitalism Failed the Arab World: The Economic Roots and Precarious Future of Middle East Uprisings*. London: Zed Books.

International Organization for Migration (IOM). 1993. 'Summary record of the 395th meeting, 23 November 1993, at 3.25 p.m.: Council 67th session'. MC/C/SR/395, 30.12.1993. Geneva: IOM.

IOM. 2012. 'Report on the 100th session of the Council (5.-7.12.2011): Council 101st session'. MC/2342/Rev.1, 27.11.2012. Geneva: IOM. Accessed 20 August 2018, https://governingbodies.iom.int/files/default/sites/iom/files/About-IOM/governing-bodies/en/council/101/MC_2342_Rev1.pdf.

IOM. 2015. *World Migration Report 2015: Migrants and Cities: New Partnerships to Manage Mobility*. Geneva: IOM.

IOM. 2017. 'Mixed migration flows in the Mediterranean and beyond: Compilation of available data and information: June 2015'. Accessed 9 August 2017, http://doe.iom.int/docs/Flows%20Compilation%202015%20Overview.pdf.

IOM. 2018. 'Missing migrants: Tracking death along migratory routes'. Accessed 7 June 2018, https://missingmigrants.iom.int/mediterranean.

Jones, B.G. 2008. 'Race in the ontology of international order', *Political Studies*, 56 (4): 907–927.

Karakayali, S. and Kleist, J.O. 2016. 'Volunteers and asylum seekers', *Forced Migration Review*, 5 (1): 65–67.

Kotsko, A. 2017. 'The prince of this world: Adam Kotsko and Patrick Blanchfield in conversation'. *The Revealer*, 25 July. Accessed 10 August 2017, https://wp.nyu.edu/therevealer/2017/07/25/the-prince-of-this-world-adam-kotsko-and-patrick-blanchfield-in-conversation/.

Mense, T. 2017. '"Jugendliche ohne Migrationshintergrund": Ethnische Identität und völkischer Nationalismus bei den "Identitären"'. In *Untergangster des Abendlandes: Ideologie und Rezeption der rechtsextremen, 'Identitären'*, edited by J. Goetz, J.M. Sedlacek and A. Winkler. Hamburg: Marta Press, pp. 227–252.

Merkel, A. 2016. 'Sommerpressekonferenz von Bundeskanzlerin Angela Merkel', 31 August. Accessed 9 August 2017, http://bundesregierung.de/Content/DE/Mitschrift/Pressekonferenzen/2015/08/2015-08-31-pk-merkel.html.

Papadopoulos, D., Stephenson, N. and Tsianos, V. 2008. *Escape Routes: Control and Subversion in the 21st Century*. London: Pluto.

Parenti, C. 2012. *Tropic of Chaos: Climate Change and the New Geography of Violence*. New York: Nation Books.

Pautz, H. 2005. 'The politics of identity in Germany: The leitkultur debate', *Race & Class*, 46 (4): 39–52.

Poulantzas, N. [1978] 2000. *State, Power, Socialism*. London: Verso.

Santer, K. and Wriedt, V. 2017. '(De)Constructing borders: Contestations in and around the Balkan Corridor in 2015/2016', *Movements*, 3 (1): 139–148.

Schiffer, S. and Wagner, C. 2011. 'Anti-Semitism and Islamophobia: New enemies, old patterns', *Race & Class*, 52 (3): 77–84.

Spiegel Online. 2015a. 'The real Merkel finally stands up', 16 September. Accessed 9 August 2017, http://www.spiegel.de/international/germany/merkel-refuses-to-apologize-for-welcoming-refugees-a-1053253.html.

Spiegel Online 2015b. 'The rise of Germany's new right', 11 December. Accessed 9 August 2017, http://www.spiegel.de/international/germany/refugee-crisis-drives-rise-of-new-right-wing-in-germany-a-1067384.html.

Swing, W.L. 2012. 'Director General's report to the 101st session of the Council: Milestones, stumbling stones and stepping stones'. 27–30 November 2012, MICEM/3/2012. Geneva: IOM.

Vieten, M. and Poynting, S. 2016. 'Contemporary far-right racist populism in Europe', *Journal of Intercultural Studies*, 37 (6): 533–540.

Wallerstein, I. 1991. 'The ideological tensions of capitalism: Universalism versus racism and sexism'. In *Race, Nation, Class: Ambiguous Identities*, edited by E. Balibar and I. Wallerstein. London and New York: Verso, pp. 29–36.

Winant, H. 2001. 'White racial projects'. In *The Making and Unmaking of Whiteness*, edited by B.B. Rasmussen, E. Klingenberg, I.J. Nexica and M. Wray. Durham, NC: Duke University Press, pp. 97–112.

CHAPTER

6

HINDUTVA, CASTE AND THE 'NATIONAL UNCONSCIOUS'

Aditya Nigam

In this chapter, I explore the troubled relationship of Marxism in India with the question of caste. I argue that though very problematic in itself, this is actually a subset of a larger problem, namely the constitution of the modern self in India, which was centrally preoccupied with the erasure of caste and a 'resolution', so to speak, of the caste question. This exploration is undertaken here in the context of the emergence of the Hindu right to political prominence and its recent ascent to power. The political formation of the Hindu right, too, is another way of negotiating the caste question in order to achieve the modern political project of a Hindu consolidation as the centrepiece of the imagined nation. In that sense, I argue, caste constitutes the 'national unconscious' of the Indian modern.

CASTE, NOT RACE

This chapter is not about race. However, it is quite centrally concerned with 'caste', which has often been thought of in terms of race. Many important late nineteenth- and early twentieth-century anti-caste crusaders, such as Jyotiba Phule in western India and E.V. Ramasamy (commonly known as Periyar) in the south, understood caste in terms of race, with upper-caste Hindus being seen as a distinct race that oppressed the subjugated castes, in turn seen as belonging to different racial stock/s (Guha 2016; O'Hanlon 2008; Pandian 1993). Periyar led a powerful movement of non-Brahmin castes in Tamil Nadu, initially known as the Self-Respect Movement, which later went on to 'merge', in a manner of speaking, with the Dravidian platform of what was once the Justice Party, which was succeeded in 1942 by the Dravida Kazhagam. The very formation of the Dravida Kazhagam by Periyar represented the coming of age of the discourse of race, in place of the earlier non-Brahmin discourse of caste that had characterised the Justice Party, where 'Dravidian' identity had played a relatively marginal role. The transformation of this ideological configuration was itself a complex process and has been mapped by some scholars in detail (Pandian 1994). The Dravidian movement's attempt to redefine south Indian non-Brahmin identity as primarily racial and as something that stood, therefore, in radical alterity to that of the Aryan Brahmin, led to a wholesale re-reading and recasting of the epics and mythological texts associated with Brahminical Hinduism, alongside a rejection of Sanskrit and a de-Sanskritisation of the Tamil language (Pandian 1996).

The position that caste is, or is akin to, race was articulated once again in the run-up to the United Nations World Conference Against Racism, Racial Discrimination, Xenophobia and Related Intolerances held in Durban in 2001. Many Dalit groups in India sought to raise the issue of continuing caste discrimination at the Durban conference, leading to a fresh debate on the relationship between caste and race. Given that 'race' itself is a category that has increasingly been subjected to intense philosophical and theoretical scrutiny in recent times and the fact that current research on caste reveals its highly complex nature, it would be a mistake if we were to once again start reading caste in terms of race. In the 1940s, B.R. Ambedkar rejected the idea and steered clear of the tendency to read caste as race. For Ambedkar, the question was twofold. In the first place, unlike the sharp Aryan/Dravidian distinction, in most contexts it was impossible to racially separate or distinguish between the Brahminical and *dvija* (twice-born) castes, on the one hand, and the oppressed Dalit Bahujan castes (to use our contemporary terminology for Ambedkar's 'Untouchables' and 'Sudras'),[1] on the other hand. Secondly, in political terms, his project of the construction of a pan-Indian Dalit identity would be jeopardised if the race question was to be foregrounded, since that identity had to be primarily political and grounded in the experience of untouchability rather than on biological difference – which is primarily how race was seen in Ambedkar's day. There is another reason why one must steer clear of the race question in discussing caste and its relationship to the Hindu right. If colonial/ Orientalist scholarship moved between viewing caste as race to seeing it as an exceptional Indian formation, it also ended up reifying it in ways that impede rather than enable a proper historical understanding of caste (Guha 2016; Metcalf 2014; O'Hanlon 2008). More importantly, within Marxist scholarship and theorisation of Indian society and politics, caste was blanked out, written over by class to the extent that one would have to look in vain at the writings of Indian Marxists to find its presence even where it was centrally visible in social reality. To take just one instance, one could cite the well-known 'mode of production' debate that concerned itself with the mode of production in Indian agriculture and continued in different scholarly journals for over a decade. Yet, it will be impossible to find any reference to caste in that entire debate, even as the protagonists debated the finer nuances of European feudalism, serfdom, second serfdom and forms of unfreedom therein. Even in relation to phenomena such as 'labour-service' and forms of agrarian unfreedom, the question of caste remained conspicuous by its absence. Indeed, if there is one common element between race and caste that Marxists might have usefully picked on and theorised, it is the question of forms of labour and unfreedom (see Menon in this volume).

It would be important to think/imagine caste and race together now, when the intellectual contexts are very different from Ambedkar's time. Today, race is not thought of as something biological; indeed, the entire push of anti-race scholarship has been towards underlining its polysemy and seeing it as an index of certain kinds of social experience. Not that this makes skin colour irrelevant but it does draw our attention to the limit cases where sharply delineated definitions cease to work. The scholarship on caste, especially the Dalit/untouchable experience, has also been moving in a similar direction away from highly essentialised notions of caste difference. Nonetheless, this body of scholarship is relatively more recent and not substantial enough at present to enable us to say anything meaningful about the history of caste and caste practices. Thinking of the two kinds of social experience of caste and race together, both in terms of how similar and dissimilar they are, could be a rewarding exercise but that falls outside the purview of this chapter, which is more about the rise of the Hindu right and the elision of caste in Marxist discourse in India. This elision of caste can be seen in a candid auto-critique by Marxist historian Sumit Sarkar, who can be counted among the few of those who became more sensitive to the issue of caste, especially since Marxists began rethinking it in the 1990s. Thus, Sarkar observed in *Writing Social History* (1997) that even though his classic *Modern India* (1983) was among the few texts that 'gave more space to caste movements' in late colonial India, he 'had kept on using phrases like "false consciousness of caste solidarity" and "sectional forms" of expressing lower caste discontent'. He then went on to observe that in revisiting early twentieth-century Bengal material, he realised that 'caste seems now to have been quite a central theme' (Sarkar 1997: 359).

The same holds true for most Marxist scholarship on Hindutva or the Hindu right, which is fundamentally marred by its attempts to understand the Hindu right in the light of the European experience and the reductive Euro-Marxist debates on fascism. Even though kindred in spirit to fascism and drawing part of its initial inspiration from it, Hindutva constitutes an entirely different phenomenon and there is little to be gained by simply reading 'fascism' into it. Though there has been some innovative thinking on Hindutva, especially since the long debate on secularism began in the mid-1980s, Marxists have, by and large, confined their interventions to reiterating the secular ideal in the face of its intense crisis. Nonetheless, it must be said that the more sophisticated among the Marxist scholars, even while defending the secular ideal, have attempted to re-examine some of the assumptions underlying it. Work by Tanika Sarkar (1991), Tapan Basu et al. (1993), Javeed Alam (1999a), Sumit Sarkar (1997) and Pradip Kumar Datta (1999) can be seen as some instances of such attempts at innovation, though it can be argued that, strictly speaking, they do not really adhere to the conventional Marxist method in their re-examination. Nevertheless, because they still remain broadly Marxist in their intellectual and political commitments, I consider their work here as part of the larger body of Marxist scholarship.

Khaki Shorts, Saffron Flags (Basu et al. 1993) is the work of a group of five Marxist scholars, who empirically investigated some of the more significant instances of communal violence in the late 1980s and early 1990s. It combines historical research into the organisation/s and ideology of the Hindu right with a contemporary examination based on interviews and popular propaganda material produced by the Hindutva organisations. This work presents a sophisticated attempt at examining what is new in the strategy and mode of address of the Hindu right organisations, including the recent mobilisation of women in the Rashtrasevika Samiti – the women's wing of the Rashtriya Swayamsevak Sangh (RSS), the central organisation of the Hindutva constellation. This research also draws on Tanika Sarkar's (1991) prior work in its novel examination of the interpellation of women as communal subjects. Datta (1999) is a more historical study of the formation of communal ideology in early twentieth-century Bengal and focuses on the ways in which colonial governmental technologies, such as censuses, contributed to the crafting of communal identities at the hands of the Bengal literati. Here and elsewhere, Datta also looks closely at the formation of communal consciousness, long before the actual emergence of the idea or ideology of Hindutva. Alam (1999a), on the other hand, represents a more political theory exercise that engages with the larger debate on modernity and secularism. While mounting a robust defence of both secularism and modernity, Alam nonetheless concedes that there is no way one can defend actually existing modernity (and by extension, secularism). He is critical of what he calls 'entrenched modernity', which he sees as bourgeois and irrevocably implicated in various kinds of violence. Against it, he posits what he calls modernity's 'unembodied surplus', where, he suggests, the philosophical resources of a different kind of modernity exist. Likewise, he sees secularism in need of being put on a different philosophical footing – away from the foundationalist understandings of the ideal that had become entrenched in modern times.

However, it is interesting that even while these scholars make significant moves in the direction of understanding the challenges posed by the onset of Hindutva, by incorporating other dimensions in their understanding of the phenomenon that are not directly reducible to class or economic factors, caste remains absent. Even the empirically rich study by Basu et al. (1993) seems to lack an adequate awareness of this question. Thus, even though the authors do provide a glimpse of the caste factor in operation at different points, these remain passing observations without eliciting adequate comment on what it might mean.[2] I say this not so much as a criticism of the scholars concerned but in order to draw attention to the fact that there was something deeply problematic not just with Marxism but, in fact, with the very constitution of the modern Indian self, which was predicated on the erasure of caste. A rare exception perhaps is a perceptive essay by Alam (1999b), which came close to acknowledging this erasure and argued that neither was an appeal to caste necessarily casteist (as in the case of oppressed castes), nor did casteism always have to resort to a caste language (as in the case of the privileged castes). The erasure of caste involved not merely its proscription or 'repression' from public discourse, in any obvious sense, rather, it was built into the formation of the self, seen as something that this 'modern Indian' had already left behind in some remote past.

I have made this argument at length elsewhere (Nigam 2006). Here, I simply want to underline that this is what I refer to when I use the term 'national unconscious' in the title of this chapter. The invisibility and unspeakability of caste in the understanding of the modern Indian self is something that was achieved through a long and tortuous process of negotiation via nationalism that installed the new, emergent nation as upper-caste Hindu. Talking about caste became anathema – and was seen as a throwback to earlier, pre-modern times, as well as being 'divisive' in terms of the nation. Parenthetically, we might note here that this is one sense in which caste can never be race – it can easily be made invisible, as indeed it has been for decades, where the visual presence of race might be impossible to erase.

What follows, therefore, is a discussion of Hindutva and its deeply problematic relationship with the Dalit Bahujan castes and the caste question in general. As will become evident throughout the chapter, the caste question lies at the heart of the Hindutva project, which along with mainstream secular nationalism had managed to silence it but is once again now out in the open, negotiating its space anew. While I have indicated the innovations that academic Marxist scholars have undertaken in their understanding of Hindutva, it will be useful to briefly refer to a wide gap that separates such scholarship from what we may call the 'party left'.[3] After a brief consideration of the official left, I will also refer to more recent developments that point to the emergence of a new left discourse, largely on the peripheries of the party left.

HINDUTVA, CASTE AND THE POLITICAL LEFT

A debate of sorts concerning the challenge posed by Hindutva took place in the party left in the second half of 2016. The debate was cast in such arcane terms that one would not spend much time on it, had it not been for the fact that it represented the terms in which communists in the major communist parties are still debating it.

Kick-starting this debate, former Communist Party of India (Marxist) (CPI(M)) general secretary Prakash Karat (2016) wrote a piece in *The Indian Express* that befuddled many. This was not an exhaustive take on the current regime but referred to it only in the context of building up a political-electoral opposition to it. Nonetheless, it does give us an idea of how the phenomenon itself is viewed by the party left in India. The current National Democratic

Alliance dispensation, led by Narendra Modi, according to Karat, is 'right-wing authoritarian' but not 'fascist'. One could have actually agreed with this supposedly fine distinction were it not meant to draw some immediate political conclusions based on a certain dated understanding about fascism. The distinction was made primarily to argue that *only under a fascist regime* is it permissible to forge the broadest possible resistance against it. Though the article was published in a mainstream newspaper, the terms of the argument clearly reflected those of an internal debate within Karat's party. At issue in the intra-party debate was the question of whether or not to ally with the Indian National Congress (hereafter, Congress) against the Modi regime.[4] What interests me here is not the actual tactical question involved but the argument that is being marshalled in order to reject any idea of a broad front against what is perhaps the most regressive, violently anti-minority and anti-democratic regime that India has ever seen.

Karat (2016) referred to something he called the 'classic definition' of fascism in order to make his point. What was simply a formulation made by Georgi Dimitrov and the Comintern, in a specific context, is turned into a definition: fascism in power is 'the open terrorist dictatorship of the most reactionary, most chauvinistic and most imperialist elements of finance capital'. From this definition, he then proceeds to make his deductions about present-day India: 'In India today, neither has fascism been established, nor are the conditions present – in political, economic and class terms – for a fascist regime to be established. There is no crisis that threatens a collapse of the capitalist system; the ruling classes of India face no threat to their class rule.'

Every bit of this statement is an instance of formulaic thinking but I cite it here because it is not just one stray comment. Rather, it represents a mode of thinking that is fairly widely prevalent across the Marxist political and intellectual spectrum. My point will appear in sharper relief if this statement is read alongside the Marxist scholarship on Hindutva and secularism referred to above. Take the following, for instance, where Karat (2016) goes on to 'define the character' of the Bharatiya Janata Party (BJP):

> There has to be clarity in defining the character of the BJP. The BJP is not an ordinary bourgeois party. Its uniqueness lies in its organic links to the Rashtriya Swayamsevak Sangh. The BJP is a right-wing party with respect to its economic and social agenda, and can be characterised as a right-wing party of majoritarian communalism. Further, given its

linkage to the RSS, which has a semi-fascist ideology, it is a party that has the potential to impose an authoritarian state on the people when it believes that circumstances warrant it.

At least two things are striking about this passage and the article more generally. First, in this delineation of the threat of Hindutva, Karat's primary focus remains on the political party (the BJP) and its 'class character', and even though he points to its connection with the RSS and its 'semi-fascist ideology', he remains blissfully unaware of the relatively minor role the BJP plays in the Hindutva configuration. A more appropriate description of the pre-Modi phase of Hindutva is 'Sanghism' – a term that underlines the centrality of the Sangh (RSS) to the configuration.[5] The story of Modi's ascent to power lends an additional dimension to the way the larger configuration has been shaped, given that neither the BJP nor the RSS were actually in favour of projecting Modi as their prime ministerial candidate. Modi's support was built on his reputation as a hard anti-Muslim leader who presided over the 2002 Gujarat carnage. This image gave Modi the support of the most viciously criminal sections of Hindutva vigilantes, many of whom might be on the fringes of even the RSS.[6] It is well known that the RSS first and then the BJP were forced into accepting Modi's candidature because of the pressure of such 'grassroots activists'. And one particular feature of this section is that it is culturally marginalised and, in that sense, anti-bourgeois. Reference to BJP's 'bourgeois' class character can in this context be highly misleading, given the range of subaltern sections it mobilises. What is important here is to understand the decisive transformation that Hindutva has undergone with Modi's rise to power, which no longer conforms even to a 1990s' understanding of the phenomenon. Second, nowhere in the entire article do we get a sense of how crucial the caste question is to Hindutva's politics and the completely new dynamic it has acquired in the present. Throughout history, Hindutva's anti-Muslim and anti-minority character has been directly tied to its effort to deal with the question of caste; it is an expression of its attempt to create a homogeneous Hindu community by invoking the fear of the Muslim. In this way, it tries to displace the internal challenge posed by the caste question, namely the potential revolt of the lower castes, on to the external enemy – the Muslim.

The RSS and other kindred organisations, such as the Hindu Mahasabha in the early twentieth century, developed on themes that were already popular, at least among the Hindu literati. Indeed, all the elements that went into the production of a 'theory' of Hindutva, as systematised by V.D. Savarkar for instance, have a much longer intellectual genealogy. This was a vastly different context from that of mass industrialisation and uprooting, of large-scale atomisation of society, for example, that had formed the backdrop of the rise of fascism in Europe. These ideas arose *in the context of colonial rule*. Through the nineteenth century, Indian intellectuals grappled with one big question: how is it that we, a large and ancient civilisation, came to be colonised by a small island state and a merchant company? In trying to answer this question, they went back to earlier waves of political aggression and 'rule by foreigners' – the Turks, the Afghans and the Mughals, all of whom came to be referred to initially as Turks and/or Yavanas, and later, as Muslims. The answer that they came up with was that 'we', the Hindus – an identity that was beginning to take shape alongside the identification of the Muslims as 'other' – were disunited. Put more explicitly, it meant the 'treachery' of the lower castes. Hindu unity came to be seen as the need of the hour, as the centrepiece of the new emergent nationalism.

'Disunity' eventually became a way of identifying the lower castes as the cause of the defeat of the ancient civilisation. How this role of the lower castes was understood by the Hindu literati and publicists of that time varied substantially. On the one hand, the Arya Samaj, established by Swami Dayanand, believed that it was the curse of untouchability and caste practices that had led to disunity. Dayanand and the Arya Samaj believed that caste was the consequence of practical distortions that had crept into Hindu society as a result of deviations from the original Vedic religion. They wanted to reconvert those who had left the Hindu order over the centuries, especially the lower castes. But this reconversion had no chance of success, Dayanand realised, as long as caste practices remained for there was always the question of what the (caste) status of such reconverted Hindus would be. The way forward, according to Arya Samaj, was to go back to the pristine Vedic religion. On the other hand, the Sanatanis (those who saw present-day Hinduism as eternal; *sanatan* meaning eternal) wanted unity but without disturbing the architecture of caste hierarchy and practices. The emergence of Hindutva as a political formation dates back to the early 1920s, when Savarkar published *Essentials of Hindutva* ([1923] 2009), which marked a break with these previous understandings, even while it continued to share some of its basic assumptions. The most fundamental break made by Savarkar was in his definition of the 'Hindu': to him it was no longer a religious category but a political one that defined nationhood. Himself an atheist and rationalist, Savarkar had no patience with what he considered irrational practices, the most important among them being caste and untouchability. Savarkar's concern was less with the question of religious identity than it was with the cultural foundations of the new nation-in-making, and he saw the abolition of caste as fundamental to the success of this project. The RSS, which later took over the entire legacy of Hindutva, became a peculiar amalgam of this Savarkarite vision, alongside various Sanatani and Arya Samajist stances.

The identification of the Muslim other, as the way of displacing the internal question of disunity on to an external entity, was, however, common to all strands. The projection of the fear of the 'rapacious Muslim' became the mode through which the more aggressively Hindu elements articulated their programme of Hindu unity. In a manner of speaking, the anti-Muslim element had rapidly become common sense in large sections of the emergent nationalist public, especially in the mid-1920s. This aspect of Hindutva is widely recognised and studied and I will not discuss this further here, except to say that the onset of Partition, and the widespread violence that followed it, entrenched the Hindu-Muslim divide as a permanent fault line in Indian politics. The caste issue, especially the Dalit issue, saw a temporary resolution in so far as Dalits found some space in the new constitutional arrangements in independent India, due, in particular, to the labours of Ambedkar, who headed the drafting committee of the Constituent Assembly and managed to ensure some safeguards and guarantees for Dalit castes. The actual dynamic of how Ambedkar and his Scheduled Caste Federation, which had been in alliance with the Muslim League (ML) until the eve of Partition, came around to make common cause with nationalism is a very complex one that I have discussed at length (Nigam 2004). Suffice it to mention that Ambedkar, who had been elected to the Constituent Assembly with ML support from Bengal (where the ML was in government), had to make complex choices as Partition approached and the nationalists attempted to wean Ambedkar away from the ML. At the time of Partition, there were still large numbers of Dalits who were influenced by Gandhi and hence brought more easily into the caste-class coalition represented by the Congress. In other words, more than the success of Hindutva, it was the relative success of the dominant nationalist project that made possible a social coalition where Dalits, too, had some space. Hindutva politics, for the most part, cannibalised on that relative success of mainstream nationalism.

This fragile balance could remain intact only as long as the Dalit masses accepted the hegemony of the upper castes, via the Congress. The powerful upper castes have never accepted any challenge to their dominance of the local structures of power and there was no way they were going to give up any of their privileges, even in the name of a putative national community. It was therefore a matter of time before the lower, Dalit and Bahujan castes would begin to assert themselves politically. From the early 1970s on, the Dalit movement started charting out its own course, challenging Brahminical dominance culturally, intellectually and politically – though it really came into its own only in the 1990s. The Dalit Bahujan assertion that began in the late nineteenth and early twentieth century has returned with a vengeance to confront the nationalist self in recent times. The Hindutva nationalists, given their self-righteous belief in their version of 'Hindu'/'national' culture have revealed themselves to be incapable of dealing with this new assertion – especially in the wake of Rohith Vemula's suicide, widely perceived to be a symptom of inbuilt institutional discrimination against Dalits, and the Hindu right's 'discovery' that 'they' eat beef and worship the demon Mahishasura.[7] Details of the Mahishasura controversy are discussed later in this chapter.

DALIT BAHUJANS CONFRONT HINDUTVA

The key issue on which the entire project of Hindutva hinged was its ability to (re)-assimilate the Dalits and other lower castes into the reconstituted Hindu order. This Hindu order, it should be underlined, was supposed to be, at least in theory, a political community of equals, with no distinction of caste; it was not – and could not have been – the mere resurrection of the old order of caste hierarchies.

The Dalit and minority question (the Muslim question, in particular), we have seen, is not incidental to the Hindutva project but lies at its very heart. Today, this is the fulcrum of the struggle against Hindutva. Attempts to appropriate and assimilate Dalits and thus isolate Muslims that had seemed to have some degree of success in the past have now begun to come apart. As the inevitable conflict between Brahminical/Manuvadi,[8] Hindutva and the cultural symbols and icons of the Dalits, and those between Dalits and over-zealous cow gangs, come out into the open, a fundamentally new situation has arisen. The question for the left is how it relates to these struggles. Many of them, such as the struggle in Gujarat, following the protests in Una (discussed later), may not have any direct or immediate bearing in electoral terms but they presage the beginning of a new politics of cultural transformation. These, along with the emergent Ambedkarite and Bahujan forces at universities, present an opportunity to rethink not just strategies of fighting Hindutva but, more importantly, of recasting the very language and imagination of left politics itself.

The ongoing revolt of the Dalit masses heralds the beginning of a new situation in Indian politics, whose implications are likely to be felt even beyond the next general elections slated for 2019. For in its most fundamental sense, the virtual civil war initiated by the cow gangs of the Hindu right (RSS/BJP being only one part of the larger constellation) represents an unprecedented rupture in the century-old project of forging a Hindu nation. At a very fundamental level, the project of Hindu Rashtra (the Hindu right's project of a Hindu nation discussed earlier) falls flat if the Dalits turn against it. This project was premised not only on a proto-fascist desire to create a nation that would be based on a reconstructed Hindu culture, it also rested on the fundamental cultural illiteracy of a Manuvadi Hindu elite about what constituted the large landmass that came to be called India. If Hindutva's most megalomaniac desire was to recreate what it thought was a once-united India (Akhand Bharat) stretching from Afghanistan at one end and Burma/Myanmar at the other – its cultural imagination about what constitutes this entity internally was utterly impoverished. So much so that it could never understand that different populations inhabited the landmass that constituted colonial and even post-Partition India, ranging from Kashmir to the north-east on the one hand, and the very different cultural practices of even the supposedly Hindu southern India, with its highly sophisticated linguistic, cultural and philosophical heritage, on the other hand – not to mention the Adivasis (tribals) and lower-caste groups. All it focused on was the proto-fascist ideal of welding this landmass and its population into one, single nation with a single culture.

What is more significant is that this cultural illiteracy of Sanghism extended equally to its knowledge and awareness of the cultural practices of the Hindus as well. So for instance, vegetarianism is not common even among the Brahmins of Bengal and Kashmir or of the hill regions of North India, for example. What the coming to power of the Modi regime has illustrated through its nationalism is that it has no understanding of the religious beliefs and practices of many lower-caste groups and Adivasi communities, even in the north. This was dramatically shown in the way in which the issue of Mahishasur worship was dealt with during the Home Ministry's RSS-inspired attack on 'anti-national activities' at Jawaharlal Nehru University (JNU).[9] The sequence in which this attack unfolded has been recorded by Pramod Ranjan (2016) in *Forward Press*. It was first *Panchjanya* and *Organiser*, RSS mouthpieces, that listed Mahishasur worship as evidence of the anti-national activities at JNU. This was followed by the compilation of a dossier by some teachers close to the RSS at JNU, who repeated this fact (among others) as evidence of anti-national activities. When Delhi police made its case against the students, it repeated, almost verbatim, these allegations of Mahishasur worship as evidence of anti-national activities. Finally, the Human Resources Development minister in a speech in parliament, in response to Mayawati, repeated the Mahishasur worship question in exactly the same fashion.

If we temporarily set aside the series of questions raised by the tragic suicide of Rohith Vemula of Hyderabad University, especially with regard to how Dalits are treated, even today, within our modern institutions such as universities and simply focus on the cultural and religious practices of different subaltern Hindu and Adivasi communities, it will be clear how, for an organisation largely dominated by Chitpavan Brahmins, these are anti-Hindu and, therefore, anti-national practices. Fundamentally, the RSS idea of what a 'Hindu' is or should be derives from a modern north Indian upper-caste rendering of 'Hinduness'. Even though it swears by the ancient texts such as the Vedas, its illiteracy extends to those texts as well. As historians have often pointed out, beef-eating was evident in Vedic times as well and Hindutva's aversion to it comes from modern identity concerns.

Its illiteracy, woven into a modernist proto-fascist project and combined with supreme intolerance of difference, has led it into other confrontations recently. That the Mahishasura episode at JNU was not an aberration is further illustrated by the fact that it led the Hindu right to hold a demonstration in Bastar in March 2016, attacking the 'offsprings of Mahishasur'. The rally was attended by BJP member of parliament Abhishek Singh and his supporters, among others. The following is an extract from a report by Sanjeev Chandan (2016) in *Forward Press*:

> The call by the Hindutvavadis to 'beat the offsprings of Mahishasur with shoes' in their 12 March rally, cost them dearly. For among the settled inhabitants of the Bastar region, Mahishasur (his local name being Bhainsasur) is worshipped. The local people naturally took this as an attack on their culture and they rose up against the drive of the Hindutvavadis towards cultural homogenization. On 30 April, they

took out a march and also got FIRs (First Information Reports with the police) registered against those who shouted slogans in the 12 March rally, although the police has not yet arrested any of the accused, allegedly because of pressure from above. Vivek Kumar [a local journalist whose Facebook post led to the storm] says, 'Hindutvavadis want to make everyone into devotees of Ram and Durga, for they care little for anybody else's culture. They cannot tolerate the fact that the local inhabitants of Bastar do not celebrate either Durga Puja or Dussehra, nor that Ravan is not set afire here.'

That vigilante groups of 'cow protectors' have sprouted up all over India and have become increasingly more brazen and aggressive in the recent past is not coincidental. Though aggressive anti-Muslim politics around cow protection has been in evidence from the late nineteenth century itself, it has acquired a particularly vicious form in recent years. Given that Modi himself introduced the cow question with high-pitched communal rhetoric in the 2015 Bihar elections – and given his complicit silence as these gangs rampage – this is not particularly surprising. That support from the highest echelons of power is what has emboldened them. Where the calculations went wrong was in the assumption that this campaign would target only Muslims and thus lead to a Hindu consolidation. They had simply assumed that this would be an easy and emotive way of whipping up sentiments against Muslims but had not anticipated that the vigilantism of the cow gangs would eventually lead to attacks on the Dalits and perhaps to the unravelling of the very project of Hindu Rashtra. Dalits, in most parts of India, have been traditionally the castes assigned various kinds of polluting work, including the removal of carcasses of animals and their disposal. Some of the castes involved in this work skin the dead animals, cows and buffaloes in particular, and are therefore also linked to leather work. In the particular instance that became the flashpoint for a major Dalit uprising, four Dalit youths were flogged by cow vigilante gangs in the presence of police personnel in Una division in Gujarat. In July 2016, these youths were skinning a dead cow when the vigilante gangs descended on them. They were taken to a police station, tied bare-bodied to a vehicle and flogged. The video went viral on social media leading to huge public outcry and a veritable uprising of Dalits.

This is where they made their biggest mistake. For the Dalit question, it needs to be reiterated, is not like any other – in it, in fact, lies the unresolved traumatic core of the modern Hindu self, and by extension, of the nationalist self. For the traditional Hindu, the Dalit was the excluded other, but whose exclusion could never be complete, for it was on the Dalit's being that the purity and being of the Hindu self was predicated and the traditionalist made no bones about it.

However, for the nationalist Hindu, the Dalit is the excess that he cannot deal with. But the promise of the nation remains hollow as long as the Dalits continue to be in the state to which traditional Hindu society has relegated them. This is what is now being militantly challenged.

THE AMBEDKAR FIGURE: A NEW MOMENT IN POLITICS

An important change is taking place in Dalit politics, on the one hand, and left politics, on the other hand. Ambedkar is no longer a name that can be kept imprisoned within the confines of history books; it has become a battle cry that has taken its stand against injustice and chicanery – a hallmark of Sanghist-Manuvadi-speak. Jai Bheem-Lal Salam (Hail Bheem [an abbreviation of Ambedkar's first name]-Red Salute) have become conjoined slogans of this moment when the Ambedkarite legacy has moved rapidly to become the voice of a universal resistance, in a manner of speaking. Marx often said that the proletariat could not achieve its own freedom without liberating society in its entirety. Nothing of that sort has occurred, but certainly, into the second decade of twenty-first-century India, it is becoming increasingly clear that the Dalit liberation struggle will be that struggle, one that will eventually break the sham unity that was foisted in the name of the nation under Brahminical hegemony during the course of the anti-colonial struggle and liberate even the upper-caste self from its secular delusions.

In his writings on democracy, Ambedkar claims that entire societies cannot be put behind bars and that law alone would never ensure the liberation of the Dalits; that in the final analysis, it would have to be the 'moral conscience' of society that would have to step in. This moral conscience was his name for a cultural-intellectual revolution in society that would draw sections of the non-Dalit, upper-caste and Bahujan masses into its fold. This is perhaps the moment of that cultural-intellectual revolution and the names of Ambedkar-Phule-Periyar are inscribed on the banner of this revolution.

This is a moment of coming together in which the mutual irritants among the left, feminism and the Dalit movement have not eroded, but it is a moment of coming together, nevertheless, as never before. To clarify, it is not that the

Dalit movement is moving close to the left movement (and the women's movement) that it has stridently criticised in the past and which remain unchanged, as it were. It is a new stirring on the periphery of the older left and the women's movement, mainly among students who have been shaped by their engagement with the discourse of the Dalit Bahujan movement, that is also producing a new discourse of left politics. The Dalit movement, too, has been moving decisively in a leftward direction, propelled by its own internal logic and its need to connect with urgent questions of the day – questions that go way beyond those of identity. Questions of identity are now articulated alongside a powerful challenge to the symbols of upper-caste cultural hegemony.

What are the implications of this new situation with all its possibilities for a Marxist project of the future? To my mind this is no longer clear. The fact that institutional Marxism continues to lag behind, in terms of coming to grips with the challenge of caste in general and the Dalit movement in particular, does not inspire hope. It is also apparent that while a certain new kind of left discourse is emerging that is able to orient itself to Dalit Bahujan politics, thus finding some common ground with simultaneously emerging radical tendencies within Dalit Bahujan politics, this may not really be 'Marxist' in the conventional sense. Marxism is certainly an important element in it and will remain so, but, strictly speaking, in order to have any serious efficacy, this discourse has to look beyond crass 'class analysis' and take on board questions of identity, dignity and self-respect. This is a moment full of possibilities and politically new solidarities are being made, new connections established. However, in theoretical terms, there is much that remains to be done on the question of caste and its relationship with labour and gender, and on finding points of synergy between the disparate 'ideological' impulses that animate these different movements.

NOTES

1 'Dalit' (literally, oppressed or ground down) refers to the new political self-description of the Ambedkarite movement of the former untouchable castes, while 'Bahujan' refers to the larger political identity of Dalits plus other lower castes, traditionally called the Sudras (also known as OBCs – Other Backward Classes, in constitutional language). Some attempts to forge a Bahujan identity in recent years have tended to include the tribal population as well as Muslims within its rubric.

2 A telling instance of this is the repeated reference, at different places in the text, to 'Harijans' – a name condescendingly given by Gandhi to the 'untouchables'. This is a name/description that has been vigorously disowned by these caste groups

as they became politically vocal, claiming for themselves the identity of 'Dalit'. In the 1970s, this identity was largely claimed by the political cultural uprising in Maharashtra in western India, known as the Dalit Panthers. By the mid-1980s, it was an identity that had made its political appearance, even in northern India.

3   It should also be clarified here that by the party left, I mean largely the mainstream communist parties – the Communist Party of India (Marxist) [CPI(M)] and the Communist Party of India (CPI). There are other, smaller parties situated on the left of these parties, which have emerged from what was known as the Naxalite revolt in the late 1960s. Some of these parties have wrestled with the question of caste in different ways for a long time with varying degrees of success, but it is not possible to discuss them in the limited space of this chapter.

4   The Congress had been in power at the centre for a decade before the rise of the Modi-led Hindu right formation, from 2004 to 2014, along with a number of other parties. This formation, known as the United Progressive Alliance (UPA), had been supported by a number of social movements and the left bloc from 2004 to 2008 and had, despite its neoliberalism, enacted some significant legislations during its first tenure (2004–2009). These legislations, which included the Right to Information Act, the National Rural Employment Guarantee Act and the Forest Rights Act, were a consequence of the fact that the UPA I actually embodied a conjunctural, if fragile, alliance with social movements and the left. The left, during Karat's general secretaryship of the CPI(M), broke with the UPA on the question of the Indo-US nuclear deal. It should also be kept in mind that in the second term (UPA II), a large number of serious corruption scandals broke out (some of them actually pertaining to UPA I) that led to discontent and anger against the UPA regime and the emergence, in 2011, of a massive anti-corruption movement against it. The Congress lost power as a result. The debate within the CPI(M) was less about the resistance to the Modi regime – fascist or not – and more about regaining power in West Bengal, where it was voted out after a 34-year stint in government.

5   The term 'Sanghism' derives from the name of the key organisation of the Hindu right, the Rashtriya Swayamsevak Sangh (literally, the National Volunteer Union). The Hindi term 'Sanghvaad' was used by the young dynamic leader of the Jawaharlal Nehru University students' union, Kanhaiya Kumar, in his speeches and slogans, especially at the time when the university was under serious attack from the current regime. I have simply rendered that term into English.

6   This can be seen in the kind of people Modi follows on Twitter and the kind of internet trolls who line up in his defence, issuing murder and gang-rape threats to Modi's opponents with complete impunity.

7   RohithVemula was a PhD student at the University of Hyderabad who came from a Dalit background. He had been active in student politics within a broadly Ambedkarite left configuration. He committed suicide on 17 January 2016 – an act that has widely been seen as a form of 'institutional murder', as something that students from Dalit backgrounds are prone to due to incessant harrassment. In July–August 2015, Vemula had been involved in protests against the death penalty for Yakub Memon, an accused in the 1993 Bombay bomb blasts and against the Hindu right's prevention of the screening of a documentary film *MuzaffarnagarBaqi Hai* at the University of Delhi. The University of Hyderabad's administration, purportedly on orders from the central government, first suspended him, along with some

other activists, and then cancelled his fellowship. It was under these circumstances that he committed suicide.

8 'Manuvad' refers to the ancient Hindu sage Manu, who is remembered primarily with reference to the *Manusmriti*, a prescriptive text that sought to lay down the law of caste duties, obligations and punishments alongside those with respect to stages of life (*varnashrama dharma*).

9 'Mahishasur' literally means the buffalo (*mahish*) demon (*asur*) and refers to the supposedly demonic character that bore this name and was killed by the Goddess Durga, widely revered and worshipped in Bengal and eastern India (but also in other parts of the country). This has been commonly accepted in 'educated' and 'cultured' society at large. In more recent times, however, the figure of Mahishasur has been reclaimed, along with many others portrayed as 'demons' in caste Hindu mythology, as revered figures of the lower orders. The claim is that there were important figures who were represented as villains in Hindu myths. Mahishasur worship was started at Jawaharlal Nehru University by a group of students. Although it came to the limelight and became an object of Hindu right-wing ire at the university, it is a fact that there have always been entire communities in different parts of the country who have worshipped Mahishasur.

REFERENCES

Alam, J. 1999a. *India: Living with Modernity*. New Delhi: Oxford University Press.
Alam, J. 1999b. 'Is caste appeal casteism? Oppressed castes in politics', *Economic and Political Weekly*, 34 (13): 757–761.
Basu, T., Datta, P., Sarkar, S., Sarkar, T. and Sen, S. 1993. *Khaki Shorts, Saffron Flags*. New Delhi: Orient Longman.
Chandan, S. 2016. 'Insulting Mahishasur costs dear: Tribals hit the streets', *Forward Press*, 29 July. Accessed 5 March 2017, https://www.forwardpress.in/2016/07/insulting-mahishasur-costs-dear-tribals-hit-the-streets/.
Datta, P.K. 1999. *Carving Blocks: Communal Ideology in Early Twentieth-Century Bengal*. Delhi: Oxford University Press.
Guha, S. 2016. *Beyond Caste: Identity and Power in South Asia*. Ranikhet: Permanent Black.
Karat, P. 2016. 'Fight against the BJP cannot be conducted in alliance with the other major party of the ruling classes', *The Indian Express*, 6 September. Accessed 4 March 2017, http://indianexpress.com/article/opinion/columns/india-nda-government-narendra-modi-bjp-right-wing-hindutva-3015383/.
Metcalf, T.R. 2014. 'The ordering of difference'. In *Caste in Modern India*, edited by S. Sarkar and T. Sarkar. Ranikhet: Permanent Black, pp. 88–112.
Nigam, A. 2004. 'A text without author: Locating the constituent assembly as event', *Economic and Political Weekly*, 39 (21): 2107–2113.
Nigam, A. 2006. *The Insurrection of Little Selves: The Crisis of Secular-Nationalism in India*. New Delhi: Oxford University Press.
O'Hanlon, R. 2008. 'Phule and the inversion of Brahman myths'. In *Caste in History*, edited by I. Banerjee-Dube. New Delhi: Oxford University Press, pp. 172–180.
Pandian, M.S.S. 1993. 'Denationalizing the past: Nation in EV Ramasamy's political discourse', *Economic and Political Weekly*, 28 (42): 2282–2287.

Pandian, M.S.S. 1994. 'Notes on the transformation of "Dravidian" ideology: Tamil Nadu 1900–1940', *Social Scientist*, 22 (5–6): 84–104.

Pandian, M.S.S. 1996. 'Towards national-popular: Notes on self-respecters' Tamil', *Economic and Political Weekly*, 31 (51): 3323–3329.

Ranjan, P. 2016. 'Bahujan discourse puts JNU in the crosshairs', *Forward Press*, 27 February. Accessed 5 March 2017, https://www.forwardpress.in/2016/02/bahujan-discourse-puts-jnu-in-the-crosshairs/.

Sarkar, S. 1997. *Writing Social History*. New Delhi: Oxford University Press.

Sarkar, T. 1991. 'The woman as communal subject: Rashtrasevika Samiti and the Ramjanmabhoomi movement', *Economic and Political Weekly*, 26 (35): 2057–2062.

Savarkar, V.D. [1923] 2009. *Essentials of Hindutva*. Republished as *Hindutva: Who is a Hindu*. New Delhi: Hindi Sahitya Sadan.

CHAPTER

7

MARXISM, FEMINISM AND CASTE IN CONTEMPORARY INDIA

Nivedita Menon

A contribution from India to a book on Marxism and race would have to be reframed in terms of caste, as Aditya Nigam's contribution to this volume explains. However, while retaining the specificity of caste, it is important not to see it as a unique phenomenon that has no resonance in other contexts. Just as we draw insights from critical race theory for caste, critical race theory could benefit from debates and discussions on caste.

It is impossible to think through Marxism outside of caste any longer in India. This realisation is relatively recent for the left and for feminism, because their politics was located in a secular modernist paradigm that rendered caste illegitimate. However, the growing assertiveness of Dalit Bahujan[1] politics over the past three decades has forced a recognition of the caste privilege engrained in what was termed as modern secular politics. This chapter will look at how this recognition of caste has played out in feminist theory and practice in India. Therefore, it engages only with one slice of a vast and complex field, and should not be taken to be an overview of Marxist–feminist theorising as such in India.

CASTE AND RACE

Frantz Fanon charges Jean-Paul Sartre with aridly *intellectualising* the *experience* of being black in 'Orphée Noir', Sartre's introduction to a collection of poetry from Francophone Africa. Fanon claims that Sartre in that essay presented Negritude as 'a minor term of a dialectical progression', as merely a transitory stage on the way towards the universal and abstract class identity. 'When I read that page,' says Fanon, 'I felt as if I had been robbed of my last chance ... Jean-Paul Sartre had forgotten that the Negro suffers in his body quite differently from the white man.' The idea that 'identity politics' is narrower than another politics that is universal, is, of course, the classic act of power, as universalism is simply a particularism that claims universality. But Fanon refuses to accept 'that amputation' conducted by Sartre. He experiences himself as black, he lives in a body recognised as black, and he will simultaneously resist the meaning the world gives to his blackness, while celebrating the solidarities it brings him (Fanon 2003: 70–71).

The painful dilemma faced by Fanon is precisely the way in which the self comes to consciousness in other forms of embodied discrimination, such as caste and gender. The term 'embodied' does not, of course, mean that the body simply exists in nature. The body in each of these instances is produced through a network of cultural material practices. The body that is deemed to be inferior is caught up in the need to recognise its difference from – and simultaneously claim similarity to – the oppressive identity that marks itself as self – whether white, *savarna* ('upper'-caste) or male.

In India, the attempt to dissolve the framework of South Asian exceptionalism, in which caste is located, has been part of the Dalit intellectual and political agenda for some time. Nigam's chapter in this volume offers an exposition of this exercise, which involves thinking of race and caste as analogues, so I will not go into it here.

Suffice it to say that the operative feature of caste that makes it central to any Marxist theorising is that like race elsewhere, caste determines labour in India, and the labouring body is marked indelibly not only by gender but by caste. Indian feminists have therefore begun to address Marxism through the critical lens of caste as well as gender.

STRUCTURE OF THE CHAPTER

This chapter will consider the engagement of feminism with Marxism under two broad rubrics, both of which are shot through by the conceptual category of caste.

The first rubric looks at feminist debates directly engaging Marxism, using conceptual vocabulary developed within the Marxist field in order to expand, rework or amend Marxism to make it responsive to questions of patriarchy, sexuality and reproduction.

The second rubric considers feminist literature that may not directly address Marxism, but is concerned with questions that should be considered significant for a Marxist analysis today, focusing, for lack of space, on two such issues – sex work and ecology.

Both these kinds of scholarship are materialist feminisms, which see bodies as located within multiple practices and structures that produce materiality – gender, class, caste, among others. The issues that post-1990s' feminism takes up, especially in India, are very much concerns that come out of a field indelibly marked by Marxism.

This chapter draws mainly on Indian scholarship, while assuming and sometimes foregrounding western literature. While debates based on western literature make universalising arguments, we of the global South use scholarship produced from our specific locations, not to *universalise*, but certainly claiming the possibility of *theorising*. Our debates speak to debates and issues in other parts of the world where capitalism, Marxism and feminism play out in a field of other identities – sexual, racial, ethnic, religious.

FEMINIST DEBATES DIRECTLY ENGAGING MARXISM

Women in 'production'

Feminist scholarship on labour insists that the 'public' and 'private' aspects of labour are intertwined. Feminists thus complicate, at its source, the Marxist conception of (public) wage labour by showing its imbrication in (private) structures of family and reproduction, and the dimension of caste here, too, is inescapable. Occupations traditionally followed by Dalits are considered to be menial, filthy and defiling, and, as Meena Gopal points out, 'technological upgradation and the benefits of modernization' remain out of their reach. Midwifery and manual scavenging are some of these labours, 'which continue to be part of social reproduction within the domestic sphere and the informal labour market' (Gopal 2013: 93). Thus, the public, the domestic and the caste orders are intimately interlinked.

Labour is not an undifferentiated homogeneous social group, but rather, as is evident when empirical material is engaged with, everyday lived experiences and practices. These can be varied and are shaped by relations of gender, caste, poverty, families and other factors, such as education and access to resources. Using life histories of women workers in an electronics factory in Tamil Nadu, Madhumita Dutta argues that women had multiple reasons for choosing to leave their homes to enter waged work. These could be 'poverty, oppressive households, violence, difficult childhoods, unpaid loans, responsibilities of taking care of siblings or illnesses in the family', but for many it was a personal sense of failure or a desire to be independent that drew them out of their homes (Dutta 2016: 2).

Dutta concludes that in a factory space, workers' responses to work may often seem 'aligned with that of the interests of the owners by working hard or competing for greater outputs', and the motivations and expectations of all workers are not the same. To understand why women consent to work in hyper-efficient and exhausting work regimes, Dutta (2016: 3) argues that one needs to look at other structures of social relations than waged work that women have to negotiate and struggle with every day.

Similarly, scholarship on unionising women workers points to how trade unions need to be involved in many other activities in order to reach women workers effectively. For instance, Chhaya Datar (1989), in her classic study of women tobacco workers in Nipani in western India, found the trade union having to take up family and individual counselling, educational services and so on. Datar finds her conclusions borne out by work in Kerala and Jamaica as well. Thus, the women workers' trade union becomes a women's organisation, too, sensitising women to patriarchy and changing their personal lives (Datar 1989: 235). But Datar also notes how the 'internalisation of patriarchy' creates tensions between the local town women and women who come for work from neighbouring villages, the former being seen as having 'loose morals' by the village women who face far stricter patriarchal controls within their communities. But at the same time, Datar found a relatively higher proportion of single women in Nipani as well as more instances of sexual freedom. What Datar terms 'partial prostitution' was common, with sex work offering an additional source of income, sometimes with the husband's knowledge. Women help each other out in this, offering their homes for short periods.

Thus, Datar's study offers a theoretical insight into the ways in which 'public' and 'private' are entwined for women workers.

Examining the labour of the traditional midwife or *dai*, in particular, Gopal sees it as part of the sexual division of labour in villages. The *dai* has an ambiguous relationship to her work (Gopal 2013). On the one hand, women of other, 'higher' castes avoid this work even though they might know how to assist in childbirth, due to the social avoidance of defiling bodily substances, which relegates stigmatising labour of this sort to Dalits. But on the other hand, the midwife herself is able to break out of this perception, because in rituals of childbirth 'the most stigmatised elements are also evoked as the most potent, and cord-cutting is seen as severing a life source in order to establish a new person' (Gopal 2013: 93). The Dalit woman herself, therefore, rejects the notion that her work is polluting, and 'maintains her transactions in the realm of skill deployment and its valuation, demanding payment and preserving the domain of her work, however meagre the remuneration may be' (Gopal 2013: 93).

Gopal points out that the modern health care system has relegated the midwife to the fringes. When the state intervened to train and upgrade skills – including access to technology for traditional midwives – this only contributed to reinforcing their low status in the social hierarchy, and by focusing on notions of cleanliness, Gopal says, highlighted their untouchability. Thus, the state as well as social structures contribute to their continuing stigmatisation, despite their significant role in social reproduction.

Caste-based labour is further complicated by religious affinity. In an ethnographic study of women of two Dalit communities in Maharashtra in western India, Smita M. Patil (2013) shows that while one community she studied, Mahars, had converted to Buddhism under Ambedkarite influence and stopped following demeaning caste-based occupations, the other, Mangs, affiliated to Hinduism, continued those occupations (making brooms, baskets and ropes) as well as moved to new forms of stigmatising jobs in urban areas, such as sex work and domestic labour. However, in the urban spaces she studied, Patil found that Mahar and Mang women were building political solidarities, giving rise to a politics of Dalit feminism. Patil (2013: 43) is critical of mainstream feminism as well as Marxism to the extent that these are unable to grapple with their own privileged location, and remain blind to 'caste-cum-class oppression'.

Rekha Raj (2013) draws on critical race theory in the US, particularly that of Patricia Hill Collins and bell hooks to understand the ways in which 'women' are assumed to be *savarna* and 'Dalits' are assumed to be male. Through a brief history of Dalit women's politics in Kerala – Dalit Christian-led movements for education and critical thinking, land struggles of Dalit and Adivasi women, the iconic Dalit woman auto-rickshaw driver, Chitralekha, who stood up to sustained violence due to both of her stigmatised identities – Raj (2013: 62) highlights 'local specificities of caste and gender and their implications for Dalit women activists in dealing with a more visible "public life" through constant interactions with their community'.

Caste, gender and labour thus criss-cross intimately in the realm of production, and Marxist–feminist theory is reshaped by this recognition.

Women in 'reproduction' and the domestic labour debate

We know that it is not a 'natural' biological difference that lies behind the sexual division of labour, but certain ideological assumptions. So, on the one hand, women are supposed to be physically weak and unfit for heavy manual labour, but at the same time, when the manual work that women do is mechanised, making it both lighter and better paid, then it is men who receive training to use the new machinery, and women are edged out. This happens not only in factories, but even with work that was traditionally done by women within the community; for example, when electrically operated flour mills replace hand-pounding of grain, or machine-made nylon fishing nets replace the nets traditionally hand-made by women, it is men who are trained to take over these jobs, and women are forced to move into even lower-paid and more arduous manual work.

The unpaid work that women perform includes collection of fuel, fodder and water, animal husbandry, post-harvest processing, livestock maintenance, kitchen gardening and raising poultry that augment family resources. If women did not do this work, these goods would have to be purchased from the market, the services hired for a wage, or the family would have to do without. However, so naturalised are assumptions about gender roles that the Indian census did not recognise this as 'work' for a long time, since it is not performed for a wage, but is unpaid labour regarding the family. Women themselves tend not to report such work because they see these as 'domestic' responsibilities. Even when their activities generate income, they may be ignored if they get wedged in between other domestic chores (Krishna Raj 1990; Krishna Raj and Patel 1982). Women's work thus remained invisible.

As a result of sustained pressure from feminist economists, in the 1991 census, for the first time, the question 'Did you work at all last year' was amended. To it was added the phrase, 'including unpaid work on family farm or family enterprise', thus enabling such work to be made visible to the state. Feminist interventions that have made such changes possible believe that the more accurate the information the state has on the kinds of work performed by women, the more fine-tuned its policies on poverty reduction and employment generation, for example, are likely to be.

The sexual division of labour has serious implications for women's roles as citizens, because every woman's horizons are limited by this supposedly 'primary' responsibility. Whether in their choice of career, or their ability to participate in politics (trade unions, elections), women learn when very young to limit their ambitions. This self-limitation is what produces the so-called glass ceiling, the level above which professional women rarely rise; or the 'mommy track', the slower track upwards, where women put aside some of the most productive years of their lives in order to look after children. The assumption that women's primary profession is motherhood drives state policy as well – the governments of France, Germany and Hungary give women three years of maternity leave, in the hope of boosting the birth rate. In 2008, the Indian government increased maternity leave for its employees to six months, as well as instituting paid leave to its female employees for a further two years (to be availed of at any time) to take care of minor children. This essentially means that only women will have to take the difficult decision of putting their career on the back burner to bring up children, while younger men race ahead of them because their child care responsibilities are fully borne by their wives.

The sex-based segregation of labour is key, not just to maintaining the family, but also the economy, because the economy would collapse if this unpaid domestic labour had to be paid for by someone, either by the husband or the employer.

Rohini Hensman (2011), establishing that the household is a site not only of consumption but of production, holds Marx's failure to identify the latter as a limitation of Marxism. She offers a summary of the debate of the 1970s, in which the key question was, does domestic labour create value? Hensman agrees with Mariarosa Dalla Costa and Selma James (1972) and Wally Seccombe (1974) whose answer was yes, it does, and demonstrates through a number of possible scenarios of working-class families in India that unpaid domestic labour compensates for the fact that part of the value of labour power is kept by capital as additional surplus value.

Hensman also considers the substitution of waged for unwaged domestic labour among middle classes and the rich, creating an unregulated informal sector of exploited labour. In wealthy states with social democratic and state socialist regimes, these services were provided by the state, but this did not eliminate the gender division of labour. Caring work remains the responsibility of women, whether paid or unpaid, and Hensman points out that feminisms, whether bourgeois or socialist or radical, also devalued caring and connectedness because of the valorisation of individual autonomy.

Of course, it should be noted that paid domestic labour cannot be understood without the dimension of caste, for the kinds of domestic labour performed, and wages allotted for it, depend on the caste position of the (generally) woman worker who performs it. Cleaning of toilets would be a Dalit's work, while Dalits would not be permitted into many Hindu middle-class kitchens. Where they are, it is not uncommon for the dishes they have washed to be ritually cleansed again by their *savarna* employers.

Hensman refers to 'this contradiction at the heart of bourgeois ideology – the fact that taken to its logical conclusion, it threatens bourgeois society with extinction [*because labour cannot be productively reproduced without non-self-interest maximising women*], and therefore the reproduction of competitive individualism depends on its opposite (the reproduction of self-sacrificing women)' (2011: 25; author's interpolation and emphasis). From the standpoint of the socialist principle of solidarity, however, in Hensman's view, an ethic of care is inescapable for any labour movement, which must therefore work towards equal sharing of nurturing between men and women and struggle towards conditions that make this possible. Most trade unions in India have engaged in collective bargaining only for their own individual members and never had a solidaristic policy, except for some exceptions such as the Chhattisgarh Mines Mazdoor Sangh, in which women were more active (Hensman 2011: 25). Hensman concedes that 'the final goals of mutually affirmative relations within the household and adequate resources for the production of labour power cannot be reached under capitalism', but it is still possible to make 'considerable progress' in that direction even within capitalist society (2011: 25–26).

'STIGMA THEORY OF LABOUR'

Whether in the realm of production or reproduction, Mary John suggests that in the context of a caste society, what operates is a 'stigma theory of labour': 'a labour theory of value stands in conflict with a caste structured society where public labour represents not value, but stigma and humiliation. Caste based labour is degrading labour and cannot be valorised like value-producing labour' (John 2013: 183).

John's argument is that such labour cannot be abstracted as 'labour power' from the caste-marked stigmatised labouring body, especially that of a woman, even if it is public labour for which a wage may be paid. Additionally, public labour is still associated with labouring out of necessity, and is stigmatic in itself, leading to an ongoing tendency to opt out of the workforce when marriage and the income of the family make that possible.

Women's labour participation in India, measured in relation to education and family income, produces a U-curve when plotted as a graph, John points out. This suggests high labour participation among the poorest as well as among the relatively well to do at the other end of the spectrum, with very low levels for large sections of women in between. This is the opposite of most other parts of the world, where women's labour participation increases with education and income. This is 'a harsh empirical reminder', says John, that counter to the dominant view, the hold of caste is not weakening in India's economy today. Significantly, this pattern does not appear to have altered to any appreciable extent with the promises of globalisation and 'inclusive growth' (John 2013: 184).

Thus, when we consider the labour theory of value in India, not only the feminist perspective but also the dimensions of caste and practices of untouchability and untouchable labour need to be understood as constitutive of the very idea of labour.

FEMINIST CONCERNS THAT SHOULD BE MARXIST CONCERNS

Sexuality

It is evident that the family as it exists, the only form in which it is allowed to exist in most parts of the world – the heterosexual patriarchal family – is key to maintaining social stability, property relations, nation and community. Caste, race and community identity are produced through patrilineally *legitimate* birth. But so, too, in most cases, is the quintessentially modern identity of citizenship. The purity of these identities, of these social formations and of the existing regime of property relations is thus dependent on a particular form of the family. The emergence of heteronormativity as a legal, moral and medical principle, around the eighteenth century in Europe and in the nineteenth century in Africa and Asia, coincides with the rise of capitalism and imperialism. While not making a functionalist argument here, this historical coincidence is significant for Marxist scholarship, or it should be.

From the 1990s in India a range of political assertions that implicitly or explicitly challenged heteronormativity and the institution of monogamous patriarchal marriage became visible. Such challenges that we could term 'counter-heteronormative' are seen in the demand for the repeal of Section 377 of the Indian Penal Code that criminalises non-heterosexual sex, and in various kinds of political action on issues related to the lives and civil liberties of lesbian, gay, bisexual and transgender people and sex workers.

It is significant that counter-heteronormative movements in India should have turned to the women's movement as a natural ally. In the 1980s, the initial response of the established leadership of the women's movement was entirely homophobic, denouncing homosexuality as unnatural, a western aberration and an elitist preoccupation. Since that time, there has been intense dialogue within the women's movements, and great shifts in perception have taken place, especially in the left. Today, it is clear that challenges to heteronormativity are an unshakeable part of the agenda of feminist politics in India. From the point of view of Marxism, anti-capitalist queer politics must be seen as central to a transformative vision that challenges existing hetero-patriarchal property arrangements and the sexual division of labour. And since the cornerstone of heteropatriarchy in India is violently enforced caste endogamy, there is a strong and visible Dalit queer politics as well today.

Sex work
Prostitution as commodification/sex work as work
The term 'commodification of the female body' refers to a form of critique that feminists have long made of certain kinds of representation of female bodies – as objects of male desire, as saleable in the market. From the scantily clad, sexualised bodies of women in advertisements for luxury items that assume a male consumer, to highly commercialised beauty contests, to women who 'sell their bodies' – that is, give sex in exchange for money – all of these have come under the framework of commodification. The term is often loosely used to suggest the pollution by market values of objects and relationships that should properly be outside of commerce.

But in a world in which everyone makes a living, or tries to make a living, by selling a faculty (intellect, musical ability, training of various kinds, physical labour) or an object (from agricultural produce to mobile phones to cheap and shiny objects at traffic lights), this kind of critique has lost its edge. Is a professor commodifying her mind when she accepts payment for teaching? And if so, why is this acceptable to feminists and not, say, a woman commodifying her body parts to advertisers, or to clients who have sex with her? One answer would be to say that the former has greater dignity and social respect than the latter, but as feminists surely we question the ways in which 'dignity' and 'social respect' are assigned to some forms of work and not others? To intellectual labour, but not to manual labour? Surely the feminist task is to upturn these values, to transform the ways in which we look at the world, and not to reaffirm the world as it is?

Perhaps we should go back and take a closer look at what Marx said about commodification, and see whether that helps in any way to rethink these paradoxes. Marx used the term 'commodity' to refer to something that has exchange value, a thing that can be bought and sold in the market. A commodity appears to be a 'mysterious' thing, said Marx, because the human labour that has gone into its production is obscured, and the commodity appears to be a purely physical object with a value that is *intrinsic* to it. Human labour is performed in a network of social relations, but this fact is hidden, and commodities appear to relate to one another directly (Marx [1887] 1965).

It is this critique of the commodity form under capitalism that has been extended by feminism to the ways in which the female body is produced as a commodity. But as the discussion above suggests, the application of this critique to human bodies is to lose sight of human agency, will, volition, or whatever one may term the fact that human beings think and make choices while objects produced by them do not.

Marx also says about the commodity: 'It is plain that commodities cannot go to market and make exchanges on their own account. We must therefore have recourse to their guardians, who are also their owners . . . In order that these objects may enter into relations with each other as commodities, their guardians must place themselves in relation to one another' (Marx [1887] 1965: 60).

This mutual recognition by guardians of one another as owning their commodities is established in capitalist society through the contract.

The idea of the contract involves the myth of two equal individual parties mutually agreeing to certain terms and conditions of exchange – of labour or commodities – for money. Marx himself has, of course, a critique of this myth, for the person selling his/her labour power is not equal in any real sense to the person who employs him or her. The equality is purely formal and legal. But as long as, and to the extent that, work is enabled under capitalist conditions, the idea of the contract is what makes possible a struggle for equitable conditions. After all, why is it preferable to be wage labour than bonded labour? Because at least theoretically, the contract assumes consent, and mutually negotiated conditions of work. And at least theoretically, these are protected by law. What after all, is the Right to Work? A demand to be brought under the capitalist contract?

This is where we come to the problem of extending the critique of commodification to women's bodies. To think of advertising, pornography or sex work as commodification is to think of the women participating in this work as 'commodities', that is, as objects owned by others, men, who are the real parties to the contract. But it is, after all, women themselves who are parties to the contract. Are they exploited? Yes of course. But all work under capitalism is 'exploitation', that is, it involves the extraction of surplus value from labour. Under capitalism, the 'choice' that the labour market offers is between more and less arduous, more and less meagrely paid work.

If women choose, then, to take up professions such as modelling, or sex work, or any other profession in which they commodify some body parts rather than others, should not feminists stand by them in demanding better conditions of work, more pay and dignity in their professions, rather than going along with misogynist values that demean certain kinds of work altogether?

Feminism has for long seen prostitution as violence against women, and many feminists still do. However, a new understanding of the practice has emerged with the gradual politicisation of people who engage in prostitution, and their voice becoming increasingly public. One of the key transformations that has come about as a result of this, is the emergence of the term sex work to replace 'prostitution'.

The understanding behind this is that we need to demystify 'sex' – it is only the mystification of sex by both patriarchal discourses and feminists that makes sex work appear to be 'a fate worse than death'.

Sex work in India

As with all labour in India, sex workers' bodies, too, are marked by caste. Earlier forms of temple prostitution were based on *devadasi* communities – traditional, matrilineal communities of 'lower'-caste women who performed music and dance in temples. The abolition of this practice during the anti-imperialist movement by social reform legislation has been understood in a complex way by feminists. The work of feminist scholars (Kannabiran 1995; Srinivasan 1985; Nair 1994) shows that *devadasis* had rights to property that other Hindu women did not have, which was ended with the abolition of the institution, often reducing former *devadasis* to the very 'prostitution' that the reform movements had claimed to rescue them from, leaving them with little control over whom they could sell sex to. In a study of Sudra and outcaste *devadasis* of Andhra Pradesh and Karnataka, Priyadarshini Vijaisri (2004) foregrounds the question of caste. She argues that within the reform movement, the relatively upper-caste (though non-Brahmin) Sudra men did not want to do away entirely with the *devadasi* institution. They, in effect, retained the institution for outcaste *devadasis*. Therefore, while the 'emasculation' of the men of Sudra *devadasi* families (due to matrilineal property rights and the relative sexual autonomy of the *devadasis*) was a central thrust of the reform movement, the masculinity of Dalit/outcaste men was not an issue for abolition politics. Thus, Vijaisri (2004) introduces an additional caste dimension to the question of *devadasi* abolition, by demonstrating that the 'reforms' in effect domesticated the relatively upper-caste Sudra *devadasis* while perpetuating sacred prostitution among the outcaste Dalits. Here we observe an analysis that does not see Dalit and Sudra politics in alliance, but rather, sees Sudras as marginalising Dalits.

In contemporary India, consider the preliminary findings of the first pan-India survey of sex workers where 3 000 women from 14 states and one union territory were surveyed, all of them from outside collectivised or organised spaces, precisely in order to bring out the voice of the un-politicised section of sex workers (Sahni and Shankar 2011). The significant finding was that about 71 per cent of them said they had entered the profession willingly.

This study establishes what feminist research on sex work has shown in that the model of *choice* versus *force* is utterly inadequate in understanding the motivations of women in sex work (Shah 2003). In fact, most sex workers have multiple work identities. The study found that a significant number of women move between other occupations and sex work. For example, a street vendor may get customers while selling vegetables and a dancer at marriages may also take clients for sex work.

Poverty and limited education are conditions that push women into labour markets at early ages, and sex work was found to be one among several options available to women in the labour market. This means that other occupations are often pursued before sex work emerges or is considered as an option. Sex work offers a significant supplementary income to other forms of labour. Many of those surveyed also worked in diverse occupations in the unskilled manufacturing or services sector for extremely poor wages.

Why did women either leave these other occupations or supplement their income from those occupations with sex work? The responses were: low pay, insufficient salary, no profit in business, no regular work, only seasonal work, not getting money even after work, or could not run their homes on that income. Quite simply, sex work is an economically attractive option (Sahni and Shankar 2011).

What this study does is force us to recognise that 'choice' is severely limited in the labour market as a whole. If people find it possible to move to work that is less exhausting and better paying, they will do so. There is no more or less agency exercised in 'choosing' to work as a domestic servant in multiple households for a pittance and with minimum dignity, or be exploited by contractors in arduous construction work, than there is in 'choosing' to do sex work – whether as the sole occupation or alongside other work. We would want that the conditions of all kinds of work should be dignified, that there should be minimum wage regulations, reasonable leisure time, and so on.

Under prevailing conditions, workers may even be prepared for more arduous hours if it means a slightly higher wage; that is, they may 'choose' this option. For instance, in India, the Karnataka state government decided in early 2011 to amend the Factories Act of 1948 to increase the daily working hours of employees from nine to ten hours in an attempt to increase productivity. It claimed the move was meant to help women workers in the garment industry, and that, in fact, the workers had themselves demanded the increase in working hours. Of course, what the workers wanted was an increase in wages, a demand they knew would not have been granted unconditionally. What this 'demand' from the workers showed was that they are grossly underpaid and so desperate to earn a little more money that they are prepared to work extra (Hunasavadi 2011).

One can see the operation of choice here – limited but still exercised within possible limits. The 'choice' to do sex work is no more or less constrained than any choice of work is under capitalism. Of course, as feminists, we should back policies and institutions that support women who want to leave the profession. Then there is the fact that sex workers often face rape and physical abuse from their clients. Decriminalisation of sex work would enable such women to take these matters to the law in the same way as any other raped woman (or person of any gender).

The growing sex workers' movement in India thus provokes us into questioning the assumption that it is better to be one man's wife, effectively subject to feudal power relations, than a sex worker, subject to a capitalist contract. An alternative way in which organised sex workers conceptualise their work is to move away from the idea of being a 'worker', a wage slave under capitalism, to a person running her own business. In many parts of India, prostitution is referred to as *dhanda* or business, and women who engage in prostitution are referred to as *dhandawali* or women in business. The Maharashtra-based organisations Sampada Gramin Mahila Sanstha and Veshya Anyay Mukti Parishad prefer this as a self-description, as opposed to Durbar Mahila Samanwaya Committee in West Bengal, which uses *jaun karmi* or sex worker. Thus, the former use the term 'people in prostitution and sex work' (PPS) to acknowledge the diverse groups covered under this term, which include *devadasis*, housewives who sell sex, women who work in brothels, streetwalkers, and male sex workers. 'Furthermore, the term PPS validates multiple identities by acknowledging people in prostitution and sex work as people first: when she is with a client she is a *dhandawali*; when she is with her children, she is a mother; when she is educating her community, she is a peer educator' (Pillai, Seshu and Shivdas 2008).

While sex worker unions are politically allied to feminist movements, a critique of this alliance emerged from some vocal Dalit feminists who see prostitution as violence. Their critique of sex worker unions comes from the position that it is largely Dalit and Bahujan women who are forced into prostitution due to either widespread poverty in these communities, or because they belong to castes traditionally identified as temple prostitutes. The argument is, therefore, that this degrading profession should not be exalted as a choice of occupation. Increasingly, sex workers' unions (including Dalit Bahujan sex workers) and non-sex worker Dalit feminists clash over this issue at public fora. Attempts are ongoing to produce a constructive dialogue on this issue.

Ecology

The most well-known eco-feminist in India, Vandana Shiva, is not Marxist, but makes her argument from a larger critique of capitalist modernity, which she sees as embodying a 'masculinist' perspective. This masculinist perspective treats forests as a resource to be exploited for its monetary value, and sets up private property in forest wealth. On the other hand, the indigenous people who have lived in these forests for generations have a feminine, life-conserving view of forests as a diverse and self-reproducing system, shared by a diversity of common views (Shiva 1999). The implicit upper-caste Hindu version of the 'feminine principle' that Shiva espouses, however, has troubled feminists writing about the environment from other perspectives, whether these are explicitly Marxist or not. Thus, Bina Agarwal's (1999) critique of Shiva's analysis points both to the essentialising of 'women' and the 'feminine', and questions Shiva's assumption that pre-colonial forms of community among forest dwellers was more democratic. Agarwal posits the term 'environmental feminism' in place of eco-feminism to address these concerns (Agarwal 1999).

An explicitly socialist feminist analysis of ecology and industrialisation is offered by Gabriele Dietrich, who has lived and worked in Madurai in southern India for decades. Dietrich is part of a socialist feminist strand in India, which is influenced by Maria Mies's reading of Rosa Luxemburg, which sees capitalism as producing several internal colonies, of which women are the 'last colony' (Mies, Bennholdt-Thomsen and Von Werlhof 1988). A socialist feminist vision in Dietrich's understanding, then, must bring women, 'the last colony', into alliances with other 'internal colonies', such as Dalits, Adivasis (indigenous peoples), unorganised sector workers and minorities. Dalits here would include communities of fisher-people displaced by capitalist transformations of the fishing industry, for example, as well as other labouring communities displaced by such ecologically unsustainable practices. Placing ecological concerns at the centre of her socialist feminism – 'the deepening ecological crisis is the deepest contradiction in the "total market" policies of global capitalism' (Dietrich 2003: 4549), Dietrich (2014) cites the example of the National Alliance of People's Movements that has worked on such alliance building.

Dietrich is thus critical of what was 'actually existing socialism in eastern Europe' for falling into a 'growth oriented paradigm of industrialism' treating nature merely as a resource to be exploited (2003: 4549). She points out that in the 1970s there were debates on the left about whether the ecological question could be solved within capitalism, suggesting a lacuna in theorising that delinked capitalism and industrialisation, thus assuming that even within socialist frames, large-scale industrialisation was necessary. It was the alliance of peace and environmental movements and the women's movements that addressed this conceptual shortcoming, pointing out that eco-socialism is the only alternative that imagines a different political economy altogether, one in which large-scale industrialisation and exploitation of nature are both rejected.

For Dietrich, then, Marxism needs to be overhauled from its heart outwards to accommodate the ecological question, and it needs to retune its modernist romance with science and technology to recognise that these are not neutral forms of knowledge but masculinist, violent and destructive of nature. Thus, Dietrich (2003: 4551) renders into an explicitly socialist feminist framework the kind of critique made by Shiva.

An added layer of complexity emerges from a Dalit perspective that sees the destruction of traditional livelihoods by capitalism as a progressive force that rescues Dalits from menial and degrading labour that is traditionally their lot (Prasad 2004). However, this kind of argument for promoting 'Dalit capitalism' is rarely made by feminists, who recognise the large numbers of Dalits displaced by processes of capitalist industrialisation. For feminists, then, in the words of Nalini Nayak, who works with fisher-people's movements on issues of livelihood and ecological sustainability, 'ecological movements are the resource base of our feminism' (Menon 2012: xi).

CONCLUSION

Returning in conclusion to critical race theory, the resonances should be clear. The identity of 'caste' is produced *sociologically* through ancient texts as well as *materially* by draconian and strict rules of endogamy and labour restrictions, a materiality reproduced and reiterated over centuries. In addition, since about the eighteenth century to the present, caste identity has also been asserted militantly by different kinds of political mobilisations. Thus, caste is both socially constructed *and* has real material manifestations. In these ways, critical race theory resonates with any analysis of caste in contemporary India.

Feminist analysis in India therefore needs to engage seriously with caste discrimination and caste identity in order to reshape itself, as well as the terrain of Marxism.

NOTE

1   Both Dalit and Bahujan are political self-categorisations. Dalit (literally 'ground down') is the term militantly adopted by the former 'untouchables' or 'outcastes', the lowest category of all in the Hindu caste order. Bahujan (literally 'majority')

refers generally to other 'lower' castes inside the caste order – 'Sudras' or Other Backward Classes (OBCs) in constitutional language. 'Dalit Bahujan' refers to a political alliance of non-Brahmin castes, coming together against the Brahminical order. However, it is important to note that Dalit and OBC/Sudras do not always come together politically, as the latter are also the proximate exploiters that Dalits face in many contexts, even more than relatively distant Brahmins. So there is often Dalit-OBC/Sudra conflict as well.

REFERENCES

Agarwal, B. 1999. 'The gender and environment debate: Lessons from India'. In *Gender and Politics in India*, edited by N. Menon. Delhi: Oxford University Press, pp. 96–142.

Dalla Costa, M. and James, S. 1972. *The Power of Women and the Subversion of the Community*. Bristol: Falling Wall Press.

Datar, C. 1989. *Waging Change: Women Tobacco Workers in Nipani Organise*. New Delhi: Kali for Women.

Dietrich, G. 2003. 'Loss of socialist vision and options before the women's movement', *Economic and Political Weekly*, 38 (43): 4547–4554.

Dietrich, G. 2014. 'Feminist-socialist transformation facing neo-liberal capitalism', *Mainstream Weekly*, LII (48) 22 November.

Dutta, M. 2016. 'Place of life stories in labour geography: Why does it matter?', *Geoforum*, 77: 1–4.

Fanon, F. 2003. 'The fact of blackness'. In *Identities: Race, Class, Gender and Nationality*, edited by L.M. Alcoff and E. Mendieta. Oxford and Berlin: Blackwell Publishing, pp. 62–74.

Gopal, M. 2013. 'Ruptures and reproduction in caste/gender/labour', *Economic and Political Weekly*, 48 (18): 91–97.

Hensman, R. 2011. 'Revisiting the domestic labour debate: An Indian perspective', *Historical Materialism*, 19 (3): 3–28.

Hunasavadi, S. 2011. 'Daily working hours for women all set to go up in Karnataka', DNA India, 23 February. Accessed 27 September 2017, http://www.dnaindia.com/bangalore/report_daily-working-hours-for-women-all-set-to-go-up-in-karnataka_1511640.

John, M. 2013. 'The problem of women's labour: Some autobiographical perspectives', *Indian Journal of Gender Studies*, 20 (2): 177–212.

Kannabiran, K. 1995. 'Judiciary, social reform and debate on "religious prostitution" in colonial India', *Economic and Political Weekly*, 30 (43): WS 61–71.

Krishna Raj, M. 1990. 'Women's work in the Indian census', *Economic and Political Weekly*, 25 (48/49): 2663–2672.

Krishna Raj, M. and Patel, V. 1982. 'Women's liberation and the political economy of housework: An Indian perspective', *Women's Studies International*, 2 (July): 16–19.

Marx, Karl. [1887] 1965. *Capital: A Critique of Political Economy: Volume I*. Moscow: Progress Publishers. See https://www.marxists.org/archive/marx/works/download/pdf/Capital-Volume-I.pdf.

Menon, N. 2012. *Seeing like a Feminist*. New Delhi: Penguin and Zubaan.

Mies, M., Bennholdt-Thomsen, V. and Von Werlhof, C. 1988. *Women: The Last Colony*. London: Zed Books.

Nair, J. 1994. 'The devadasi, Dharma and the state', *Economic and Political Weekly*, 29 (50): 3157–3167.

Patil, S.M. 2013. 'Revitalising Dalit feminism: Towards reflexive, anti-caste agency of Mang and Mahar Women in Maharashtra', *Economic and Political Weekly*, 48 (18): 37–43.

Pillai, S., Seshu, M. and Shivdas, M. 2008. 'Embracing the rights of people in prostitution and sex workers, to address HIV and AIDS effectively', *Gender & Development*, 16 (2): 313–326.

Prasad, C. 2004. *Dalit Diary: 1999–2003: Reflections on Apartheid in India*. Chennai: Navayana Publishing.

Raj, R. 2013. 'Dalit women as political agents: A Kerala experience', *Economic and Political Weekly*, 48 (18): 56–63.

Sahni, R. and Shankar V.K. 2011. 'The first pan-India survey of sex workers: A summary of preliminary findings'. Accessed 27 September 2017, http://sangram.org/Download/Pan-India-Survey-of-Sex-workers.pdf.

Seccombe, W. 1974. 'The housewife and her labour under capitalism', *New Left Review*, 1 (83): 3–24.

Shah, S. 2003. 'Sex work in the global economy', *New Labor Forum*, 12 (1): 74–81.

Shiva, V. 1999. 'Colonialism and the evolution of masculinist forestry'. In *Gender and Politics in India*, edited by N. Menon. Delhi: Oxford University Press, pp. 39–71.

Srinivasan, A. 1985. 'Reform and revival: The devadasi and her dance', *Economic and Political Weekly*, 20 (44): 1869–1876.

Vijaisri, P. 2004. *Recasting the Devadasi: Patterns of Sacred Prostitution in Colonial South India*. New Delhi: Kanishka Publishers.

Racism After Apartheid

PART TWO

AGAINST RACISM IN SOUTH AFRICA

CHAPTER

8

THE REPRODUCTION OF RACIAL INEQUALITY IN SOUTH AFRICA: THE COLONIAL UNCONSCIOUS AND DEMOCRACY

Peter Hudson

The objective in what follows is to analyse the status of colonialism under contemporary South African conditions after the democratic breakthrough of 1994.

The notion of a democratic breakthrough is (by itself) too blunt to capture what has happened vis-à-vis the articulation of colonialism and democracy in South Africa. In particular, it fails to rule out the thesis according to which the reproduction of colonialism in South Africa can be reduced to an effect of the *inertia* of the past, with colonialism itself already *neutralised in the present*, cut off from any structural motor and thus eventually vanishing. All the conceptions of colonialism that identify it as a residue of the past, of apartheid/colonialism, or even of an earlier articulation of modes of production (Wolpe 1988), thus also subscribe to the inertia thesis. Across the left, from the Tripartite Alliance to the Economic Freedom Fighters, the United Front and the National Union of Metal Workers of South Africa, there is agreement that South Africa is still a colonial society. At the same time, reference is made to the democratic breakthrough of 1994 (Turok 2011: 247). This understanding of the current relationship between colonialism and democracy pulls in two opposing directions – one emphasising the break with colonialism and the other the latter's resilience. But what we are not offered is any conceptualisation able to hold these together. Attempts to invoke (see Turok 2011: 234) the form (democracy)/content (colonialism) distinction get us nowhere because they merely repeat the problem in the guise of a solution. What is not confronted is the question of just how colonialism lives on in the democratic state, that is to say, of how democracy is able simultaneously to repress and accommodate – if not legitimate – colonialism.

It is argued here that post-1994 colonialism does not disappear but is repressed and unconscious. This does not, however, prevent it from continuing to structure social practice. It does this without seeming to disrupt the democratic non-racial order by inserting itself in an ambivalence at the heart of capitalism.

Colonialism is inserted into democracy via capitalism, with the result that it accedes to the place of capital and its correlative powers that are unconsciously in the service of the reproduction of colonialism. It is thus argued that in order to account for *capitalist* practice in South Africa today, the hypothesis of the colonial unconscious has to be invoked.

It is proposed that only by approaching colonialism today as unconscious can its status after the democratic breakthrough be precisely articulated. Far from being the mere effect of an earlier structure, as claimed by the inertia and residue argument, colonialism is constantly reproduced in the present by the intervention of the colonial unconscious into the structure of democratic life.

THE UNCONSCIOUS IS HISTORY

Subsequent to its discursive turn, the psychoanalytic (concept of the) unconscious is a set of practices of signification that produce meaning and subjectivity.[1] This decentred and differentially constituted subject is the subject of the unconscious. In other words, it is the subject of the signifier, which, since Saussure, we have known as negative and relational. The signifier does not constitute itself but depends entirely on its difference from other signifiers, on what it is not. The unconscious is therefore *relational* in its structure, not self-centred and self-sufficient – it is neither individual nor collective substance but structured practice (Eagleton 2016; Tomsic 2015).

It is only in the contingent and arbitrary practice of articulating signifiers that meaning, the signified, and lived experience, are produced. The order of the signifier is a formal autonomous order of difference that produces and does not reproduce or express social objectivity: neither God, Nature, History nor the Economy is the foundation of the order of the signifier.

The process of the production of meaning is structurally absent from consciousness by virtue of its relational character, which makes it impossible for it to be transparent to consciousness. If the articulation of signifiers productive of meaning were transparent to consciousness, the effect of meaning would not be produced. Thus 'false consciousness' is a pleonasm – all consciousness is false (Tomsic 2015). The result is that consciousness itself is fetishised and represses its structural determination. The absence of the structural cause has as its correlate the effect of fetishism (Althusser 1972; Rancière 1967; Tomsic 2015).

The concept of the unconscious flows directly from the theory of the signifier in so far as this involves the distinction between the signifier and the signified. The differential structure of the signifier means that its subject is not the unified and centred subject of consciousness but the relationally structured subject of the unconscious; this is repressed by the subject of consciousness, which takes itself as *causa sui*.

The unconscious refers then to those relationally structured practices that sustain and account for the fetishism of the imaginary, of lived experience.

Another way of putting this is to say that because the Big Other does not exist (being nothing but untotalisable difference), the subject is split between consciousness and differential value, the structural cause. The Saussurian bar that separates the signifier (value) from the signified (meaning) says it all already – signifier and signified are not aligned, that is, there is no immanent link between them, and the unconscious/consciousness distinction is the necessary effect of this lack of a relation.

The unconscious is thus both historical and political. It is not a timeless universal or symbolic transcendental, but refers to antagonisms, tensions and torsions within determinate social formations, and the concept of the unconscious thus has explanatory traction in social and political analysis. As Samo Tomsic (2015) says, 'the unconscious is history pressing in on itself' and manifesting in symptomatic disturbances of the dominant order.

COLONIALISM AND THE COLONIAL UNCONSCIOUS

'The Black man does not exist; anymore than the White man.'
– Frantz Fanon, *Black Skin, White Masks*

Frantz Fanon's revolution in the theory of colonialism is twofold. Firstly, he introduces modern structuralism by focusing on the *relation* between black and white as the structural cause of both: white and black become signifiers, neither of which has meaning independently of the other, with the pure difference between them constitutive of both.[2] Colonialism is an autonomous formal order of difference, which constitutes forms of subjectivity and of lived experience, the imaginary. The black/white relation is, then, an arbitrary and contingent relation between signifiers without an external foundation.

In a second move (which has to be read carefully), Fanon (1968) ontologises the colonial differential: white is equated with plenitude and black with lack, non-existence. But, remember, this is the ontology of a determinate articulation of signifiers, thus arbitrary and contingent. This black alienation and negativity is not constitutive – the necessary consequence of the subject's dependence on the signifier – but historically, that is, colonially, constituted (see Tomsic 2015 on the constitutive/constituted distinction). Colonialism, in other words, constitutes the white as a full Althusserian ego-subject and the black as a non-subject lacking self-possession and 'subsisting at the level of non-being' (Fanon 1968: 131).[3] In this sense, colonialism for Fanon amounts to a specific distribution of being, of lack and plenitude, with the white subject minimally out of joint and the black subject maximally so.

As non-existent and indescribable (Fanon 1968), the black non-subject is the internal condition of possibility of the self-centred and full white subject. Here, the figure of the black colonised complements, i.e., sutures and totalises, whiteness. At the same time, however, its very heterogeneity prevents it from being digested by the colonial order, and, as a bone in the throat, it functions as the condition of *im*possibility of this order, as *antagonism*.

Understood as a formal difference, as having the structure of a signifier, colonialism immediately involves the unconscious. All those practices of signification fixing white and black comprise the colonial unconscious, and the colonial subject is unconscious of them in virtue of their relational, hence absent, character. Colonial subjectivity is thus unaware of its structural cause and takes itself as *causa sui*. Racial fetishism is the objective form necessarily, that is, structurally, assumed by the colonial antagonism.

The colonial unconscious is, thus, the differential and antagonistic subject of the colonial signifier.

THE CAPITALIST UNCONSCIOUS AND THE COLONIAL UNCONSCIOUS

Under capitalism, the antagonistic class signifier, the irresolvable antagonism between capital and the proletariat, is repressed by its own product, fetishised subjectivity. Classes only ever appear objectively as homo economicus, and class antagonism and struggle as competition. As Glyn Daly (2011: 373) puts it: 'Class functions as a kind of objectified unconscious: the collective markers of the constitutive repression inherent in the reproduction of capitalism.' The class antagonism thus *objectively* appears as a relation of equality between autonomous individuals: homo economicus is the form taken by fetishism under capitalist conditions. Marx famously showed, in the chapter on 'Simple Reproduction' in *Capital, Volume 1*, how, because they exist as relations of commodity exchange, capitalist relations of production are *experienced* as between free and equal individuals. This effect of fetishisation occultates the antagonism constitutive of capitalism, which comprises its unconscious. Note, however, that the relations of production, the separation of the working class from the means of production, cannot on their own produce the experience of free subjectivity. The intervention of the ideological and juridico-political instances is decisive here. What democracy produces vis-à-vis capitalism in South Africa is, therefore, the realisation of the process of capitalist fetishisation, that is, the occultation of the exploitative and antagonistic relations of production by the *objective* appearance of free subjectivity. It does the same for colonialism.

The colonial antagonism is not repressed in the same way as the capitalist antagonism. Under capitalism, the antagonism is repressed by the exchange of equivalents between autonomous subjects.[4] The specifically capitalist effect of fetishism erases antagonism from the capitalist imaginary. Under colonialism, the colonial signifier bleeds into the colonial signified with the result that colonial fetishism does not bar antagonism: in other words, racial antagonism is integral to the colonial imaginary itself (the so-called immediacy of colonial antagonism). Therefore, under colonialism, the lacking black subject is never anything other than a bone in the throat of the system. Capitalism represses and reproduces itself via an 'antagonism-free' imaginary, colonialism via a 'fetishised antagonism'. Under the conditions of colonialism *stricto sensu*, only the discursive processes that produce subjectivity are repressed and unconscious: the fundamental antagonism between white plenitude and black lack is fetished but not removed from the theatre of consciousness: the antagonism between white being and black non-being is not repressed but is a category of experience. Only when we move from colonialism *stricto sensu* to colonialism under conditions of democracy is the colonial/racial antagonism itself repressed and colonial forms of subjectivity made unconscious.

THE COLONIAL UNCONSCIOUS AND LIBERAL DEMOCRACY

> 'They do not know it, but they are doing it.'
> – Karl Marx, *Capital*

The capitalist unconscious – the practice of class antagonism – produces and is repressed by the fetishisation of homo economicus. The combination of capitalism with liberal democracy has the effect of repressing the class antagonism under the democratic regime of individual liberty and equality. However, liberal democracy has a different relationship to and effect on colonialism and the colonial unconscious. Bear in mind that colonial lived experience is shot through with racial antagonism (the immediacy of colonialism) whereas the capitalist imaginary occultates antagonism. Democracy does not have to repress the product of the capitalist symbolic, that is, homo economicus, it complements it, but it does have to repress the product of the colonial symbolic, that is, self-identification in racially antagonistic terms. Under democratic conditions, the colonial unconscious must then be understood as referring to not only the discursive production of racist beliefs but to those beliefs (the signified of the colonial unconscious) as well. In this sense, colonialism becomes unconscious when it is displaced by a set of relations, practices and subject positions incompatible with it.

Even before 1994, colonial subjectivity was not fully conscious in that colonial subjects took themselves 'seriously', that is, as self-sufficient, with the symbolic relations and mechanisms responsible for their constitution (the colonial symbolic) remaining unknown to them. In this sense, all colonial subjects are unconscious, that is, cut off (in the imaginary) from their real structural cause. But the point being made here is that before 1994, whites were conscious of themselves as 'white', even if unconscious of the mechanism producing this effect of subjectivity. After 1994, they are still unconscious of their symbolic construction but now they are *also* unconscious of being 'white' because their dominant identity is as 'citizen'.[5] Now, they are constituted by two mechanisms, both unconscious, but one of whose effects (democratic egalitarian subjectivity) is conscious of itself. And note that the repression of colonial consciousness is fundamentally structural here in that the self-consciousness of a subject cannot simultaneously be colonial and democratic – to the extent it is one, the other just is repressed. However, if it is repressed, how do we know it exists and is active?

Here we need to refer to the specificity of the psychoanalytic transcendental turn – psychoanalysis sets out to derive the conditions that involve 'the gaps in the phenomena of our consciousness' (Freud 1940: 119). Thus, 'the oldest and best meaning of the word unconscious is the descriptive one; we call unconscious any process the existence of which we are obliged to assume – because we infer it from its effects' (Freud 1933: 63).

Slavoj Zizek (2004) then uses this transcendental argument for the unconscious as correlative to the 'gaps in consciousness' for the purpose of social analysis in an account of anti-Semitism. He firstly points out the concept of the unconscious transforms the standard opposition of subjective and objective:

> It subverts the standard opposition of subjective and objective. Of course, fantasy is, by definition, not objective (in the naïve sense of existing independently of the subject's perceptions). However, it is also not subjective (in the sense of being reducible to the subject's consciously experienced intuitions). Rather, fantasy belongs to the bizarre category of the objectively-subjective – the way things actually, objectively, seem to you even if they don't seem that way to you. (Zizek 2004: 94)

So, here, the unconscious is not really 'hidden away' at all but present, 'embedded' in social practice, in all those instances where social normativity 'breaks down' and one does or says something that interrupts the 'normal' flow of practice and meaning: it is in its practice that the subject 'bears witness' to how things 'effectively' appear to it, as opposed to how they 'immediately' appear to it. The (Freudian) unconscious thus refers to 'the knowledge which doesn't know itself', the 'unknown knowns', 'the disavowed beliefs and suppositions we are not even aware of adhering to ourselves' but which still govern our practice (Zizek 2004: 94–95).

The anti-Semite

The 'anti-Semite' consciously defines himself as universalist – and experiences himself in his interactions with others in purely egalitarian terms. He insists he is not an anti-Semite and he is being sincere. But in his social interaction with others *we* can discern – even if he cannot see it – a pattern of, for example, aggressively bumping into Jews or turning away from Jews when he should not by the norms of etiquette to which he consciously subscribes. From this we conclude that he must believe Jews to be as defined in anti-Semitism – even if – as is the case – he is unconscious of holding this belief: we have to posit it, otherwise we cannot account for his social practice. This unconscious belief is not hidden away from us, only from him. He can deny we are interpreting his behaviour correctly, but, there it is – we can pick it out – even if he cannot – an objective pattern – which compels us to attribute to him *qua* subject, beliefs of which he is unconscious, that is, he is not aware of how Jews 'really seem to him' (Zizek 2004: 95).[6]

And as we have pointed out, the standard 'subjective/objective' distinction is crossed several ways here – this unconscious is subjective but not consciously subjective; it is objective too, but in so far as it is, it is also immediately subjective.

Zizek goes further in the elucidation of the status of this unconscious when he points out where it is to be located vis-à-vis consciousness by underlining its reflexivity. In this sense, it is 'equivalent' to the Cartesian cogito. What this subject does not know is what he thinks about what he thinks. Here at this point of self-reflexivity is to be located the 'unknown knowns', which are responsible for the unconscious judgement he passes on what he consciously thinks 'is the case' and 'is to be done'. Far from being 'beneath' thought, expressing some 'primitive substrate', some substantial instinct, this unconscious, that is, these disavowed beliefs, relates to consciousness as the site where its reflexivity breaks down, where it cannot access what it thinks about its thought (Zizek 2012: 554).

THE COLONIAL UNCONSCIOUS AND CAPITALISM: 'COLONIALISM OF A (VERY) SPECIAL TYPE'

The colonial unconscious is on display in contemporary South Africa everywhere; the texture of democratic life is ambivalent enough for this unconscious to appear without openly defying the non-racial democratic imperative. Capitalism is one such site of weakness in the fabric of democracy.

Under capitalism, a class relation of antagonism is occluded by the exchange of equivalents by free and equal individuals. Capitalism *objectively* appears to comprise free exchanges between equals but this conceals the exercise of class powers. Capitalist relations of production and class are, as Marx insisted, 'invisible'. Here is the *ambiguity* in capitalism that gives the colonial unconscious its entry point, viz-à-viz this two-sidedness. The capitalist in South Africa can thus objectively appear to treat individuals as free and equal, and, at the same time, because he is still in thrall to the colonial unconscious, be the vector of a specifically colonial/racial distribution of assets and opportunities. Occupying the place of capital, the colonial unconscious intervenes in the texture of democratic, non-racial egalitarianism to impose and reproduce colonial inequality and colonial relations of production without *objectively appearing to do so*. It is this ambiguity of capitalism, combined with the property powers of capital, that enable the colonial unconscious to determine the distribution of assets, resources and opportunities *silently and invisibly*. It is precisely because the class powers of capital are concealed by the fetishism of man and the commodity, that is, objectively appear as relations among individuals/subjects, that the colonial unconscious, via its occupancy of the place of capital, can distribute resources and opportunities along colonial/racial lines while seeming to obey the imperatives of homo economicus.

The capitalist objectively and systematically privileges whites across all aspects of his practice – investment, procurement, management and employment. That he does this is not something that can be empirically doubted. However, it passes under the democratic radar – with the effect of reproducing the colonial distribution of assets, income and opportunity, colonial relations of production. Capitalist practice in South Africa has not changed, it is as colonial as ever. All that has changed is that it is now unconscious of its colonial character because this is now occultated by the combination of capitalism and liberal democracy.[7]

The South African capitalist subject maintains he is non-racial and that if he favours whites in his practice that is only because he is acting in a context where there is already a racial distribution of capital and competence. He might be reproducing this through his practice, but this is just a by-product of the apartheid distribution of resources and opportunities that governs his economic decisions. He is not influenced by race itself, in fact he does not see race – it has been effectively excluded from his consciousness and he is governed exclusively by the non-racial law of accumulation.

This is the inertia theory of the reproduction of colonial inequality in South Africa. On this colonial inequality in the present is an effect of colonial inequality in the past – apartheid lives on although it has been displaced by democracy and survives without the intervention of colonialism in the present. The critique of the inertia thesis that follows has political implications in that what it argues is that colonialism is not the by-product and vanishing effect of the past, but unconsciously structures the present; and this, in turn, has implications for how we understand inter alia the democratic breakthrough of 1994.

Although he disavows it, the capitalist really is (unconsciously) acting like a colonial subject. He claims he only gravitates towards whites because whites are historically advantaged but what he does not see, however, is that this historical advantage exercises no independent causality over him: its meaning depends entirely on how it is symbolically framed. The white-skill nexus, by which he claims to be objectively constrained, depends entirely on the colonial symbolic of white plenitude and black lack. Unless framed in these terms, historic advantage will not be taken as a *given* but will be transformed.

Only if one believes in it, that is, unconsciously believes in the colonial fantasy, will white historic advantage be allowed to constrain practice. Only if the subject of the colonial signifier is still producing an effect of whiteness will white historic advantage be taken as a given.

There is no neutral position vis-à-vis historic advantage: it always has to be framed by symbolic coordinates. If it is framed in non-racial democratic terms it immediately becomes the object of a transformative practice. To the extent to which this does not occur, the colonial unconscious is effective, underwriting the ontological permanence of white plenitude. The inertia theory does not hold up because the hypothesis of the colonial unconscious has to be invoked to account for objective capitalist practice in South Africa today.

The capitalist unconscious never works alone. In the South African case, it is articulated with the colonial unconscious. How are these two unconscious forms of practice articulated in South Africa today? To start with, what can we tell in this regard from the *effect* of their articulation? It is clear that colonialism constitutes the dominant axis of inequality and resource distribution; on the other hand, it is dominant because it occupies the place of capital, that is, because the colonial unconscious exercises the extensive range of powers constitutive of capitalism. If colonialism did not occupy the place of capital it would not be able to exercise the powers of capital and through this impose a specifically colonial form of inequality.

In fact, capitalism as a socio-symbolic system is not an essence or substance that is self-sufficient and can fully occupy its own place. Hence, the capitalist universal is never pure. We can only ever have deformations of capitalism. Capitalism cannot, by definition, exist outside its over-determination by other social relations. It is never present as such, but only ever as impure, that is, some particular always and necessarily intrudes in the capitalist universal and commodity relations are themselves, thus, as a matter of structural necessity, always mediated: the fantasy of capital is that it can shake off extraneous conditions in order to achieve maximum self-realisation. Class antagonism is an absent, purely differential cause, always covered over by and inseparable from its actualisation (Zizek 2012: 488). Thus, the contingent conditions of the existence of capitalism are its very conditions of possibility and are internal to and constitutive of it; capitalism always functions through its outside, through some other social relation.

South Africa is no exception to this law of structure – and thus to say that colonialism is dominant in South Africa is not to say it is determinant. On the other hand, this same structural law entails that it (colonialism) is a *sui generis* antagonism *and* that it structures social practice.

Democracy represses colonialism but because democracy accommodates capitalism, colonialism, by occupying the place of capital, is able to exercise its class powers while appearing to respect equality.

Thus, owing to the ambivalence of capitalism – simultaneously a regime of free and equal individual subjects and of class antagonism – colonialism is able to elude the censorship of the democratic imperative and circumvents repression by playing on an ambivalence. Here capitalism is ambivalent and colonialism can only structure social practices under democratic conditions because this ambivalence allows it objectively to appear not to.

Because the capitalist regime of abstract individual equality is the flip side of class antagonism, whose place is occupied by the colonial unconscious, the latter can exist and disturb the logic of democracy without appearing to do so. Democracy constitutes individuals as free and equal and the South African capitalist subject also treats individuals as free and equal – he coerces no one, erases race and pursues only the law of accumulation. However, as we have seen, what his practice attests to is that he must be simultaneously obeying the law of the colonial unconscious.

What is the warrant for introducing the hypothesis of the colonial unconscious – what is it about the conduct of non-racial economic subjects that cannot be explained in its own terms, as homo economicus? Is there anything left over that needs to be accounted for? As before, the unconscious is inferred from practice, that is, as an attempt to account for those instances that deviate from the rules – it is not a matter of arbitrarily affixing the adjective unconscious or the adverb unconsciously to some set of practices, but of indicating how this performs an explanatory function.

The argument here is that capitalism, in particular the powers of property and the managerial prerogative, the class powers of capitalism, concealed by the objective appearance of equality and freedom, allow those whites unconsciously in thrall to colonial whiteness to enact this identity, to treat whites as whites and blacks as blacks. The latitude enjoyed vis-à-vis investment, procurement, remuneration and employment, makes it possible for the capitalist subject to unconsciously favour whites and impose the colonial dichotomy in all these areas, as all these decisions fall under the parameters of the authority of ownership.

Our capitalist subject will deny it; like the anti-Semite, he will insist his decisions involve only and strictly non-racial economic rationality – he has acted as homo economicus that is all. We, on the other hand, can grasp that mechanisms of social closure do not have to be conscious to be effective. Homo economicus can be white without this being apparent to him, without him being conscious of this. He denies he is racist but we can see that in his practice, unconsciously, he repeatedly and systematically enacts colonial whiteness quite legitimately in the terms of capitalism because nothing he does exceeds the powers ownership confer on him. Nothing has gone wrong from the point of view of the logic of capitalism – the gap is in the consciousness of the subject who defines himself as non-racial. This unconscious exclusion/closure is the mechanism via which colonialism operates today, and this explains the reproduction of colonial relations of production and inequality in South Africa.

We have to assume that our capitalist subject really is non-racial, that he genuinely subscribes to a generic humanism and that it really is the case that as far as he is concerned he does not even see race. We assume, in other words, that liberal democracy is not mere decoration, but constitutes specific forms of lived experience and subjectivity. Only then does a gap open up between his consciousness, his self-consciousness, and his practice, and only then is there any need to go any further in accounting for his practice.

The gap in his consciousness is that he does not see that he is systematically excluding blacks *because they are black*. He is not doing what he thinks he is doing; the gap in the consciousness of our subject is formally identical to that of the anti-Semite. His practice exceeds his consciousness – he thinks he is doing what capitalists do but, unconsciously, he is doing what *colonial* capitalists do.

Notice the novelty of this argument in relation to the debate about the articulation of capitalism and colonialism in South Africa. The *liberal position* merely poses capitalism and colonialism as two external and antagonistic logics and fails to come to grips with the complexity of this relation. The colonial unconscious, as subverting democracy via capitalism itself, resists incorporation in any liberal problematic that is constitutively unable to get to grips with colonialism in South Africa today.

Marxists might be familiar with the determinant/dominant distinction but colonialism is reduced in Marxism to an effect that has an effect – an effect of capital accumulation that has an effect on capital accumulation, and this falls short of acknowledging the *sui generis* character of colonialism as a formal autonomous difference that produces its own forms of the subject and of experience. This is related to the conception that colonialism is a residue of an earlier articulation of modes of production and regimes of accumulation (see Wolpe 1988). In this sense, then, Marxism may be said to subscribe to the inertia thesis discussed above. However, saying colonialism is a residue expressing only the inertia of apartheid fails to account for its structural dominance as well as the reproduction of colonial inequality in South Africa. In South Africa, capitalist practice itself enjoins us to invoke the hypothesis of the colonial unconscious. Restricted to the horizon of consciousness and by its reductionist conception of colonialism, Marxism, too, is at a loss when it comes to South Africa today.

NOTES

1   This account is indebted to Tomsic (2015). For an earlier attempt to conceptualise the colonial unconscious, see Hudson (2013).
2   'What we will observe in what follows is an attempt to analyse the black-white relation' (Fanon 1968: 9). Fanon's epistemological break with Sartrean theoretical humanism only goes so far, however, because when it comes to the white subject he sometimes 'abstracts from circumstances' (Fanon 1968) and ends up treating the white subject as a transcendental subject and not as a subject constituted to take itself for a transcendental subject (see Hudson 2015).

3   There are two positions to be avoided here. One takes black non-being as itself ontological, as inscribed in social being itself and irredeemable (see Wilderson 2008). The other sees in black non-being a form of subjectivity already free from the grip of the symbolic and already in between symbolic determinations. What risks being missed here is that symbolic failure for the black – who is by definition the subject of anxiety – is how colonialism is constituted and reproduces itself. This does not mean that under colonialism antagonism is domesticated but the opposite, i.e., under colonialism reproduction is immediately antagonised. From this it does not follow, however, that the colonised black non-subject is already free from the grip of the colonial symbolic. *The subject must free itself from its colonial non-being to become a subject* and this act of self-constitution/destruction is not performed by the condition of colonial non-being itself.

4   Is the exchange of commodities necessarily between juridically free and equal individuals and can we refer to capitalism in the absence of such a form of exchange? These questions have an obvious bearing on the dispute between liberals and Marxists over the relationship between capitalism and colonialism in South Africa. The point to be stressed is that the specifically capitalist form of fetishisation, homo economicus, never operates alone but always in combination with other effects of fetishisation, including the juridico-political constitution of subjectivity, none of which are reducible to structural effects of capitalism. Before 1994, capitalist relations of production do not objectively appear as relations between free and equal individuals and are not experienced as such. This does *not* entail that capitalist relations of production and exploitation do not exist under such conditions, which is the liberal claim. It is only if one essentialises capitalism and understands it as a self-sufficient totality with its own *necessary* forms of subjectivity, that one can claim it does not exist in the absence of liberal democracy.

5   Whites are understood, in what follows, to have sincerely jettisoned their identities as colonial whites and to have embraced the identity of a non-racial citizen. Their colonial whiteness still sticks to them, however, but now, in an unconscious mode. At the level of their conscious lived experience, they are no longer white in the colonial sense but citizens; unconsciously they remain colonial subjects, however. Unless we assume this, their (disavowed) racial practice remains inexplicable.

6   As Chabani Manganyi (1981: 77) reminds us, we need to avoid the connotation classically associated with the concept of the unconscious "... of energy, location and place."

7   The grip of the colonial unconscious on the South African economy has been resisted since 1994 via the implementation of black economic empowerment and employment equity policies. These, it needs to be noted, are made necessary by only white incalcitrance, strenuously disavowed by whites themselves.

REFERENCES

Althusser, L. 1972. *Reading Capital*. London: New Left Review Books.
Daly, G. 2011. 'The terror of Zizek', *Revue de Philsophie*, 66 (261): 359–379.
Eagleton, T. 2016. *Culture*. New Haven: Yale University Press.
Fanon, F. 1968. *Black Skin, White Masks*. London: Paladi.

Freud, S. 1933. 'New introductory lectures on psychoanalysis'. In *The Standard Edition of the Complete Psychological Works of Sigmund Freud*, Volume 22, translated and edited by J. Strachey. London: Hogarth Press and the Institute of Psychoanalysis, pp. 1–267.

Freud, S. 1940. 'An outline of psychoanalysis'. In *The Standard Edition of the Complete Psychological Works of Sigmund Freud*, Volume 23, translated and edited by J. Strachey. London: Hogarth Press and the Institute of Psychoanalysis, pp. 1–312.

Hudson, P. 2013. 'The colonial unconscious and the state', *Social Dynamics*, 39 (2): 263–277.

Hudson, P. 2015. 'The concept of the subject in Fanon'. Fanon seminar series, 2–6 October, University of the Witwatersrand.

Manganyi, N.C. 1981. *Looking Through the Keyhole*. Johannesburg: Ravan Press.

Rancière, J. 1967. *Lire Le Capital III*. Paris: Maspero.

Tomsic, S. 2015. *The Capitalist Unconscious* (Kindle edition). London: Verso.

Turok, B. (ed.). 2011. 'Building a national democratic society: Strategy and tactics of the ANC'. *Polokwane Document 2017*. Johannesburg: Jacana, pp. 224–262.

Wilderson, F.B. III. 2008. 'Biko and the problematic of presence'. In *Biko Lives! Contesting the Legacies of Steve Biko*, edited by A. Mngxitama, A. Alexander and N.C. Gibson. New York: Palgrave Macmillan, pp. 95–114.

Wolpe, H. 1988. *Race, Class and the Apartheid State*. London: James Currey, OAU Inter-African Cultural Fund and UNESCO Press.

Zizek, S. 2004. *Organs without Bodies*. London: Routledge.

Zizek, S. 2012. *Less than Nothing*. London: Verso.

CHAPTER

9

DEMOCRATIC MARXISM AND THE NATIONAL QUESTION: RACE AND CLASS IN POST-APARTHEID SOUTH AFRICA

Khwezi Mabasa

The current development impasse in South Africa has incited public debate and analysis. Many commentators have traced its origins to the transition during the early 1990s and subsequent policies implemented by the ruling party. Positive accounts describe the transition as a miracle while critics view it as an elite pact (Bond 2000: 16). The latter perspective has been used to explain the underlying structural causes of the post-apartheid socio-economic crisis (Bond 2000; Freund 2013; Terreblanche 2012). This situation is exacerbated by the glaring race, class and gender inequalities that characterise post-apartheid society. The 'rainbow nation thesis' is being challenged by persistent levels of social differentiation, which have reignited the historical debate on resolving the race question (Gumede 2014; Mashiqi 2014).[1]

Contemporary public discourse has been gripped by various accounts of institutionalised and anecdotal racism. These incidents have incited two dominant ideological responses. The first is the liberal tradition, which locates race relations within an ideational framework. Advocates of this view argue that the persistence of racism is caused by irrationality and degradation of liberal political values established during the democratic transition (Maloka 2014: 205–206). They also point out that racism distorts the neutral rational logic of capitalist development in a liberal democratic polity. The second perspective, inspired by reductionist black nationalist theories, reduces racism to institutionalised white supremacist mental paradigms (BLF 2017).[2] Proponents of this view focus solely on epistemological and ontological racism without relating both phenomena to the political economy power nexus.

This chapter will argue that both these explanatory approaches are insufficient to explore the complexity of the national question in post-apartheid South Africa. It will highlight the limitations of these accounts by advancing a democratic Marxist interpretation of post-apartheid race relations. This approach will draw from black and global South Marxist traditions, which question some of the fundamental assumptions of the classic tradition. The argument is premised on the following underlying propositions: (a) specific historical epochs shape the nature and form of race relations. Therefore, it is illogical to view race or racism as a static and predetermined phenomenon; (b) racism in South Africa is inherently linked to the evolution of a racialised capitalist social order and the power relations it produces. Thus, it is impossible to understand racism outside evolving class-power relations in the political economy; and (c) democratic Marxism, which appreciates historical specificities, provides a suitable analytical framework for characterising racism in the country. The point of departure will be a discussion on the national question debate that developed during the twentieth century.

THEORETICAL BACKGROUND

The historical discussion on race and class in South Africa has been centred on the colonialism of a special type (CST) thesis. It emerged from debates about the nature and base of authoritarian rule in South Africa during the first half of the twentieth century. The early Marxist proponents of CST were Michael Harmel and Rusty Bernstein, who were leading theoreticians of the Communist Party of South Africa (CPSA) (Maloka 2013; Mawbey 2014). These activists were influenced by the international communist discourse on the transition to socialism in colonial underdeveloped states.[3] The South African case was at the heart of this debate in the 1920s, and was resolved through what is popularly referred to as the 'native republic thesis'. This term was drawn from the resolution adopted by the Third Communist International, which stated that the CPSA should be 'calling for an independent native South African republic as a stage towards a workers' and peasants' republic with full, equal rights for all races' (SACP 1928). The theoretical underpinnings of CST were that South Africa is a peculiar colony, characterised by the existence of two political societies: a highly developed white capitalist community with imperial links, and a subjugated African polity that existed as a colony of the former. The peculiarity in this case was the coexistence of these states within a single geographic territory, and the coloniser's inability to exterminate the indigenous population (Jordan 1997; SACP 1962). This meant the socialist struggle could not be advanced outside the broader movement for independence. Additionally, the first objective was to eradicate race-based oppression, and then proceed to a class struggle for a socialist egalitarian society. Revolutionary nationalism was guided by this incremental strategy commonly referred to as the two-stage theory. The development of the Freedom Charter as a political programme illustrated the commitment to this approach. In sum, the national and class questions were inherently interrelated, and this required Marxists to form alliances with multiclass formations agitating for national liberation. This school of thought has dominated the political outlook of the South African Communist Party (SACP) and the African National Congress since the 1950s. However, various academics, activists and writers have challenged it.

REVISITING COLONIALISM OF A SPECIAL TYPE

Critics have pointed out the following shortcomings of the CST thesis. First, it did not explore the political economy of racism and white supremacy sufficiently. Harold Wolpe (1972; 1975) argued that the CST thesis fails to adequately link racial superiority to the socio-economic power structure that reproduces it. This, in turn, reduces the debate on national oppression to race-relations theory (Hart 2007; Masondo 2007; Wolpe 1975). Racial superiority is isolated and viewed as an independent phenomenon. It is removed from the racialised capitalist political economy that shapes and structures social relations to reproduce exploitative economic relations. The logical conclusion of this line of thinking is developing nominal plural society political solutions, which overlook the economic underpinnings of white supremacy. According to Wolpe (1975: 8), the only way to resolve this is to create an analytical framework that is 'on the one hand, a description of the ideology and political practices of the ethnic, racial, and national groups, and on the other, an analysis of how they relate to the mode of production and social formation in which they are located'.

Second, the CST thesis was supported by a mechanistic linear interpretation of the two-stage theory. This was drawn from Lenin's ([1906] 1980, [1917] 1980) work on the necessity of advancing a multiclass national democratic bourgeoisie struggle – popularly referred to as the national democratic revolution (NDR) – before proceeding to a socialist revolution (Lenin [1917] 1980). This first stage was essential for developing capitalism, which created 'class demarcation' ideal for advancing political contestation required for the ultimate transition to socialism (Neocosmos 1993: 17–18). Moreover, it was assumed that the establishment of a democratic non-racial polity would elucidate the fundamental exploitative class relations in society. This explains why early proponents of CST argued that non-racialism would elevate the class struggle in South Africa. John Mawbey (2014: 23) states that Bernstein believed the 'end of the race versus race issue would expose the underlying class nature of society'.

This linear conception of the two-stage theory also downplayed the internal contradictions within the national liberation movement. The NDR in South Africa has been the subject of intense debate among activists (Hart 2007; Masondo 2007). According to David Masondo (2007: 75), this discourse has been anchored on two main views: a socialist and a non-racial capitalist perspective on democracy. The first places primacy on eradicating capitalism, which is dependent on race-based authoritarianism and the super-exploitation of cheap black labour; while the second emphasises the creation of a non-racist form of democratic capitalism. This perspective views the emergence of a black bourgeoisie as a progressive step towards de-racialising capitalism. The main aim is not to obliterate capitalist relations of production but rather, to establish a political system that is conducive for removing racial biases in the development of capitalism in South Africa. This view ironically converges with the liberal political economy ideology, which perceives racism as an impediment to the objective rational logic of capitalist development.

These debates are not confined to theory, but also inform political strategy and agency. According to Michael Burawoy (2006), they represent two contending political programmes that coexisted in the broader national liberation movement. The CST thesis ignored these subjective political interests, and collapsed them into a unified struggle against what was perceived to be a peculiar form of imperialist rule. Furthermore, the mechanistic conception of the two-stage theory has limited political agency. The working-class movements that follow this paradigm have curtailed the scope and extent of activism, as a result of waiting for particular stages of political struggle to develop. The uncritical acceptance of stagist dogma has paralysed the working class at certain historical conjunctures when it should have led genuine anti-capitalist struggles. Moreover, stagism supported perverted conceptions of Marxism, which justify colonial capitalist dispossession by stating that it is necessary for the transition to socialism. The SACP recognised all these shortcomings in the early post-apartheid era, and developed a third view on revolutionary stages. This was expressed through the slogan of 'socialism is the future, build it now'. The ninth national congress analysed this slogan by arguing: 'In South Africa we are in the phase of advancing, deepening and defending the national democratic revolution. But there is no Chinese wall between this phase and the consolidation of socialism' (SACP 1995).

The third drawback of CST is related to the development of an inadequate theory of transition. Proponents presupposed that the establishment of an independent republic would lay the basis for dismantling racialised capitalism in South Africa. This assumption was based on a nationalistic conceptualisation of anti-imperialism, informed by a narrow conception of political self-determination. The underlying argument was that formal political independence was sufficient for establishing egalitarian social relations. Advocates of CST ignored how national liberation is undermined by developments in the imperial global capitalist political economy. Moreover, the detailed transition to a 'workers' and peasants' republic with full, equal rights for all races' was not spelt out (SACP 1928). The SACP's reformed perspective on revolutionary stages failed to develop an elaborate theory of transition, and paid minimal attention to the central task of building mass-based political agency for attaining socialism. Frantz Fanon (1963) highlights this shortcoming in *The Wretched of the Earth*. He argues that post-colonial political transitions have been undermined by the overemphasis on nationalistic conceptions of freedom, which do not sufficiently explore the material basis of imperialist relations. This is exacerbated by the absence of an adequate theory on transforming the political economy in national liberation movements. As Fanon (1963: 121) explains: 'The objective of nationalist parties as from a certain given period is, we have seen, strictly national. They mobilise the people with slogans of independence, and for the rest leave it to future events. When such parties are questioned on the economic programme of the state that they are clamouring for, or on the nature of the regime which they propose to install, they are incapable of replying because, precisely, they are completely ignorant of the economy of their own country.'

Fanon's post-colonial critique is also related to the fourth shortcoming: the inability of CST to deal with the reconfigured class-race nexus in a post-apartheid society. The relationship between class and race is altered by the evolution of capitalism over various epochs. This point is well captured by Stuart Hall's (1980) notion of articulation. He describes this as 'a connection or link which is not necessarily given in all cases, as a law or fact of life, but which requires particular conditions of existence to appear at all, which has to be positively sustained by specific processes, which is not eternal and has to constantly be renewed, which can under some circumstances disappear or be overthrown, leading to the old linkages being dissolved and new connections – re-articulations – being forged' (Hall 1980: 323).

The transition to democracy slightly reformed the nature of the relationship between class and race in South Africa. Roger Southall (2010) describes the South African democratisation process as a reform coalition. It was centred on an elite pact, which accommodated the emerging black petite bourgeoisie into existing economic structures dominated by white capital. This coincided with an agreement to use social redress policy as an instrument for expanding the black middle class (Southall 2010; Terreblanche 2012). By 2008, the government had succeeded in adding 2.7 million African households into the overall national category of middle-class citizens (Visagie 2011: 8). This figure expanded to 4.2 million by 2012 and recent estimates suggest that there are close to five million black households in this category (Southall 2016; Visagie 2013). However, it should be noted that estimates vary depending on variables used to define middle class. In addition to the above, black economic empowerment policy has created a small African capitalist class over the past 20 years (Southall 2010). State procurement policy and the restructuring of public enterprises have contributed immensely to this drive of creating a black bourgeoisie. The Sunday Times 2016 Rich List pointed out that 45 of the 250 most affluent individuals in South Africa are African. It also revealed that there are nine black individuals in the top 100 earners' rankings.[4] The state has played an active role in reforming capitalism and creating a more complex class-race power nexus (Van der Walt 2015: 40–41).

These dynamics of class formation clearly illustrate that the articulation of race and class has been slightly altered in the democratic era. Therefore, we have to revisit and rethink how this phenomenon should be conceptualised in contemporary Marxist discourse on race. The starting point should be an acknowledgement that the CST thesis is insufficient to understand this new nuanced articulation of the race-class power nexus. Moreover, it is integral to challenge the reductionist liberal and minimalist black nationalist perspectives, which reduce this debate to the primacy of race outside the socio-economic context. This is particularly important at this historical conjuncture, characterised by the prevalence of racism in all spheres of society. The first step is developing an adequate tool of analysis, which this chapter describes as democratic Marxism.

DEMOCRATIC MARXISM

There is no precise or strict definition of a democratic Marxism. However, this approach to Marxism is based on the following central prescripts that reform and provide alternatives to the economic reductionism of the classic tradition. The first is related to debunking dogmatic conceptions of Marxism that ignore historical specificity, and the subsequent divergent experiences of working-class exploitation. Various lessons drawn from black and global South Marxists are crucial for achieving this. Secondly, democratic Marxism seeks to understand various forms of revolutionary political agency that coexist with the reconfiguration of global capitalism over different historical epochs. Thirdly, this approach attempts to develop a nuanced dialectical relationship between class and race relations. It avoids the unproductive primacy debates associated with what Hancock (2007) describes as 'oppression olympics', and rather explores divergent forms of interconnection. Lastly, democratic Marxism must explore and challenge some key tenets of the classical tradition. This point is related to the following key themes explored in the next two sections: first, historicising systemic structural racism, which deals with the centrality of race in the development of both South African and global imperial capitalism, and second, historicising conjunctural racism, which explores conditions shaping racist politics in the context of a particular class project such as neoliberalism. This section also examines the various forms of socialist political agency that seek to challenge racialised capitalism.

HISTORICISING SYSTEMIC RACISM

Racism and the origins of capitalism

The point of departure for a democratic Marxist approach is a historical materialist analysis of racism. It is grounded on connecting oppressive race relations to structural dominance in the economic and political spheres over various epochs. Racist social ordering is embedded in the genealogy of global capitalist development. Authors such as C.L.R. James (1963) and Eric Williams (1944) have illustrated that African working-class (broad sense: includes coercive labour) exploitation was central for developing various forms of global imperial capitalism. For example, merchant capitalism coincided with the emergence of the Atlantic slave trade (James 1963; Rodney 1972). Moreover, the strength of the European mercantilist bourgeoisie-led trading empires was based on coercive slave labour (James 1963: 50). James's (1963: 48) historical account on the development of the French bourgeoisie supports this last point when he states that 'the capital from the slave trade fertilised them; though the bourgeoisie traded in other things than slaves, upon the success or failure of the traffic everything else depended'.

In this context, both colonial and apartheid capitalism are inherently linked to white supremacy and black super-exploitation. Steve Biko (1981: 133) expresses this point succinctly by stating that 'there is no doubt that the colour question in South African politics was originally introduced for economic reasons'. The nature of this race-based subjugation is embedded in the peculiar form of capitalist development in the South African context. Capitalist accumulation is not monolithic. It develops in various forms, especially in colonial societies (Magubane 1996: 342–343).

Hall's (1980: 310) historical account on the nature of capitalist development in South Africa is a good starting point. He argues that the introduction of capitalism in the country was based on colonial dispossession and the implementation of racist authoritarian labour regimes. The nature of the transition from the pre-capitalist political economy incorporated the 'African working class into the capitalist system in ways which preserve rather than liquidate its racial character' (Hall 1980: 310). For example, racist labour laws created internal stratification among the black and white segments of the workforce in South Africa. Therefore, it is essential that Marxist historical analysis of the class-race nexus avoids what Bernard Magubane (1996: 4) describes as an 'abstract class analysis', which 'liquidates the national question and ignores the crucial differences in the exploitation of black and white workers which are due specifically to racism'.

This analysis is central for historicising the development of the class struggle in South Africa beyond the confines of classical Marxism. More importantly, it challenges the ideational and cultural theories of racism promulgated by both liberalism and reductionist black nationalism. Race is conceptualised within a context that appreciates its relation to the reproduction of socio-economic exploitation. It is not reduced to innate feelings or ideas of racial superiority. This ultimately develops a more nuanced sociological understanding of racism as a phenomenon created and reproduced by structural power. Racial superiority cannot be eradicated without restructuring the exploitative socio-economic base that appropriates social assets as a means of legitimising and sustaining white supremacy. Historicising racism within this methodological framework grounds the national question in a discourse on substantive power relations. More importantly, it limits the possibility of being confined to a normative reductionist political identity debate.

HISTORICISING CONJUNCTURAL RACISM AND LEFT POLITICAL AGENCY

Revolutionary political agency

Classical Marxist theory places primacy on the industrial proletariat as the most revolutionary class in society (Engels 1894; Marx and Engels 1848). This stratum is elevated because of its strategic location in the production process and its experience of exploitation, which lays the basis for social revolution. The emergence of this social group is also associated with the development of a modern capitalist industrial society. This explains the negative perspective that classic Marxists have on other social strata, which form part of the broader working class. The peasantry and other segments of the working class are viewed as being inherently backward. They are associated with underdevelopment, and have limited knowledge on developing alternatives to capitalism. In sum, classical Marxism dismisses the political agency of other segments of the working class on the basis of backwardness (Jacobs 2010; Maghimbi, Lokina and Senga 2011; Moyo, Jha and Yeros 2013).

The above-mentioned line of thinking is informed by a Eurocentric conception of modernisation and political agency, drawn from the experiences of nineteenth-century Europe (Robinson 2000). Cedric Robinson (2000: xxix) expresses this succinctly when he states that Marx 'tossed slave labour and peasants into the imagined abyss signified by pre-capitalist, non-capitalist and primitive accumulation'. This perspective overlooks the historical revolutionary agency exercised by the slaves, peasantry and other working-class strata located in other regions of the world (Cabral [1979] 2007; Fanon 1963; Mao 1980). This broader working-class agency has been documented by black and global South Marxists such as James (1963), Robinson (2000) and Magubane (1996).

Furthermore, Moyo, Jha and Yeros (2013) specifically point out that African and Asian peasants played a key role in challenging colonial capitalist conquest in the global South. The dispossession associated with the introduction and expansion of capitalist agriculture developed what Hannah Wittman (2009: 806–807) describes as 'agrarian citizenship'. This concept refers to various acts of resistance carried out by the peasantry against the establishment of racialised capitalist relations. These forms of political agency have been articulated by several Marxist thinkers writing about the development of capitalism in colonies. Fanon (1963), Mao (1980) and Amilcar Cabral ([1979] 2007) also emphasise the centrality of the peasantry in the revolutionary struggle against colonial capitalism.

Moreover, contemporary working-class struggles in post-apartheid South Africa are not led by a powerful, highly organised proletariat (Buhlungu 2010; Cosatu 2012; Naledi 2014). The country has a high unemployment rate (36 per cent), and the labour market is dominated by precarious forms of work. Statistics South Africa's (2014, 2015) Quarterly Labour Market Surveys illustrate this exploitation by pointing out that 53 per cent of workers' salary increases were determined unilaterally by employers. It also highlights the fact that only 22 per cent of the labour force was represented by unions during salary negotiations, and 6 per cent of workers had no consistent increment. In 2015, 56 per cent of workers had their salary increments determined unilaterally by employers. And 5 per cent of employees had no regular salary increment. More importantly, only 29 per cent of the labour force is unionised. The super-exploitation of the proletariat is exacerbated by its declining structural power as a result of years of deindustrialisation (Bond 2010; Marais 2011).

All this evidence illustrates that the over-reliance on a developed proletariat to wage anti-capitalist struggles is not sustainable in the contemporary era. It also explains the emergence of various social movements that are made up of working-class strata in communities across South Africa. Their membership includes the unemployed, precarious workers and citizens engaged in survivalist activities in black working-class communities (Greenberg 2006; Madlingozi 2014; Nieftagodien 2015).

These organisations mobilise around key pro-poor demands, such as equal access to public goods, and protest against the expansion of privatisation. The movements are not governed by traditional vanguard organisational principles.

However, their struggles are embedded in challenging some of the fundamental neoliberal policy prescripts associated with accumulation by dispossession (Madlingozi 2006; Von Holdt 2013).

A democratic Marxist approach should support and form linkages with these movements. This is particularly important in the South African context because racist conservative groupings characterise these organisations as movements led by backward and barbaric individuals. Supporters of this view rely on arguments derived from racist beliefs and doctrines. These include conservative theories of social behaviour, which conceal the underlying interests of preserving the hierarchical racialised socio-economic order. Thus, it is essential to develop a counternarrative that elucidates the principled social justice and transformative politics driving these movements. This can only take place if Marxist conceptions of political agency are altered to include all working-class strata.

The debate between Guy Standing (2016) and Erik Olin Wright (2015) on understanding class formation in the current capitalist epoch is a good starting point. Standing (2016: 192) argues that 'there has been class fragmentation, so that the old nomenclature is no longer fit for understanding the dynamics of class struggle. Another way of putting this is that differences within bloc concepts, such as the bourgeoisie/capitalist class and working class, have grown to the point of splitting them.' He explains his argument by introducing a non-classical schema of class categorisation in the modern era (Standing 2016: 192). This mapping includes new conceptual categories such as 'precariat', which he argues have distinct features. Wright (2015: 173) concurs with this analysis on intra working-class social differentiation; however, he points out that the various groupings within the broader category do not constitute distinct classes. Both authors pay minimal attention to other crucial factors that influence class formation, such as race, neo-imperialism and gender. This is partially caused by the limitations of the three variables used in the debate. Nonetheless, this discourse provides the necessary nuance for more pluralistic, modern class analysis. But it has to be augmented by other historical scholarly work, which explores the question of revolutionary political agency beyond the canon of classic Marxism.

Modernisation theory and neoliberal rationality

Both liberals and conservatives always present modernisation as a class- or race-neutral process of social transformation. Orthodox Marxists argue that it is essential for developing the modern capitalist political economy, which ultimately creates the social conditions conducive for accelerating the socialist revolution. The advancements associated with modernisation are viewed as crucial for creating new forms of technology and production methods. This, in turn, accelerates capitalist development and the subsequent class exploitation, which finally leads to social revolution.

Socialist proponents of this linear interpretation of scientific Marxism have overlooked how the stagist approach to modernisation has supported racialised forms of capitalist exploitation. This applies to both colonial and apartheid capitalism in the South African context. Architects of both social systems have used the modernisation argument to systematically dispossess and exploit the black working class. The paternalistic form of modernisation is driven by a rationale of coercively co-opting perceived 'underdeveloped' social groups into capitalist relations (Magubane 1996: 13–14). This development logic continues today, and informs what David Harvey (2004) describes as 'accumulation by dispossession'. Multinational companies still accumulate profit by displacing the rural and urban black working class. The minerals–energy complex, which drove both racial colonial and apartheid capitalism, still persists in the context of globalised adjustment and restructuring. It is mediated by a slightly different modernisation discourse grounded on neoliberal developmentalism within a democratic state. Both politicians and representatives of these enterprises argue that this capitalist expansion is integral for creating de-racialised modern systems of local economic development. However, modern neoliberal developmentalism has largely sustained the racial inequality associated with colonial and apartheid capitalism. The discourse and the rationale underpinning market-led development is derived from the same racist premises as classic colonial modernisation theory. Racist neocolonial capital relations are concealed by a slightly different jargon of appropriation, promulgated by the markets. The only key difference is that this is taking place within a politically democratic context. Peter Hudson's chapter in this volume provides a succinct description of this phenomenon by stating:

> The capitalist objectively and systematically privileges whites across all aspects of his practice – investment, procurement, management and employment. That he does this is not something that can be empirically doubted. However, it passes under the democratic radar and as allowed – with the effect of reproducing the colonial distribution of assets, income and opportunity – colonial relations of production. Capitalist practice in South Africa has not changed, it is as colonial as ever. All that has changed is that it is now unconscious of its colonial character.

Moreover, neocolonial capitalism has created specific conditions for class formation, which require a nuanced analysis. The state-capital nexus has been slightly reconfigured, with government facilitating the internationalisation of South African monopoly capital. How race works and articulates with this process is a crucial analytical task for democratic Marxism.

Racist doctrines have always been used to support this socio-economic subjugation in the process of modernisation. A democratic Marxist approach should reject this mechanistic interpretation at the heart of most racist theories on development. It should rather advance forms of economic development that appreciate existing knowledge on production. Democratic Marxism should also question models of development that dispossess the black working class. This is essential for challenging the prevalence of race-based capitalist gentrification, which is legitimised by policy directives of building modern cities. In sum, it is integral to bring class-race nexus power politics back into the modernisation discussion, especially in a society like South Africa, which has clear lines of social differentiation formed by racialised capitalism.

Labour and the crisis of social reproduction

Classical socialist political economy studies have explored power relations between capital and formal labour (Engels 1894; Marx and Engels 1848). This orthodox Marxist emphasis on relations of production has been, for the most part, gender-blind. It has ignored other forms of labour, which support the reproduction of capitalism. Moreover, orthodox approaches overlook how social relations in other institutions shape resource allocation. Feminist scholars and activists have highlighted this omission in historical accounts of racialised capitalism in South Africa. The most succinct criticism has been raised by feminist scholars working on the agrarian question. They argue that the contribution of reproductive labour, which supported the transition to capitalist agriculture, is omitted in classical accounts (Razavi 2011; Tsikata 2015). This unpaid labour (care work) in the household is essential for reproducing workers for capitalist agriculture, and exacerbates exploitation by decreasing the value of wages (Wolpe 1972).

The unpaid labour was not only beneficial for the agricultural sector. Wolpe (1972) points out that the mining sector, which was at the centre of apartheid capitalism, benefited the most from African women's reproductive labour. Reserves functioned as a form of social security for super-exploited male mine workers. The burden of this unpaid social security fell solely on females because of the gendered division of labour in the house. Black females in rural areas performed household duties to support male workers who had lost their jobs because of ill-health and other work-related reasons. Moreover, their subsistence farming served as a buffer against hunger. Apartheid wages were low and could not ensure socio-economic security within households. In sum, black working-class female unpaid labour has subsidised the historical development of racialised capitalism in South Africa.

This phenomenon continues in the contemporary epoch. All the data on socio-economic inequality clearly points out that African females are the most marginalised social group in post-apartheid South Africa. For example, the experience of food insecurity among African women residing in rural and informal urban areas is higher than among their male counterparts (Earl 2011; Jacobs 2010; Molestane and Reddy 2011; Oxfam 2014). Furthermore, the structure of the South African economy remains largely unchanged. It is still reliant on the core and periphery spatial development model characterised by the phenomenon of male-dominated black migrant labour (Alexander 2013; Chinguno 2015). African women still support this system through unpaid work (Benya 2015: 546–547).

Moreover, the crisis of social reproduction has been exacerbated by neoliberal developmentalism. The precariousness is caused by restructuring, and market-led development has negative implications for 'child birth and rearing; reproduction of the labour force through household and education institutions; and the provisioning of social infrastructure to provide for care and the social needs of citizens' (Satgar and Williams 2017: 46). Asanda Benya (2015) argues that black female labour still serves as a 'cushion' for the crisis of social reproduction in the contemporary era because state interventions are not adequate. Her account on black women's experiences during the Marikana crisis illustrates that the struggle was not solely based on wages. According to Benya (2015: 547), 'the platinum strikes of 2012 were not only a response to low wages or the crisis of production. They were also a response to the crisis of social reproduction, for the struggle for a living wage, which would enable workers and their families to reproduce themselves on a daily basis under increasingly harsh economic conditions.'

A democratic Marxist approach should transcend the classic formulation of labour. It must acknowledge and appreciate other forms of labour, which contribute to the reproduction of racialised capitalism. This point specifically applies to the unpaid labour of African working-class women. Both colonialism and apartheid capitalism were based on the super-exploitation of this social stratum. This socio-economic subjugation continues in the post-apartheid capitalist era. Thus, any attempt to challenge the fundamental basis of racial subjugation must be gendered. More importantly, class analysis must be broadened and deepened so that it appreciates the crisis of social reproduction. Socialist scholars and activists must link struggles in production sites to experiences in black working-class households and communities. The point of departure should be the adoption of a materialist intersectional approach. Delia Aguilar (2015: 212) describes this framework as one that recognises that 'these identity categories are activated as a mechanism to facilitate exploitation in the context of capitalist social relations'. This means that unequal gender relations are invoked and sustained to reproduce racialised capitalist socio-economic exploitation. Therefore, democratic Marxists should embed themselves in materialist intersectional analysis. This point on identity is linked to the final task of the democratic Marxist approach: challenging narrow identity-based solutions to racism. The most prominent of these are black bourgeoisie nationalism and chauvinism.

Black bourgeoisie nationalism and chauvinism

Black bourgeoisie nationalism espouses the creation of an African capitalist class that will replace white capital. This argument is presented in the context of an emancipatory project for all Africans. It relies heavily on an identity-based nationalist economic development paradigm. Proponents of this view argue that the creation of a black bourgeoisie – through gaining access to assets of white capital – will lay the basis for black economic emancipation and political superiority. Black bourgeoisie nationalism draws heavily on developmental state literature that places emphasis on creating nationalistic capitalists. This logic ignores the inherent exploitative nature of racialised capitalist relations of production, and seeks to re-establish economic privilege mediated by a different form of identity politics. Moreover, it does not deal with the three fundamental characteristics of racialised capitalism: the reproduction of mass, marginalised, cheap black labour, the systemic dispossession of black working-class and poor communities, and the historic appropriation of communal assets required for social reproduction. Black bourgeoisie nationalism seeks to re-invent these phenomena with only one slight alteration: the ascendance and co-option of African economic elites into the higher echelons of racialised capitalist structures.

Another tenet of black bourgeoisie nationalism is to reduce social transformation to identity. Advocates of this approach argue for the reformation of institutions on purist diversity grounds. They do not explore the underlying systemic socio-economic causes, which reproduce institutionalised unequal race relations in the first place. The emphasis is on aesthetic changes without addressing fundamental structural power relations. These middle-class black nationalist social movements argue for meritocratic rewards within the confines of a racialised capitalist society. Institutional reform is then divorced from organic black working-class struggles, and focuses on integrating privileged Africans into established white-dominated, middle-class structures of power. The debate on establishing egalitarian race relations becomes an avenue for preserving social privilege, rather than articulating the interests of the African working class.

Neville Alexander (1986) highlights an additional danger associated with essentialist chauvinist identity politics. He expresses this point by stating that 'the fundamental problem with the two-nation thesis and any other many-nation thesis in the South African context is that it holds within it the twin dangers of anti-white black chauvinism and ethnic separatism' (Alexander 1986: 83). Black chauvinism stems from a vulgarised conception of Black Consciousness, which relies on supremacist racial political ideals. It argues that black emancipation can only be established through the subjugation of other racial groups. This view contradicts the writings of authoritative Black Consciousness exponents such as Biko (1981). He described Black Consciousness as a school of thought that 'expresses group pride and determination of the black to rise and attain the envisaged self' (Biko 1981: 137). However, this is not aimed at establishing a black chauvinist society.

Biko (1981: 135) explains this well by arguing: 'The thesis is in fact a strong white racism and therefore the anti-thesis to this must, ipso facto, be a strong solidarity among blacks on whom this white racism seeks to prey. Out of these two situations we can therefore hope to reach some kind of balance – a true humanity where power politics will have no place.' The humanity described by Biko is different from the ideals promulgated by chauvinists. It is not based on the politics of racial superiority and subjugation. Proponents of chauvinism have presented a perverted expression of this philosophy, which presupposes that embracing black identity and solidarity always coincides with the exploitation of other social groups. My main contention here is that the race question in South Africa can only be addressed by dismantling the socio-political and economic structures of white supremacy. The logical conclusion of this process will lay the basis for a non-racist society – not the establishment of a new racialised capitalist social hierarchy.

The democratic Marxist approach seeks to highlight the limitations of these perspectives by elucidating their underlying bourgeoisie class politics, and exposing their authoritarian tendencies. This is achieved by linking the question of political identity to structural socio-economic power, and examining any solution based on its ability to obliterate the fundamental characteristics of authoritarian racial capitalism. Black bourgeoisie nationalism cannot deal with the structural causes of racism because of its obsession with the political economy framework that reproduces exploitative race relations in the first place. Chauvinism is also not suitable, as it promotes a politics of superiority instead of emancipation. This logic is not helpful in obliterating racism in society. Moreover, its essentialist rationale reduces social behaviour to predetermined human characteristics and beliefs.

CONCLUSION

In discussing the national question, the main objective of this chapter was to examine a democratic Marxist response to the persistence of racism in post-apartheid South Africa. Democratic Marxism provides a more nuanced conception of racialised capitalist development that appreciates historic and contextual specificity. Moreover, it challenges socialist analysis to acknowledge the political agency exercised by other segments of the subaltern and broader working-class category over different historical epochs. This includes engaging new forms of anti-capitalist political agency in the twenty-first century.

This approach was developed to counter both liberal and reductionist black nationalist theories on race. It illustrated that race relations should not be interpreted in a deterministic manner because they evolve and manifest themselves differently during various historical epochs. Therefore, any attempt to obliterate racism has to start with an analysis of how race is shaped by the specific characteristics of the sociological context.

The chapter also argued that racism in the South African context is inherently linked to the evolving racialised capitalist political economy. It connects unequal race relations to historical and contemporary capitalist socio-economic exploitation. Thus, anti-racist struggles have to challenge the power relations in the political economy that reproduce these exploitative social relations. Democratic Marxism is presented as an important starting point to engage in this endeavour.

NOTES

1   The national question in South Africa is inherently linked to race relations because of the history of colonialism and apartheid.
2   See also A. Mngxitama, 'Penny Sparrow: Racism's sacrificial lamb, *Mail & Guardian*, 8 January 2016.
3   The case of the US was also a key factor in these debates. African Americans were experiencing intersectional oppression: race and class. Du Bois (1933) attempts to tackle this question in his article 'Marxism and the Negro problem'.
4   R. Henderson, 'Here are the black South Africans on the 2016 Rich List', *Sunday Times Live*, 12 December 2016.

REFERENCES

Aguilar, D.D. 2015. 'Intersectionality'. In *Marxism and Feminism*, edited by S. Mojab. London: Zed Books, pp. 203–220.
Alexander, N. 1986. 'Approaches to the national question in South Africa', *Transformation*, 1: 63–95.
Alexander, P. 2013. 'Marikana, turning point in South African history', *Review of African Political Economy* 40 (138): 605–619.
Benya, A. 2015. 'The invisible hands: Women in Marikana', *Review of African Political Economy*, 42 (146): 545–560.
Biko, S. 1981. 'Black Consciousness and the quest for a true humanity', *Ufahamu: A Journal of African Studies*, 11 (1): 133–142.
BLF (Black Land First). 2017. 'The black agenda'. Accessed 2 August 2017, https://blf.org.za/policy-documents/black-agenda/.
Bond, P. 2000. *Elite Transition: From Apartheid to Neoliberalism in South Africa*. London: Pluto Press.
Bond, P. 2010. 'South Africa's developmental state distraction', *Mediations*, 24 (1): 9–28.
Buhlungu, S. 2010. *A Paradox of Victory: COSATU and the Democratic Transformation in South Africa*. Pietermaritzburg: University of KwaZulu-Natal Press.
Burawoy, M. 2006. 'From liberation to reconstruction: Theory and practice in the life of Harold Wolpe'. In *Articulations: A Harold Wolpe Memorial Lecture Collection*, edited by A. Alexander. Trenton, NJ: Africa World Press, pp. 3–36.
Cabral, A. [1979] 2007. *Unity and Struggle*. Pretoria: UNISA Press.
Chinguno, C. 2015. 'Strike violence after South Africa's democratic transition'. In *COSATU in Crisis*, edited by V. Sagtar and R. Southall. Johannesburg: KMM Review Publishing, pp. 246–267.
Cosatu (Congress of South African Trade Unions). 2012. 'Socio-Economic Report to the 11th Congress of South African Trade Unions', September, Johannesburg.
Du Bois, W.E.B. 1933. 'Marxism and the Negro problem'. Accessed 15 September 2016, http://credo.library.umass.edu/view/full/mums312-b211-i091.
Earl, A. 2011. 'Solving the food crisis in South Africa: How food gardens can alleviate hunger amongst the poor'. MA research report, University of the Witwatersrand.
Engels, F. 1894. 'The peasant question in France and Germany', Volume 3 of the Selected Works. Accessed 26 September 2016, https://www.marxists.org/archive/marx/works/1894/peasant-question/index.htm.

Fanon, F. 1963. *The Wretched of the Earth*. London: Penguin.
Freund, W. 2013. 'Swimming against the tide: The macro-economic research group in the South African transition 1991–1994', *Review of African Political Economy*, 40 (138): 519–536.
Greenberg, S. 2006. 'The Landless People's Movement and the failure of post-apartheid land reform'. In *Voices of Protest: Social Movements in Post-Apartheid South Africa*, edited by R. Ballard, A. Habib and I. Valodia. Pietermaritzburg: University of KwaZulu-Natal Press, pp. 133–154.
Gumede, V. 2014. 'Racial inequality in post-apartheid South Africa'. Accessed 15 October 2016, http://www.vusigumede.com/content/2014/ACADEMIC%20PAPERS%202014/Working%20Paper%20(August%202014).pdf.
Hancock, A. 2007. 'Intersectionality as a normative and empirical paradigm', *Politics & Gender*, 3 (2): 248–254.
Hall, S. 1980. 'Race, articulation and societies structured in dominance'. In *UNESCO, Sociological Theories: Race and Colonialism*. Paris: UNESCO, pp. 305–345.
Hart, G. 2007. 'Changing concepts of articulation: Political stakes in South Africa today', *Review of the African Political Economy*, 111: 85–101.
Harvey, D. 2004. 'The new imperialism: Accumulation by dispossession', *Socialist Register*, 40: 63–87.
Jacobs, P. 2010. 'Household food insecurity, rapid food price inflation and the economic downturn in South Africa', *Agenda: Empowering Women for Gender Equity*, 24 (86): 38–51.
James, C.L.R. 1963. *The Black Jacobins*. New York: Random House.
Jordan, P.Z. 1997. 'The national question in post-apartheid South Africa'. Accessed 6 November 2016, https://www.marxists.org/subject/africa/anc/1997/national-question.htm.
Lenin, V. [1906] 1980. 'The stages, trends and prospects of the revolution'. In *Revolutionary Thought in the 20th Century*, edited by B. Turok. London: Zed Books, pp. 62–63.
Lenin, V. [1917] 1980. 'The April theses'. In *Revolutionary Thought in the 20th Century*, edited by B Turok. London: Zed Books, pp. 63–65.
Madlingozi, T. 2006. 'Legal academics and progressive politics in South Africa: Moving beyond the ivory tower', *Pulp Fictions*, (2): 5–24.
Madlingozi, T. 2014. 'Post-apartheid social movements and legal mobilisation'. In *Socio-Economic Rights in South Africa: Symbols or Substance?* edited by M. Langford, B. Cousins, J. Dugard and T. Madlingozi. New York: Cambridge University Press, pp. 92–130.
Maghimbi, S., Lokina, R. and Senga, M. 2011. 'The agrarian question in Tanzania? A state of the art paper'. Current African Issues Report No. 45. Uppsala: Nordiska Afrikainstitutet and Dar es Salaam: University of Dar es Salaam.
Magubane, B.M. 1996. *The Making of a Racist State: British Imperialism and the Union of South Africa, 1875–1910*. Trenton, NJ: Africa World Press.
Maloka, E. 2013. *The South African Communist Party: Exile and After Apartheid*. Johannesburg: Jacana.
Maloka, E. 2014. *Friends of the Natives: The Inconvenient Past of South African Liberalism*. Durban: 3rd Millennium.

Mao, T. 1980. 'The Chinese revolution and the Chinese Communist Party'. In *Revolutionary Thought in the 20th Century*, edited by B. Turok. London: Zed Books, pp. 73-89.

Marais, H. 2011. *South Africa Pushed to the Limit: The Political Economy of Change*. Cape Town: University of Cape Town Press.

Marx, K. and Engels, F. 1848. 'Manifesto of the Communist Party'. Accessed 26 July 2016, https://www.marxists.org/archive/marx/works/1848/communist-manifesto/.

Mashiqi, A. 2014. '20 years of democracy: Race narratives in South African society', *Journal of the Helen Suzman Foundation*, (72): 12-15.

Masondo, D. 2007. 'Capitalism and racist forms of political domination', *Africanus*, 37 (2): 66-80.

Mawbey, J. 2014. The unresolved national question in left thinking: Seeking lineages and hidden voices. Paper presented at Chris Hani Institute Workshop, Johannesburg.

Molestane, R. and Reddy, V. 2011. *The gendered dimensions of food security in South Africa: A review of the literature*. Human Science Research Council Policy Brief.

Moyo, S., Jha, P. and Yeros, P. 2013. 'The classical agrarian question: Myth, reality and relevance today', *Agrarian South: Journal of Political Economy*, 2 (1): 93-119.

Naledi (National Labour and Economic Development Institute). 2014. 'Findings of the COSATU Workers' Surveys, 2012'. Accessed 15 September 2016, http://www.cosatu.org.za/docs/reports/2012/final%20workers%20surveys%20results%20August%202012.pdf

Neocosmos, M. 1993. *The Agrarian Question in Southern Africa and Accumulation from Below*. Uppsala: Nordic Africa Institute.

Nieftagodien, N. 2015. 'Reconstituting and re-imagining the left after Marikana'. In *New South African Review 5: Beyond Marikana*, edited by G. Khadiagala, P. Naidoo, D. Pillay and R. Southall. Johannesburg: Wits University Press, pp. 18-33.

Oxfam. 2014. *Hidden Hunger in South Africa*. Oxford: Oxfam.

Razavi, S. 2011. 'Agrarian debates and gender relations: "Now you see them, now you don't"'. In *Du grain à moudre: Genre, développement rural et alimentation*, edited by C. Verschuur. Geneva: Actes des colloques genre et développement, pp. 47-58.

Robinson, C.J. 2000. *Black Marxism: The Making of a Radical Tradition*. Chapel Hill, NC: University of North Carolina Press.

Rodney, W. 1972. *How Europe Underdeveloped Africa*. London: Bogle-L'Ouverture Publications.

SACP (South African Communist Party). 1928. 'The South African question'. Accessed 15 September 2016, https://www.marxists.org/history/international/comintern/sections/sacp/1928/comintern.htm.

SACP. 1962. 'The road to South African freedom: Programme for the South African Communist Party'. Accessed 15 September 2016, https://www.marxists.org/history/international/comintern/sections/sacp/1962/road-freedom.htm.

SACP. 1995. 'Socialism is the future, build it now! SACP strategic perspectives adopted and amended by the SACP Ninth National Congress, April 1995'. Accessed 2 August 2017, http://www.sacp.org.za/main.php?ID=1649.

Satgar, V. and Williams, M. 2017. 'Marxism and class'. In *The Cambridge Handbook of Sociology, Volume 2*, edited by K. Odell Korgen. Cambridge: Cambridge University Press, pp. 41-50.

Southall, R. 2010. 'The South African developmental model: Hitting against the limits', *Strategic Review of South Africa*, 32 (2): 69–92.
Southall, R. 2016. *The New Black Middle Class in South Africa*. Johannesburg: Jacana.
Standing, G. 2016. 'The precariat, class and progressive politics: A response', *Global Labour Journal*, 7 (2): 189–200.
Statistics South Africa. 2014. 'Quarterly Labour Market Survey'. Accessed 27 August 2018, http://www.statssa.gov.za/?p=2652.
Statistics South Africa. 2015. 'Quarterly Labour Market Survey'. Accessed 27 August 2018, https://www.statssa.gov.za/publications/P0211/P02111stQuarter2015.pdf.
Terreblanche, S. 2012. *Lost in Transformation: South Africa's Search for a New Future Since 1986*. Johannesburg: KMM Review Publishing.
Tsikata, D. 2015. *The social relations of agrarian change*. IIED Working Paper. London: IIED.
Van der Walt, L. 2015. 'Beyond white monopoly capital', *South African Labour Bulletin*, 39 (3): 29–42.
Visagie, J. 2011. The development of the middle class in South Africa. Paper presented at the Micro-Econometric Analysis of South African Data Conference, University of KwaZulu-Natal.
Visagie, J. 2013. 'Who are the middle classes in South Africa? Does it matter for policy?' Accessed 2 August 2017, http://www.econ3x3.org/sites/default/files/articles/Visagie%202013%20Middle%20class%20FINAL_0.pdf.
Von Holdt, K. 2013. 'South Africa: The transition to violent democracy', *Review of African Political Economy*, 40 (138): 519–536.
Williams, E. 1944. *Capitalism and Slavery*. Chapel Hill, NC: University of North Carolina Press.
Wittman, H. 2009. 'Reworking the metabolic rift: La Vía Campesina, agrarian citizenship, and food sovereignty', *Journal of Peasant Studies*, 36 (4): 805–826.
Wolpe, H. 1972. 'Capitalism and cheap labour-power in South Africa: From segregation to apartheid', *Economy and Society*, 1(4): 425–456.
Wolpe, H. 1975. 'The theory of internal colonialism: The South African case'. Accessed 27 January 2018, http://www.wolpetrust.org.za/main.php?include=texts/theory.html.
Wright, E.O. 2015. *Understanding Class*. London: Verso.

CHAPTER

10

SEVEN THESES ON RADICAL NON-RACIALISM, THE CLIMATE CRISIS AND DEEP JUST TRANSITIONS: FROM THE NATIONAL QUESTION TO THE ECO-CIDE QUESTION

Vishwas Satgar

It has become commonplace, in the current conjuncture, to attack 'non-racialism' and argue for new identities, African nationalism and the importance of Black Consciousness. Moreover, within popular consciousness, despite non-racialism being a founding constitutional principle, there are banal and ahistorical conceptions of non-racialism at work merely reducing it to being colour blind, with no definitional content. This chapter takes issue with the onslaught against non-racialism and the increasing shallow, popular understandings of non-racialism. 'Radical non-racialism' is defended in this intervention and an argument is made for its re-affirmation. This is different from the official non-racialism of the African National Congress (ANC), which has morphed into different inflections of state-centred nationalism during different phases in post-apartheid South Africa, to include 'rainbowism', Afro-neoliberalism and resource nationalism. Official non-racialism is in crisis in the context of the unravelling of ANC-led national liberation hegemony and the degeneration of the ANC itself.

The defence of radical non-racialism affirms a crucial principle and practice for prevailing anti-racism, in dialogue with some currents within contemporary Black Consciousness, and as part of the renewal of left politics in South Africa. The argument made in this chapter is that official ANC non-racialism, tied to a contingent political-economy analysis and within the frame of the national question approach, is outdated, in crisis and discredited. It is dying with the ANC-led Alliance. At the same time, this chapter argues for replacing the national question with the eco-cide question, in the context of the existential threat posed by the climate crisis to human and non-human life. The eco-cide question is central to a post-national liberation, post-neoliberal and renewed left politics, as the basis for radical, non-racial nation building to sustain life. This perspective is set out in seven theses below.

THESIS 1

Radical non-racialism is central to a people's history of struggle and achieved a hegemonic location in the national liberation struggle against apartheid. Its challenge to racialised exploitation, white supremacy, gender oppression and oppressions in general, because of its deep humanist impulse, defined its radicalism.

Does non-racialism, as a political principle and practice, belong to the ANC? In the mythologised history of the ANC, in the construction of its post-apartheid hegemony and in its official practices as a ruling party, it would seem the ANC has proprietary claims on non-racialism.[1] As the party of national liberation and the dominant ruling party for over two decades, it has constructed and articulated post-apartheid nation-building nationalism, in which non-racialism has been a crucial ideological element. This has been part of its project to rule a capitalist South Africa and has impacted on its approach to economic transformation, state building, state-civil society relations and international relations. Various presidents of the ANC and the country have also imbued official non-racialism with particular discursive elements and practices. For instance, Nelson Mandela was the fulcrum of a 'rainbow' nationalism, Thabo Mbeki harnessed 'rainbow' nationalism for deep globalisation, black economic empowerment and the indigenising of neoliberalism as Afro-neoliberalism, and Jacob Zuma has brought in an element of resource nationalism linked to a corrupt transactional politics. The success of these nation-building efforts is a separate question; suffice to note that the ANC's articulation of official non-racialism is in crisis.

On the other hand, radical non-racialism as part of a peoples' history of struggle does not belong to the ANC.[2] Three defining moments of national liberation struggle in the twentieth century affirm radical non-racialism as an orientation in mass politics, as part of popular struggles and as belonging to the people. The first was the formulation and adoption of the Freedom Charter in 1955 at the Congress of the People, including its embrace of the idea that South Africa belongs to all who live in it, black and white. The initiative to formulate the Freedom Charter was not an initiative of the ANC exclusively but of the Congress Alliance, made up of the ANC, the South African Indian Congress, the South African Coloured People's Organisation and the South African Congress of Democrats. Moreover, the process to formulate the content and ideas of the Freedom Charter gave primacy to grassroots dialogue, input and registering the voice of the people.[3] Essentially, the participation and input of the people is what gave the Congress of the People and the Freedom Charter its legitimacy. While the Freedom Charter became a programmatic basis of national liberation politics, it reflected the aspirations of the people, including the idea of an inclusive non-racial democracy and nationalism. This does not belong to the ANC.

The second crucial moment was the emergence of militant black trade unionism from 1973 onwards, propelled by the powerful Durban strikes. The rise of independent trade unions, their growth and eventual merger into the Congress of South African Trade Unions (Cosatu) in 1985 was crucial for affirming radical non-racialism within the organised working class in South Africa. Cosatu embraced non-racialism and the Freedom Charter after serious internal debates. Various affiliates of Cosatu also carried firm commitments to the principles of non-racialism and socialism.[4] Cosatu did not belong to the ANC and was an independent, worker-controlled labour federation. The third crucial moment was the resurgence of mass resistance against apartheid in the 1980s, spurred on by the student uprising of 1976. The mass movement that rose in the 1980s, under the banner of the United Democratic Front (UDF), brought together sport, cultural, faith-based, youth, women, student, union and civic organisations, as well as various other formations. These organisations were not controlled by the ANC, although there might have been ANC sympathisers, underground operatives and members in some of them. Moreover, some in the UDF leadership also openly affirmed the importance of the link to the ANC.[5] However, the embrace of the Freedom Charter by the UDF strengthened the impulse of mass, radical non-racialism. This impulse did not belong to the ANC.

But what is the content of radical non-racialism, a people's non-racialism? It has been first and foremost about solidarity and unity. It was about countering the racialised differences of apartheid by constituting strategic unity within and between race groups as concrete expressions of 'people's power', advancing a programmatic unity of all forces to overcome apartheid and the building of powerful people's organisations. The idea of people's power ('the people shall govern'), inscribed in the Freedom Charter, is about deep democracy and was central to Mandela's political thought in the 1950s.[6] This process of strategic unity was forged in different racialised spatial and sectoral contexts and went through various conjunctural phases since the 1940s. In organisations, such as the Communist Party and the black trade union movement, non-racialism was taken further in terms of different races being part of the same organisation and playing a leadership role. The ANC, on the other hand, remained an African organisation into the 1960s, and non-African leadership was elected into its structures much later. Second, radical non-racialism was deeply anti-capitalist. It married a critique of racial oppression to a critique of capitalism. The Freedom Charter, while a people's document, was also a product of its time in terms of its imagination and horizons. It was a document deeply imbued with a state-centric perspective, shaped by Soviet socialism, revolutionary nationalism and social democracy. As a people's document, the Freedom Charter was anti-capitalist. Moreover, the non-reductionist conception of racialised and gendered class understandings expressed itself in Communist Party thinking, in trade union organising and in mass organisations, such as the UDF, with principled commitments to working-class leadership. Class and race were linked in theory and in mass organisations against capitalism and its racialised structures.

The third aspect of radical non-racialism was that it was not anti-white but it was anti-white supremacy. Apartheid (1948–1994) was a white supremacist social order, which had a history going back to the early colonial encounter. Apartheid imbued whiteness with a racialised superiority against the subhuman non-white. It was a social order that brought together racialised economic relations with political and ideological relations to affirm white superiority through Afrikaner nationalism. The radical non-racial tradition embraced those whites who consciously stood against white supremacy and supported the national liberation struggle. In the Communist Party, in the trade union movement, in faith-based organisations and in the UDF, this was certainly the case. The fourth aspect of radical non-racialism was its recognition that race as a group attribute and racism as a form of discrimination had no scientific basis for its existence in social relations. This was not about being colour blind in a facile sense, but was grounded in a deep humanist and universalist commitment to see and live beyond colour, as part of the struggle for a new society. While apartheid constructed a racist society and organised society through racialised relations, which impacted on all South Africans, our individual and collective challenges were to overcome these racialised social relations and its consequences. Racism in South Africa stole the humanity of the oppressed but it also tried to install a socially engineered racist in all of us, to keep the people divided. The brutalised humanity and racist consciousness, among the oppressed, also had to be confronted. The radical non-racial principle was a crucial guide on this existential journey. Many biographies and autobiographies of radical non-racial activists tell this story and are important resources of existential phenomenology.[7]

In all four respects, radical non-racialism is still relevant in South Africa – as a basis for strategic unity and solidarity for democratic people's power, as an anti-capitalist critique and practice, as anti-white supremacy and as an existential guiding principle to achieve a humanised society and world. Radical non-racialism is crucial, now more than ever, for a new left politics grounded in addressing the eco-cide question. This will be developed further below.

THESIS 2

Radical non-racialism shares important common ground with Black Consciousness but also goes beyond it in significant ways to achieve a future South Africa beyond skin colour.

The Black Consciousness movement made an important contribution to the liberation struggle in the 1970s. Its most prominent intellectual leader, Steve Biko, as part of this movement, left behind a powerful legacy, which impacted on philosophy, culture, black feminism, psychology, community-empowerment practices, black theology and a critical engagement with liberalism.[8]

Black Consciousness still resonates in the present. A rough typology of post-apartheid Black Consciousness suggests there are three articulations, each with different approaches to South Africa's future, and includes: (i) academic Black Consciousness, (ii) populist Black Consciousness and (iii) Africanist Black Consciousness. Academic Black Consciousness has produced some important interventions in our national conversation about continued racial oppression, the relevance of black identity and key solutions for the way forward for the country. Xolela Mangcu, for instance, argues, following Biko, for a joint culture among different groups of people, based on race-transcendent leadership and a public philosophy. He argues against the ANC's non-racial inequality.[9] While Frantz Fanon would be uncomfortable with the essentialist underpinnings of both Biko's and Mangcu's understandings of culture, a joint culture premised on the lived experience of the people and born out of struggle to build a deeply democratic society shares common ground with radical non-racialism. Zimitri Erasmus posits a new humanism for South Africa. She suggests love as a political practice, which brings together friendship, imaginative co-creativity, care for the Other and transformative politics as crucial for emancipation.[10] Erasmus's politically engaged humanism shares much ground with the existential journey central to the practice of radical non-racialism, which has been at the frontline of overcoming racial domination in South Africa. Radical non-racialism is a deeply political humanism that exists and does not have to be invented. It has to be further elaborated.

Populist Black Consciousness is best expressed in student politics today. With the rise of #RhodesMustFall and subsequently #FeesMustFall in 2015, student politics quickly lost its radical non-racial character and became explicitly Black Consciousness-orientated. While this shift has its own explanations, it also had its own implications for student unity, as the pain of the aspirant or already existing black middle-class child was exalted in performative ways. Moreover, two crucial intellectual ideas stand out, decolonising the university and intersectionality.[11] The populist version of decolonising the university would mean removing all white academics and all intellectual work by white academics. This is akin to a 'Pol Pot approach' to the university, smacks of adventurous millenarianism and is deeply racist. On the other hand, decolonising the university, as an epistemological and decolonising project, shares important ground with radical non-racialism in terms of not being anti-white but resisting white supremacy in all its forms. Moreover, intersectionality, as an analytical category, is not new to radical non-racialism and its non-reductionist understandings of class, race and gender related to capitalism. Also, it just might be that radical non-racialism has a much richer analytical tradition around the challenge of simultaneous oppressions which is home-grown. Intersectionality, understood as a concept of political practice to build solidarities among workers, women, students and society, also shares ground with radical non-racialism in terms of advancing strategic solidarities. While there might be different language registers at work and discursive distance, radical non-racialism has come to appreciate this challenge in the course of decades of mass resistance against apartheid oppression and capitalism.

An Africanist Black Consciousness is expressed through the resurgent Pan African Student Movement and the Economic Freedom Fighters (EFF), a breakaway political party from the ANC that is led by Julius Malema. These are political forces whose political practice is premised on generalised and essentialised understandings of race and racism. Their dialectical of change is simple: African versus the rest. With the crisis of the ANC's official non-racialism, these forces have been capitalising on this to argue that the entire non-racial tradition is irrelevant and they have been gaining important ground in some sections of society. As African nationalists, their future for South Africa is exclusionary, populist and based on a dangerous proclamation of racialised difference to advance revenge. It clashes directly with radical non-racialism.

THESIS 3

Radical non-racialism was defeated in the transition to democracy and was displaced by 'rainbowism', an Afro-neoliberal approach to nation building and the authoritarian corruption of the Zuma regime. Radical non-racialism is not the same as 'rainbowism', liberal democracy or narrow black nationalism.

The ANC-led Alliance has disarticulated radical non-racialism since 1994.[12] This means that the official non-racialism of the ANC-led Alliance and state, at the level of ideological relations and articulation, has eviscerated it. The ideological framing of non-racial politics was remade and this occurred in the context of electoral politics, state policy making, shallow nation building and managing the globalisation of a capitalist economy. This means that national and class struggle, race and class, were not articulated in national liberation political practice against, with and beyond post-apartheid capitalism. The programmatic content of national liberation, as contained in the Freedom Charter, was abandoned. Instead, a deeply racist capitalist society was embraced as the means to achieve national liberation. Non-racialism became about normalising the requirements of a globalising capitalism, including racialised labour processes, accumulation and new logics of commodification. The dialectic of working-class solidarity, mass power and radical non-racial unity was surrendered to the power of domestic and global capital. ANC-led Alliance ideological hegemony, through radical non-racialism, was remade against the interests of the historical subjects of liberation struggle, the oppressed black majority (African, coloured and Indian) and the working class.[13] This profound revision in the ideological imagination, articulation and practice of national liberation in the post-apartheid period has to be located in the following material and ideological conditions.

First, reconciliation, national unity and nation building were ideologically uncoupled from radical non-racialism. Instead, nationalism in post-apartheid South Africa became about a fuzzy 'rainbowism'. We were a country in which racialised difference and oppression was dissolved in the hues and shades of a fictive and re-imagined rainbow nation. We were all the rainbow, the rainbow was us. To dissent from and resist was to stand against the beauty of who we all were as a rainbow nation. The Truth and Reconciliation Commission, the government of national unity, the Mandela factor, the role of sport including the Rugby and Soccer World Cups, were all marshalled to address the deep historical fault lines of racial oppression, class exploitation and sexism. A country ravaged by dehumanisation was now meant to be living the rainbow dream, a new normalcy. The deep racial structures of formal apartheid were also dismantled to prop up this re-imagined nation. A progressive and new constitutionalism was crucial in this regard. Non-racialism was reduced to the celebration of racial diversity in the rainbow. We moved from apartheid racial classification to post-apartheid racial classification.

Second, the ANC-led Alliance and state, despite some intra-alliance quibbles, embraced another ideological element as part of post-apartheid national liberation: neoliberalism. Transnational neoliberalism was central to US-imperial hegemony and international relations over the past few decades. Not only did it seek to lock in the power of US financial markets across the globe, it also sought to remake the functions of the nation-state to serve the market and weaken the power of labour. For the ANC's rainbowist nationalism, this meant the state and economy were to be de-racialised but not fundamentally transformed through radical non-racialism. A de-racialised state amounted to being an African state. This is not a capable, non-racial, nation-building state directing, disciplining and reallocating capital. It is not a state capable of leading a nationally determined and driven development project. Despite the rhetoric of constructing a 'developmental state', the post-apartheid state merely appeases African nationalism and for more than two decades has been about subordinating this state to the power of global finance. The state has been an Afro-neoliberal state, managing a deeply globalised and financialised economy. The ubiquitous market has squeezed and disciplined the state. With the Zuma project, the state has been squeezed through corruption and rent seeking. The formal authority of the state has been increasingly undermined and an informal, shadow state has emerged. Market-driven and financialised black economic empowerment has been supplemented by state-driven, transactional black economic empowerment. A new parasitic black capitalist class has been in the making in the nexus of the state–market–ruling party. All of this is consistent with a neoliberalised global capitalism that is deeply corrupt and driven by an accumulation logic centred on increasing inequality. In this context, black capital and white capital have become the champions of an ostensible non-racialism to ensure harmonious race relations and radical economic transformation in the rainbow nation. A society led by capital has become the linchpin of national liberation practice and ideology.

Third, radical non-racialism has also been supplanted by marrying nationalism to 'liberal constitutionalism'. Ironically, the ANC-led alliance has always maintained that historically, the national liberation struggle has never been narrowly about civil and political rights. This was a struggle for fundamental transformation of the racist political economy. Despite this, South Africa's transformative constitutionalism has been reduced to a liberal constitutionalism articulated with national liberation ideology and its commitment to being a well-governed Afro-neoliberal state. An abstract citizenship has rendered all equal before the law; every South African is now the bearer of rights and a custodian of voting electoral power every five years. In the economy, every citizen is free to sell their labour power and harness the 'free market' for wealth acquisition. This liberal fiction, imagined as part of the rainbow nation, stands in stark contrast to the lived experience of precariousness among workers, deep inequality, widespread hunger, high unemployment and extremely high costs to access the courts in South Africa.[14] South Africa's imagined liberal democracy works only for a minority; hence between electoral cycles there are widespread social protests and increasingly violent civic struggles to gain recognition for the suffering in the everyday lives of the people. Shallow change, without fundamental transformation based on the constitution, has made South Africa a dangerous rainbow nation with a minority inside the imagined liberal democracy and the black majority outside.

Fourth, the centrality of the working class and working-class leadership was also a pivotal element in national liberation ideology, nationalism and the politics of radical non-racialism. The rise of powerful black trade unions in the 1970s and the formation of Cosatu in the mid-1980s gave a crucial organised expression to the working class in the South African national liberation struggle. The organised power of labour was also an important democratising force. Workers were actively engaged in their communities, as well as building popular organisation and constituting mass power prior to 1990. Today, in the context of the ANC-led Alliance, Cosatu has been split, it has lost its strategic capacity to shape South African politics, unions have been bureaucratised and there is growing social distance between organised workers and society.[15] Moreover, the Afro-neoliberal accumulation regime has introduced racialised and gendered precariousness, apartheid-style labour relations persist on farms, fragmentation of unions has taken root and worker control in unions has been replaced by a growing business unionism linked to black economic empowerment. South Africa's working class has been defeated by African nationalism. The erasure and denial of radical non-racialism reinforces both white and black privilege for a minority. This is what the 'radical economic transformation' agenda of the ANC really means.

THESIS 4

The ANC's embrace of deep globalisation, the unravelling of its hegemonic project and its populist call for 'radical economic transformation' has unleashed new conjunctural racisms in South Africa, undermining the future of the country.

The roots of racism run deep in South Africa and the making of a racialised social order extends to the colonial encounter of conquest, dispossession, slavery, genocide, segregation, proletarianisation in the context of agricultural modernisation and industrialisation, and institutionalised apartheid. The racial structures of society have articulated with class and gender in different historical moments and conjunctures in the development of capitalism. Post-apartheid South Africa inherited these racialised structures and relations of oppression. The ANC's embrace of Afro-neoliberalism and corrupt capitalist accumulation has unleashed both de-racialising and re-racialising dynamics as part of the rainbow nation. De-racialisation has been led by market and transactional class forces producing a black capitalist class and a sizeable black middle class.[16] This is sometimes referred to as the 30 per cent solution and has not laid the basis for a viable transformative democracy and social order.

Moreover, re-racialisation of social relations has also emerged in the context of the thin veneer of rainbowesque nation building evaporating as perceptions and insights into corruption at the heart of the ANC-led state have become more visible. The Zumafication of corruption has given licence to looting at various levels of the state and has grown grotesque since the ANC's vaunted Polokwane conference, which brought Zuma to power at the helm of the ANC and then the country. The Nkandla scandal, Gupta leaks, revelations about state capture in the Public Protector's report, corrupt dealings in relation to mega-government spend, the compromising of criminal justice institutions together with failed service delivery have fed into the deepening legitimacy crisis of the Africanised state. All these realities have rolled back nation-building efforts and have fuelled racist tropes and stereotypes about the ANC state in everyday common sense. The ANC's commitment to non-racialism is now in question as it no longer represents the interests of society but the interests of corrupt factions seeking looting opportunities in processes of parasitic accumulation. The ANC's calls for radical economic transformation ring hollow, given how criminalised its politics has become and how the deep legitimacy crisis of the state re-racialises South Africa. Authoritarian populism will merely further divide the country.

At the same time, the land and agrarian challenge has not been addressed in South Africa, and this is an emotive issue given the historical injustices related to land dispossession. The ANC's approach to land reform has been modest and has actually not worked in several instances. On its current trajectory, the ANC would take at least another 40 years to achieve even its modest target of 30 per cent land reform. The lack of a proper agrarian transformation strategy (except the use of liberalisation and marketisation since 1994), policy failure and a narrow productivist approach to agricultural development, through agri-business hubs and export-led agriculture, has again produced a class of small black farmers, connected to the dominant white-controlled and globalised agrarian economy while undermining the potential for more broad-based small black farmer development.[17] At the same time, the land question has become deeply racialised. White farmers still control 73 per cent of agricultural land in South Africa.[18] They are insecure and fearful of the populist direction of the ANC. At a recent demonstration concerning murders of white farmers, called #BlackMonday, a reactive and reactionary Afrikaner chauvinism came to the fore. The old apartheid flag was raised in some quarters and the new South African flag was burnt. These were deeply inflammatory and provocative moves. The African nationalist EFF, through their fiery leader, Malema, has an extremely populist approach to land reform. They have vaunted the Zimbabwe experience of land grabs and have also staged a few land occupations. Malema's EFF has a profoundly Africanist politics on the land question and he positioned himself as the voice of African nationalism against the Afrikaner chauvinism of #BlackMonday. He further racialised the national discourse, polarising the country even more. The land question has to be resolved but without a populist-engendered race war and in the context of failing corporate-controlled food systems. How the land question is dealt with can be an opportunity to build a new, resilient and food-sovereign system that advances radical non-racialism.

Another crucial expression of conjunctural racism is the rampant xenophobia in society (see Ekambaram in this volume). It is becoming increasingly incontrovertible that state practices and the state's policy approach to the migration regime are deeply xenophobic. This is contrary to the human rights framework of the country and the country's international relations commitments to the continent. State xenophobia has also contributed to divisions among the working class. Over the years, many of the violent flare-ups against non-South Africans have occurred in black working-class communities. These communities experience high levels of hunger and unemployment. The competition for economic opportunities is intense, given the crisis of social reproduction and the inability of the state to dynamise a labour-absorbing growth path. State xenophobia has certainly fuelled this situation. Moreover, working-class organisations such as unions, informal trader organisations, civic organisations and faith-based organisations have not done enough to build solidarities and support for migrants/immigrants in these communities. The once deeply solidaristic, radical non-racialism has again been further undermined by the crisis of national liberation ideology, state practice and the re-racialising dynamics of ANC leadership in South African society.

THESIS 5

The climate crisis threatens the existence of humans and non-human life forms. Eco-imperialism and capital, as a geological force, are driving the climate crisis in the context of the Anthropocene.

On a planetary scale, capitalism has undermined various natural cycles of the Earth's ecosystem. The assumption of endless capitalist accumulation, as part of fossil fuel and natural resource extractivism, globalised production patterns and wasteful mass consumerism has overshot various planetary limits. Resource peak, widespread pollution and ecological destruction are commonplace. The central contradiction in this context is the climate crisis.[19] The climate crisis, involving the heating of the planet, poses the gravest threat to human and non-human life. We have crossed a one-degree Celsius increase in planetary temperature since pre the industrial revolution and are heading rapidly to overshoot 1.5 degrees in the next two decades or sooner. Many scientists also predict that we will cross the two-degree increase in planetary temperature in this century. These increases unleash dangerous feedback loops and extreme shifts in Earth's ecosystem. There are already indicators of the awesome destruction and unbearable living conditions resulting from a heating planet. Hurricanes, droughts, heat waves, floods, rising sea levels threatening island states and low-lying areas, and freak extreme weather events are becoming the new normal. In this context, the conditions to sustain life on planet Earth, including South Africa, are being undermined. To make sense of the human impact on the planet, scientists, particularly geologists, have declared that we have left behind almost 11 000 years of stable climatic conditions, known as the Holocene, and are now entering a new stage in planetary history known as the Anthropocene.

This means humans are a causal factor in shaping planetary conditions such as climate change. This is a scientific fact. On the face of it, this approach to the climate crisis makes sense. However, from the standpoint of Marxist ecology, the Anthropocene is really about imperial eco-cide, that is the role of the US as the dominant imperial power refusing to let the world take the climate crisis seriously, given that a decarbonised civilisation requires fundamental systemic transformation, including going beyond capitalism, if we are to survive. In addition, capital as a geological force is responsible for global carbon extraction, for burning fossil fuels and driving global carbon-based accumulation, including production, consumption and everyday patterns of living that are carbon-centric, wasteful and destructive to planetary ecosystems. Capital as a geological force has for 150 years enlisted the role of rich industrialised countries in the global North, petro states and carbon-addicted ruling classes.

Of late, industrialising countries such as China and India are also contributing, in aggregate, to global emission levels. Similarly, South Africa is a carbon-intensive economy and has extremely high levels of aggregate carbon emissions in the world.[20] Global leadership has failed in multilateral institutions and at the state level. The UN Paris Climate Agreement brings too little, too late, and has already been undermined by the Trump administration. Vulnerable island states are challenged by increasing sea levels and climate shocks, such as hurricanes. In 2017, hurricanes Harvey, Irma and Maria left a trail of destruction in their wake and extremely high costs for reconstruction. South Africa is a carbon-addicted society. Our economy is heavily invested in coal and the government has flirted with a nuclear deal that would bankrupt the state. South Africa's carbon capitalist forces are also driving a resource nationalism that would lead to fracking in parts of the country with fragile ecosystems and gas/oil exploration of our coastlines through Operation Phakisa. These extractive initiatives aim to yield complex hydrocarbons that will worsen the climate crisis and also involve extending and deepening the carbon-based minerals–energy complex. South Africa is a carbon criminal state seeking to make a few super-wealthy, through carbon capitalism, while the rest of society bears the brunt of climate shocks. This is the terminus of the ANC-led Alliance approach to the national democratic revolution. It is not about sustaining life but about destroying it.

THESIS 6

The ANC-led Alliance approach and, more generally, the orthodox Marxist approaches to the national question are outdated in the context of the dangerous climate contradiction and the deepening planetary ecological crisis. The national question has to be replaced by the eco-cide question.

The ANC-led South African state is a carbon criminal state and a failed climate crisis state. It is undermining the right to life of present generations and generational justice for future generations. South Africa's drought, since 2014, has been one of the worst in the history of the country. It has had dramatic impacts on food prices, hunger (14 million South Africans went to be bed hungry before the drought), water systems and food production. Cape Town has experienced acute water stress and could become the first major urban conglomeration that might not be viable because of water shortages linked to climate change. South Africa's drought is linked to the El Nino effect but also to a heating planet. Moreover, the Knysna fires of 2017, wave-surge flooding in the city of Durban and freak weather events (extreme downpours or cold spells during the onset of summer 2017) all portend a climate-driven South Africa and world. In this context, more droughts, flooding, heat waves and other extreme climate shocks should be expected. More climate shocks also mean more costs for society related to infrastructure, health, food and adaptation. A fiscally constrained state, due to mismanagement and corruption, is already a failed state.[21] With climate shocks, such a state will not survive. The South African state thus far has not been able to factor in the costs of these climate shocks and is failing to appreciate the death spiral of society due to climate change. Instead, the state is preoccupied with preventing the Eskom 'death spiral' by trying to save South Africa's corrupt coal-driven electricity monopoly at the expense of society. This is all about return on investment in the context of bad policy decisions, state capture and a worsening climate crisis. South Africa should be leaving Eskom behind as a stranded resource and transitioning to socially owned renewables at local government and community level.

The climate crisis is merely the expression of the deeper eco-cidal logic of global capitalism. More sharply, the climate crisis reveals how capitalism, including post-apartheid capitalism, is incapable of solving the most serious existential threat faced by human and non-human life. Instead, capital, while it is causing the climate crisis, is also undermining the conditions that sustain life, leading to a sixth planetary extinction. This is the crux of the eco-cide question. Yet the ANC-led Alliance in South Africa has embraced carbon-driven capitalist modernity, neoliberal globalisation and its eco-cidal logic. The argument that more carbon-based energy or even nuclear power is required for industrial development is a false argument, given that there are cheaper renewable energy sources that can power the country at scale and meet its development needs. The national question in South Africa, as I have argued, has been resolved contra the interests of the workers, the poor and the majority. Class and race, in the ANC's non-racialism, has been about class formation for the few, as part of African nationalism. This has become the dominant agenda of national liberation. Such social forces are incapable of leading deep social change and transformation.

This prompts a serious question: why has the national question ideological approach to liberation ended up in such a degenerate, politically bankrupt and eco-cidal place with a fundamental disregard for the most dangerous contradiction facing human and non-human life? Part of the answer relates to the kind of Marxism that has provided the intellectual scaffolding, template, imagination and tools to think through the national question and which has brought South Africa to this destructive turning point. South Africa's embrace of the national question approach to understanding racial oppression has its origins in Lenin's thesis on the right to self-determination, which was further elaborated by Stalin. It was imported into South Africa through the South African Communist Party (SACP) (then called the Communist Party of South Africa) and became central to ANC-led national liberation discourse to understand national oppression.[22] This framework evolved from the 1950s on, and became an analytical tool to understand class, race and capitalism as part of 'colonialism of a special type'. The SACP's approach to understanding settler colonialism through positing and analysing colonialism of a special type, from its beginnings in modern economic relations through its vicissitudes of segregation and apartheid, became the hegemonic understanding of the national question in the ANC-led Alliance. It articulated a dualistic understanding of a coloniser/colonised society, in which the oppressor and oppressed shared a common territorial space. Similarly, Trotskyists evoked the political economy concept of racial capitalism.[23]

All the Marxist approaches to the national question in South Africa are marked by a deep productivism, which means that they did not bring into perspective the dimension of nature in historical materialism and in their understandings of South African capitalism. A crucial premise for these Marxisms was the idea of dominating nature, and even the envisaged socialist modernisation, with its state-centric relations of production, was about the march of the forces of production. Soviet modernisation was the answer, despite its extremely destructive ecological relations. Today, China has such an attraction as well with its growth-driven political economy. This is an anthropocentric and Promethean Marxism, marked by a fetish for eco-cidal industrial development. Whether married to a first or a second stage of revolutionary change, these frameworks are deeply flawed from an ontological point of view.

In addition, the national question approach is based on an 'additive model of change'. Thus, while a non-reductionist approach to class and race were the primary contradictions in the national liberation struggle, this was then extended to include the women's question and oppression. A hierarchy of oppressions was set up within the national liberation canon and this was mediated by the contingencies of the struggle within the national democratic revolution. However, this can easily degenerate into a static understanding of society such that the complexities, contradictions and dynamics of change in a social formation are not fully grasped. Looking at the Freedom Charter, the cornerstone programmatic basis of the ANC-led national liberation movement, and post-apartheid policy documents of the ANC, there is no ecological thrust in these documents that makes the connection between race, class, gender and ecological relations. National liberation thought has no conception of the ecological, even on the terms of its 'additive model of change'. While climate determinism will register and will probably be added to the national question roster of contradictions, this will largely be an add-on that is reactive to a changing reality and not based on a deeper understanding of how it relates to the making of an eco-cidal capitalism in South Africa. This will not be an effective basis to shift society and can easily be about green climate capitalism, a false solution.

Finally, South Africa's vanguardist national liberation forces (the ANC-led Alliance) are the real custodians of the national question, not the people. These forces are firmly entrenched in a carbon capitalist trajectory and the reproduction of South Africa's minerals–energy complex, revealing another fundamental weakness of the national question approach to the dangerous climate contradiction and eco-cide. Theory and theoretical analysis, as the basis to guide revolutionary practice, cannot be the preserve of ideologues and vanguardist forces that proclaim to have the monopoly on the truth. Vanguards lose their way and are not the guarantor of 'revolutionary success', even for the resolution of the national question. History has repeatedly shown this to be the case, including in contemporary South Africa. Put differently, South Africa's vanguardist forces, such as the ANC and SACP, are historically exhausted, have failed and cannot be the basis to address the eco-cide question. An alternative politics is required to address the eco-cide question and challenge.

While the national question framework has had a decisive impact on the national liberation struggle, it is outdated, discredited and incapable of dealing with the life-threatening challenge of the climate crisis contradiction within global and South African capitalism. As it stands, the national question framework is married to carbon capitalism in South Africa and an avaricious resource nationalism in practice. It might take on elements of a green climate capitalism but this will not be enough. The national question framework is part of the problem. The climate crisis and more generally the eco-cide question has to be the basis for a new emancipatory, deeply democratic and transformative politics. The time for the eco-cide question is now.

THESIS 7

Securing a future and overcoming the eco-cidal logic of capitalism lies in a democratic eco-socialist nation-building project. Such a project has to confront the climate crisis through deep just transitions, grounded in radical non-racialism, mass transformative politics and the reclamation of our sovereignty to sustain life.

The eco-cide question is the question of our time, for present and future generations and for human and non-human life forms. We cannot sustain life on planet Earth, including South Africa, with runaway global warming and worsening ecological crises. This is not about catastrophism, eco-fatalism or end of times millenarianism. The doomsday clock is ticking but there is still time to act. A fundamental shift in planetary consciousness is required to deal with and overcome the logic of capitalist eco-cide. As I have argued, global leadership in multilateral institutions and in national states are not up to this task. Actually they have failed. In this regard, crucial political imperatives have to be advanced and realised, noting that these imperatives are emerging from grassroots mass movements, radical intellectuals, progressive think tanks and activists engaged with the challenge of sustaining life.[24] These imperatives include the following:

- Scientific evidence produced by the UN, NASA and the World Meteorological Organisation, geologists and Earth scientists are compelling in enabling us to understand the scale, pace and current and prospective impacts of the climate crisis. Embracing the science of climate change and other ecological crises has to be the basis for

understanding the eco-cide question and has to be made understandable to all in the public sphere.
- Planetary eco-cide is about understanding how ecological relations have been racialised, classed, gendered and imbricated in various forms of oppressions. It has been central to supremacist whiteness and is about understanding the political economy of 500 years of destruction of human and non-human life in the making of capitalism's eco-cidal logic. Genocides, slavery, species extinction, colonialism, industrial-scale violence, apartheid and human brutalisation are central to this history of the origins and making of capitalism. These relations can no longer be reified and ignored as part of capitalism's 'endless accumulation' logic. Moreover, with climate change, there are and will be disproportionate impacts on workers, the poor, indigenous peoples, black lives, women peasant farmers and more generally the poorer and darker nations of the world. Capital's eco-cidal logic is deeply racist and anti-life, more generally. Confronting planetary eco-cide is also about confronting supremacist whiteness and advancing decolonisation as part of radical non-racialism.
- Radical non-racialism has to be re-engaged as the basis for renewing and building mass people's power to confront capitalism's eco-cidal logic. This means the anti-capitalism, anti-racism and anti-oppression thrusts of radical non-racialism have to be harnessed to unite social forces, build alliances (of workers, the landless, peasants, women's organisations, the permanently unemployed, radical intellectuals, students and middle classes) and advance movements to sustain life. These movements are already on the march at the frontlines of confronting carbon extractivism, land grabs, protecting the water, seed and forest commons, protesting against nuclear energy, fighting for decent work and more. Such movements are engaged in finding transformative and systemic alternatives to the contradictions of eco-cidal capitalism in local, national, regional and global spheres. The imperative is to bring out the best of humanity, including human consciousness, solidarity and collective endeavour to scale up these alternatives and sustain life in South Africa and beyond.
- Deep just transitions and democratic eco-socialisms are the horizons and visionary concepts of anti-eco-cide politics. The system change logic of systemic alternatives, such as food sovereignty, the solidarity economy, climate jobs, indigenous knowledge systems, rights of nature, socially

owned renewable energy, mass renewable energy public transport, zero waste, universal basic income grants, water commoning, democratic planning and more, are about deep just transitions beyond capitalism, from within and outside. It is about harnessing deep democracy at the household, community, village, town, city and country level to constitute transformative power from below. At the same time, such deep democracy practices assist with reclaiming, re-embedding and transforming the state so that the people can govern. It is about affirming an eco-centric ethics in our relationship with human and non-human life, while meeting human needs. Simply, the democratic eco-socialism project is about ending the capitalist war with nature and affirming human life, black and white, as part of renewing nation building in South Africa.

NOTES

1 Frederikse (1990) argues for the official unbreakable thread of non-racialism as central to the ANC. See Everatt (2009) for a more complexified history on the origins of non-racialism.
2 A people's history of struggle and radical non-racialism still has to be written in South Africa beyond the mythologies of the ANC's official non-racialism or big-man histories.
3 See Suttner and Cronin (1986) for an important history of the Congress of the People campaign and how the Freedom Charter was put together through peoples' demands and ideas from below.
4 The National Union of Mineworkers adopted the Freedom Charter. The National Union of Metalworkers of South Africa, the most left-wing affiliate of Cosatu, adopted the Freedom Charter as well as committed to developing a more explicit working-class programme. See Forrest (2011: 418).
5 See Seekings (2000) for an 'instrumentalist history' of the UDF, in which the ANC made it all happen and was determining. This is another example of official non-racialism in the historiography of South Africa's struggle, which needs to be challenged through a people's history of liberation. Of course, this is not to argue that the ANC did not have influence but to over-exaggerate its role in history is propagandistic. It also takes away from the agency of the people and people's organisations.
6 This is the Mandela that has to be read and reclaimed for our contemporary period. See Mandela (1994), particularly the chapter 'The Struggle is My Life'.
7 See Mandela (1994), Sisulu (2002), Kathrada (2004), Reddy (1991), Meer (2002), Bernstein (1999), Simons (2004), among others.

8   See Mngxitama, Alexander and Gibson (2008) and Pityana et al. (1991). Both are important collections reflecting on the legacy and impact of Black Consciousness.
9   See Mangcu (2015).
10 See Erasmus (2017: 141).
11 See Chinguno et al. (2017), which is a compilation of reflections and analyses by students involved with Fallist politics and student protests at Wits University.
12 Stuart Hall (1980), building on Gramsci, assists us to think about the contradictory, non-deterministic and contingent ways in which ideology operates. His method of articulation and how ideologies are constituted through various elements, linked to power and material conditions, is instructive.
13 I have covered this ground in other work, which I draw on for this part of the argument. See Satgar (2008, 2009, 2012, 2014, 2015).
14 According to Statistics South Africa (2017a), the unemployment rate was at 27.7% in 2017 and income inequality was at 0.68 (2017b), with sharp increases in income per capita inequality among whites and Indians. Both the unemployment rate and per capita income inequality are among the highest in the world.
15 The crisis of Cosatu is well documented in Satgar and Southall (2015) and Bezuidenhout and Tshoaedi (2017).
16 Southall (2016: 42) provides a crucial analysis of the new black middle class. He also looks at the size problem covered in the various studies that deal with this issue. The largest measurement suggests the new black middle class comprised 9.3 million, in 2008, as part of the population.
17 See Jara (2014) and Hall and Kepe (2017).
18 A land audit done by Agri-SA suggests that white farmer ownership of agricultural land declined from 85.1% in 1994 to 73.3% in 2016. See J. de Lange, 'Who owns SA's land?' *City Press*, 29 October 2017, p. 8.
19 The science and urgency of the climate crisis is also covered in the previous volume in this series. See Satgar (2018).
20 EDGAR (2016) highlights that South Africa was 40th in the world in 2015 in terms of carbon emissions per capita and was 18th in global ranks in 2015 in terms of aggregate emissions.
21 South Africa's debt to GDP ratio is increasing and is currently at about 56%. State-owned enterprises are highly indebted and if these institutions default the entire fiscal system could be brought down. At the same time, looting of public resources is inducing tax fatigue and a massive leakage of public finance.
22 Mzala (1988) provides a useful account of the intellectual genealogy and itinerary of the national question approach. It should be noted that Marxism has also had other approaches to racism and colonialism. See chapter 1 in this volume.
23 Other Marxists utilised neo-Poulantzian structural analysis, racial Fordism and modes of production approaches. See two useful collections that capture the national question approach in South Africa: Van Diepen (1988) and more recently Webster and Pampallis (2017). What is striking about the latter collection is the complete absence of any recognition of the corporate-induced climate crisis and its eco-cidal implications by the contributors.
24 See also Satgar (2018) for more in-depth engagement with democratic eco-socialist systemic alternatives, practices and pathways.

REFERENCES

Bernstein, R. 1999. *Memory Against Forgetting: Memoirs from a Life in South African Politics 1938–1964*. Johannesburg: Penguin.

Bezuidenhout, A. and Tshoaedi, M. (eds). 2017. *Labour Beyond Cosatu: Mapping the Rupture in South Africa's Labour Landscape*. Johannesburg: Wits University Press.

Chinguno, C., Kgoroba, M., Mashibini, S., Masilela, B., Maubane, B., Moyo, N., Mthombeni, A. and Ndlovu, H. (eds). 2017. *Rioting and Writing: Diaries of Wits Fallists*. Johannesburg: Society, Work and Development Institute (SWOP).

EDGAR (Emission Database for Global Atmospheric Research). 2016. 'Emissions time series'. Accessed 27 November 2017, http://edgar.jrc.ec.europa.eu/overview.php?v=CO2ts1990-2015&sort=des2.

Erasmus, Z. 2017. *Race Otherwise: Forging a New Humanism for South Africa*. Johannesburg: Wits University Press.

Everatt, D. 2009. *The Origins of Non-Racialism: White Opposition to Apartheid in the 1950s*. Johannesburg: Wits University Press.

Forrest, K. 2011. *Metal That Will Not Bend: National Union of Metalworkers of South Africa 1980–1995*. Johannesburg: Wits University Press.

Frederikse, J. 1990. *The Unbreakable Thread: Non-Racialism in South Africa*. Johannesburg: Ravan Press.

Hall, R. and Kepe, T. 2017. 'Elite capture and state neglect: New evidence on South Africa's land reform', *Review of African Political Economy*, 44 (151): 122–130.

Hall, S. 1980. 'Race articulation and societies structured in dominance'. In UNESCO, *Sociological Theories: Race and Colonialism*. Paris: UNESCO, pp. 305–345.

Jara, M. 2014. 'The solidarity economy response to the agrarian crisis in South Africa'. In *The Solidarity Economy Alternative: Emerging Theory and Practice*, edited by V. Satgar. Pietermaritzburg: University of KwaZulu-Natal Press, pp. 227–248.

Kathrada, A. 2004. *Memoirs*. Cape Town: Zebra Press.

Mandela, N. 1994. *Long Walk to Freedom: The Autobiography of Nelson Mandela*. New York: Little, Brown and Company.

Mangcu, X. 2015. 'What moving beyond race can actually mean: Towards a joint culture'. In *The Colour of our Future*, edited by Xolela Mangcu. Johannesburg: Wits University Press, pp. 1–16.

Meer, I. 2002. *A Fortunate Man*. Cape Town: Zebra Press.

Mngxitama, A., Alexander, A. and Gibson, N.C. (eds). 2008. *Biko Lives! Contesting the Legacies of Steve Biko*. New York: Palgrave Macmillan.

Mzala, C. 1988. 'Revolutionary theory on the national question in South Africa'. In *The National Question in South Africa*, edited by M. van Diepen. London: Zed Books, pp. 30–55.

Pityana, N.B., Ramphele, M., Mpulwana, M. and Wilson, L. (eds). 1991. *Bounds of Possibility: The Legacy of Steve Biko and Black Consciousness*. Cape Town: David Philip.

Reddy, E.S. (compiler). 1991. *Monty Speaks: Speeches of Dr G.M. (Monty) Naicker 1945–1963*. Durban: Madiba Publishers and Cape Town: UWC Historical and Cultural Centre.

Satgar, V. 2008. 'Neoliberalised South Africa: Labour and the roots of passive revolution', *Labour, Capital and Society*, 41 (2): 38–69.

Satgar, V. 2009. 'Global capitalism and the neoliberalisation of Africa'. In *A New Scramble for Africa? Imperialism, Investment and Development*, edited by R. Southall and H. Melber. Pietermaritzburg: University of KwaZulu-Natal Press, pp. 35–55.

Satgar, V. 2012. 'Beyond Marikana: The post-apartheid South African state'. *Africa Spectrum*, 47 (2–3): 33–62.

Satgar, V. 2014. 'South Africa's green developmental state?' In *The End of the Developmental State?*, edited by M. Williams. London: Routledge and Pietermaritzburg: University of KwaZulu-Natal Press, pp. 126–153.

Satgar, V. 2015. 'Marxism and the crisis of labour in post-apartheid South Africa'. In *Cosatu in Crisis: The Fragmentation of an African Trade Union Federation*, edited by V. Satgar and R. Southall. Johannesburg: KMM Publishers, pp.134–161.

Satgar, V. (ed.). 2018. *The Climate Crisis: South African and Global Democratic Eco-Socialist Alternatives*. Johannesburg: Wits University Press.

Satgar, V. and Southall, R. 2015. *Cosatu in Crisis: The Fragmentation of an African Trade Union Federation*, edited by V. Satgar and R. Southall. Johannesburg: KMM Publishers.

Seekings, J. 2000. *The UDF: A History of the United Democratic Front in South Africa 1983–1991*. Cape Town: David Philip.

Simons, R.A. 2004. *All My Life and All My Strength*. Johannesburg: STE Publishers.

Sisulu, E. 2002. *Walter and Albertina Sisulu: In our Lifetime*. Cape Town: David Philip.

Southall, R. 2016. 'White monopoly capital: Good politics, bad sociology, worse economics'. Accessed 27 November 2017, http://theconversation.com/white-monopoly-capital-good-politics-bad-sociology-worse-economics-77338.

Statistics South Africa. 2017a. 'Quarterly Labour Force Survey: Quarter 3: 2007'. Accessed 27 November 2017, http://www.statssa.gov.za/publications/P0211/P02113rdQuarter2017.pdf.

Statistics South Africa. 2017b. 'Poverty trends in South Africa: An examination of absolute poverty between 2006 and 2015'. Accessed 27 November 2017, http://www.statssa.gov.za/publications/Report-03-10-06/Report-03-10-062015.pdf.

Suttner, R. and Cronin, J. 1986. *30 Years of the Freedom Charter*. Johannesburg: Ravan Press.

Van Diepen, M. (ed.). 1989. *The National Question in South Africa*. London: Zed Books.

Webster, E. and Pampallis, K. 2017. *The Unresolved National Question: Left Thought under Apartheid*. Johannesburg: Wits University Press.

CHAPTER

11

FOREIGN NATIONALS ARE THE 'NON-WHITES' OF THE DEMOCRATIC DISPENSATION

Sharon S. Ekambaram

In the context of this chapter, migration and movement of people includes refugees fleeing conflict and violence in fear of persecution, but it also includes people fleeing unliveable conditions created by economic crises in the cases of Zimbabwe, Mozambique and Malawi, among other countries in Africa.

It is argued that policy shifts currently being implemented in South Africa go against the ethos and vision of the constitution, which frames a rallying call for transformation and redress of the wrongs of capitalist apartheid. 'Our constitutional design is emphatically transformative. It is meant to migrate us from a murky and brutish past to an inclusive future animated by values of human decency and solidarity. It contains a binding consensus on or a blueprint of what a fully transformed society should look like' (Moseneke 2014: 4).

South Africa should be championing an approach that protects basic human rights and respects the human dignity of vulnerable people fleeing to this country. Instead, South Africa is notorious for its xenophobic violence in all its forms, which include state practices, public perception, hate speech and media stereotypes.[1] The practice of the Department of Home Affairs in itself displays characteristics of institutional xenophobia in its response to migrants and refugees. This practice has been explained as a product of the apartheid past (Möser 2016).

This chapter highlights the crisis facing migrants and refugees, predominantly from the African continent, coming to South Africa. It is a critique of the current policy and practice of the South African government and the Department of Home Affairs, in particular. It locates the current crisis affecting migrants and refugees (foreign nationals) in the context of the apartheid era, globalisation and post-colonial neoliberal economic restructuring, centred on continuing racialised forms of exploitation through the ubiquitous market.

I outline a worrying trend that sees the South African government aligning itself to the policies and practices of the rich governments of the North in scapegoating migrants and refugees and blaming them for social ills (see Georgi in this volume). This policy shift, which is based on exclusion, encampment and seeing migrants and refugees as a security risk, is examined. Moreover, this shift effectively denies accountability of the state and its constitutional obligation to provide decent, adequate basic services for all as enshrined in the bill of rights.

Looking critically at the Refugees Amendment Bill and the White Paper on International Migrants, this chapter exposes how these policy shifts are couched in arguments of migrants being a 'security threat' and a political presence against the 'national interest', reflecting the influence of reactionary international practice as witnessed in Europe, the US and Australia, among others.

The current crisis and collapse of the asylum system and state of chaos of Refugee Reception Offices of the Department of Home Affairs is brought into view. The chapter outlines how human dignity is trampled on and the disrespect with which people from predominantly African countries are treated as they struggle to gain access to the asylum process, which is near impossible under current conditions.

It is argued that our democratic dispensation places a constitutional obligation on the executive to ensure that policies and their implementation take into account the racist repressive past, and have transformation and redress as their objective. In light of this obligation, policy on international migration has to take into account the history of the migrant labour system, which saw the exploitation, through a capitalist economic system, of black labour institutionalised and enforced through the divide and rule polices of the system of apartheid. Dating back to 1886, with the discovery of gold on the Witwatersrand, systems to control African labour were put in place, with strict regulations to prevent them from settling permanently in South Africa (Bakewell and De Haas 2007).

Xenophobia and the manner in which migrants are treated, together with the policy shifts proposed, cannot be the practice of a revolutionary progressive movement that fought for the liberation of black oppressed people of South Africa.

This policy of exclusion and building of walls affects people fleeing from the global South and from so-called developing nations. The racial oppression and ideology manifesting in this has historical roots in the barbaric system of slavery and, more recently, has continuities in a racialised neoliberal globalisation.

MAKING THE ARGUMENT FOR RACIST PRACTICE

UNHCR and UN conventions: Protecting vulnerable refugees

The United Nations High Commissioner for Refugees (UNHCR) was established in 1950 with a core mandate to protect refugees (UNHCR 2010). UNHCR's initial task was to help millions of uprooted peoples in the aftermath of the Second World War, and to seek permanent solutions for them. The convention obliged states not to expel or forcibly return an asylum seeker to a territory where he or she faced persecution.[2]

The response to the refugee crisis post the Holocaust in Europe was admirable. 'There is a lot to be learned from history. European states were the architects of the modern refugee regime. They negotiated the 1951 Refugee Convention in the aftermath of the Holocaust. It is a legacy we should be proud of and seek to preserve. It was a moment at which Europe collectively understood that people fleeing persecution should have a right to seek refuge in order to access fundamental human rights' (Alfred 2015: 2).

Why was there greater empathy and support for refugees fleeing after the Second World War compared to the way in which South Africa and the international community is responding to a similar crisis today? Is the fact that it is predominantly people from the South, and more specifically people from the African continent that are moving, which make migrants a 'security risk' and a 'threat to the national interest'?

Countries on the African continent are hosts to the largest population of refugees. According to UNHCR, out of a total population of 13 024 491 refugees in 2014, Africa took responsibility for 3 670 630, while Europe and the US hosted 329 891 and 501 335 respectively (UNHCR 2017). It is argued that over the last decade Europe has exaggerated figures of migrants reaching its shores, when in fact the figures are an undercount.[3]

Refugees today no longer have geopolitical value

The post-Second World War era saw the US on the offensive to impose a new world order. Movements on the African continent that were formed to overthrow their colonisers were met with counter-revolution by US-supported forces. Vishwas Satgar (2009: 45) highlights how 'the counter-revolution in Africa destroyed countries, dislocated populations and shattered the lives of millions of ordinary people'. In Africa, the forced movement of people out of their communities and countries was largely a result of global geopolitical rivalry in the twentieth century, which played itself out in Africa.

Post-Second World War, Russia and the US engaged in conflict in the era of the cold war by providing economic and military aid to strengthen the countries that supported communist or imperialist ideology. Refugees fleeing communist countries were supported and had value in as far as they strengthened the agenda and propaganda of US imperialism, and vice versa. This is what gave refugees value and resulted in financial support and protection. The propaganda value of accepting refugees fleeing communism remained central to US policy (Tempo 2015).

POVERTY AND UNDERDEVELOPMENT ON THE AFRICAN CONTINENT: WHO ARE THE PERPETRATORS?

Where is our outrage? Not against the vulnerable people seeking refuge in South Africa but against political and economic instability and conflict that forces people to uproot themselves and embark on perilous journeys, not out of choice. Journeys that expose men, women and children to dangers, often including death. Is it because it is black people from Africa who are fleeing that the response is not informed by the dire need for them to be offered protection? Achille Mbembe speaks about the unequal redistribution of the capacities to negotiate borders on a global scale. He also makes reference to 'the anti-immigrant racism' that is on the rise in the North (Mbembe 2017). Those deemed 'non-European' or 'non-white' are subjected to overt and not so overt forms of violence and discrimination. Racism is rooted in the origins of capitalism, which is intertwined with the history of slavery where the black human body was turned into a commodity to be sold to the highest bidder (see Manji as well as Mabasa in this volume).

The White Paper on International Migration calls for the further decolonising of South Africa's immigration policy, and addressing the bias that favours immigrants from Europe over African countries (DHA 2017). It contextualises the history of migration and documents the fact that Africans were classified as 'Natives' and consigned to the migrant labour system that maintained colonial economies across southern Africa. It also admits that 'the 1999 White Paper opened our borders to Africa and the world but reserved the right to immigrate largely to those with high levels of skills or capital. Workers with low to mid-level skills from SADC [Southern African Development Community] countries can only be recruited by farmers, the mines and other companies under temporary Corporate Work Visa that has roots in the migrant labour system' (DHA 2017).

The xenophobia experienced today is a legacy of our colonial and apartheid history. White supremacist and racist world views involving divide and rule, 'othering' (what appears to be borders in the head) and labelling were institutionalised in the apartheid system in South Africa and extended to the colonial political economy.

Colonisation was a brutal invasion, driven by European rivalries, but based on the subjugation of civilisations, predominantly in Africa. This was justified through demonising African people as uncivilised and referring to Africa as the 'Dark Continent'. Black people were seen as subhuman, inferior and uncivilised, needing to be saved by the civilised European (see Manji in this volume). The looting of raw material was the real objective, which was extracted largely through slave wages and the exploitation of black labour and used to fuel the industrial revolution. Europe's manufacturing industry used the raw materials to manufacture cloth, jewels and other products, stimulating their economies and creating wealth. Looking at development and underdevelopment on the African continent, Walter Rodney debunks the myths that colonisation was about bringing civilisation to the African continent. He systematically sets out how the wealth and resources from the continent were siphoned off to Europe. 'Colonialism was not merely a system of exploitation but one whose essential purpose was to repatriate the profit to the so called "mother land"' (Rodney 1972: 177). This historical experience of a brutalising and racist capitalism has defined the basis of systemic racism between the imperialist countries of the global North and Africa. This systemic racism has also impacted on Africa in the current conjuncture of globalisation and neoliberalisation.

FAILURE OF THREE DECADES OF STRUCTURAL ADJUSTMENT AND DEEP GLOBALISATION

Satgar (2009: 34) makes reference to the concept of transnational neoliberalism to describe the post-colonial era: 'During this period the increasing international mobility of capital, further integration of the global market and the restructuring of global production have re-organised global capital.' The World Bank and the International Monetary Fund imposed what was referred to as Structural Adjustment Programmes, forcing states seeking loans to implement austerity measures. To qualify for a loan, states had to cut back on social spending, including health and education. Privatisation, liberalisation and public-private partnerships in a globalised economy resulted in increased levels of impoverishment of poor and working-class communities. State cutbacks on social spending and related service delivery through the privatisation of essential services resulted in impoverished working-class communities that could not pay for basic services.

Ashwin Desai (2015) provides a detailed overview and analysis of how successive leaders of the African National Congress (ANC) failed to implement economic policies to alleviate the abject poverty in which most South Africans were living. The outcome is chronic systemic unemployment with high and ever-escalating levels of poverty and inequality. A racialising and market-centred neoliberalisation has further created conjunctural conditions, for both the African continent at large and South Africa as a country on the continent, that have led to labour mobility in search of dignity, security and the means to ensure social reproduction. This desperate search, however, has exposed the myths and assumptions about open, seamless and accessible economies in the age of neoliberal globalisation. The flow and mobility of labour and decent work has not happened alongside uneven trade and investment in countries.

XENOPHOBIA, RACIAL OTHERING AND ISLAMOPHOBIA

As is the case today in South Africa and in Europe, the narrative about the threat that refugees and migrants pose is narrow and nationalist. In other words, support and solidarity for the plight of migrants is not in the national interest. Migrants and refugees are scapegoated for failed policy implementation by states. Walls are being built and refugees are being blocked from entering

Europe. During his candidacy announcement speech in June 2015, Donald Trump campaigned: 'I will build a great wall – and nobody builds walls better than me, believe me – and I'll build them very inexpensively. I will build a great, great wall on our southern border, and I will make Mexico pay for that wall. Mark my words' (Gunderman 2014).

A racialised border regime is at work in Europe to deal with the migration crisis (see Georgi in this volume). South Africa is no different.

The declaration of a 'war on terror' by the US has resulted in specific populations being seen as a security risk. This marks a distinct shift in how many states internationally and predominantly in the North are responding to the humanitarian crisis of people fleeing from persecution and for their very survival.

From an era of cold war to an era defined by George W. Bush (2001) in an address to a joint session of Congress and the American people: 'Either you are with us, or you are with the terrorists. From this day forward, any nation that continues to harbour or support terrorism will be regarded by the United States as a hostile regime.'

The US would have no regard for bringing democracy to Iraq or Afghanistan if there were no interest in oil. 'There has been so massive and calculatedly aggressive an attack on the contemporary societies of the Arab and Muslim for their backwardness, lack of democracy, and abrogation of women's rights that we simply forget that such notions as modernity, enlightenment, and democracy are by no means simple, and agreed-upon concepts that one either does or does not find like Easter eggs in the living-room' (Said 1979 [2014]: xix).

RISE OF XENOPHOBIA

According to the online Oxford English Dictionary, xenophobia is defined as 'a dislike of or prejudice against people from other countries'.

The outbreak of xenophobic violence in 2008 and then again in 2015 in South Africa are just blips on the radar that catch the attention of the international media as a sensational story of bloody faces and dead bodies – headlines that sell newspapers. This xenophobic violence is meted out on a daily basis to foreign nationals, predominantly poor, working-class people seeking refuge and an opportunity to survive horrific circumstances by coming to South Africa. A documentary called *Voetsek! Us, brothers?* was commissioned by Lawyers for Human Rights (LHR) in 2017.[4] It looks at the timeline of violence through the lens of socio-economic inequalities and documents the unsubstantiated reckless statements made by political leaders in South Africa and related outbreaks of violence in townships and informal settlements in the country.

Xenophobic violence can be traced to as early as a few months after the first democratic elections of 27 April 1994. In December 1994 in Alexandra township, 'armed youth gangs destroy[ed] foreign-owned property and demand[ed] that foreigners be removed from the area' (Misago, Laundau and Monson 2009). Evictions, looting of property and even killings were reported elsewhere in the country. The frequency of such events gradually increased, with an unprecedented level of violence reached in May 2008. Between January 2008 and the May 2008 riots, at least 13 foreigners were killed, shops were burnt down and many were made homeless. Violence was also reported in the Eastern Cape, the Western Cape, Gauteng, KwaZulu-Natal and the Free State (Duponchel 2009).

FAILED ASYLUM SYSTEM

The Refugee Appeal Board and the Standing Committee for Refugee Affairs is desperately under-staffed and under-resourced. These are bodies that are responsible for decision making with respect to applications for refugee status by asylum seekers coming to South Africa. The quality of decision making has come under criticism from civil society. In a presentation to the Parliamentary Portfolio Committee for Home Affairs in March 2016, the Department of Home Affairs announced that there was only a four per cent acceptance rate of refugee claims in 2015 (Amandla.mobi n.d.). The Musina Refugee Reception Office had a zero per cent acceptance rate. In the context of regional conflicts, including the ongoing problems in Somalia, violent presidential elections in Burundi, crackdowns on opposition in Zimbabwe and a presidential crisis in the Democratic Republic of Congo, it is hard to believe that not one 'genuine' refugee has passed through the Musina office since 2016. Roni Amit (2011) documented the low quality of decisions from the refugee status determination officers. The only conclusion that one can come to is that decision-makers are stuck in a system that is intended to reject as many people as possible.

Families are forced to travel repeatedly across the country from their homes, jobs and support communities to renew permits and go through processes in a struggle to get documented. Those few who are lucky enough to get through are often rejected at their first arrival. Rejected asylum seekers face arrest, detention and deportation, with few alternatives available to them.

Asylum seekers are left in limbo with little access to services and protection. Refugee Reception Offices have been closed (even in violation of court orders) and corruption remains a principal barrier to South Africa fulfilling its obligations under international law.

Refugee clinics run by LHR in different parts of the country receive clients who face major levels of frustration just accessing the different Refugee Reception Offices. Some of the problems include individuals who fail to receive any form of documentation as these offices do not issue and renew their permits on the same day. This leaves undocumented foreign nationals vulnerable to arrest, detention and deportation. Research conducted by Amit (2012) found that almost two-thirds of respondents did not receive an asylum permit the first time they came to the office to apply. This means that at great financial cost and often at the risk of losing temporary work, foreign nationals have to go to the Refugee Reception Office on many occasions before gaining access. In addition, the long queues have created opportunities for crime and corruption (Amit 2015).

SHIFTS IN POLICY: THE REFUGEES AMENDMENT BILL

The Refugees Amendment Bill informs current shifts in policy, especially with regard to refugees and migrants, and goes against the ethos of South Africa's progressive constitution. The cornerstone of South Africa's bill of rights is equality and respect for human dignity for all who live in South Africa and not just its citizens. But the Department of Home Affairs is currently pushing through legislative changes in policy, which marks a deviation from the urban refugee policy that embraces protection and integration into communities for refugees and asylum seekers. A Green Paper on International Migration was published in the Government Gazette on 24 June 2016. Significant amendments are also proposed to the Refugees Act (130 of 1998). The Green Paper is now the White Paper on International Migration. While there are progressive elements to the White Paper, they come at the expense of asylum seekers and refugees who face lengthy periods of immigration detention (Ekambaram 2017).

Department of Home Affairs officials have a tendency to exaggerate the figures to give the impression that South Africa is under siege and flooded by an influx of foreign nationals post-1994. Based on unsubstantiated statements and unverifiable figures, reactionary policy changes are proposed that play into conservative populist perceptions. In public discourse such changes are justified and validate populist, majoritarian, vote-catching 'action' by the crisis-ridden ruling party.

A few years ago, the Department of Home Affairs made claims that there were millions of asylum seekers in the country. According to the Department, at the end of 2016 there were 309 342 people of concern in the country, of which 91 053 were recognised refugees and 218 299 asylum seekers.[5]

A number of changes are proposed in the Refugees Amendment Bill. Two of these are of serious concern: one is the proposal to take away the asylum seekers' right to work; and the other to establish 'processing centres'.

As mentioned, the Department of Home Affairs initially tabled the Green Paper and then the White Paper on International Migration and also tabled proposed amendments to the refugee policy. Civil society formations have engaged in this process, calling for the withdrawal of the amendments to the Refugees Bill and denouncing what is clearly a reactionary (and unconstitutional) shift in policy, especially with respect to the establishment of camps at the border and taking away asylum seekers' rights to work. An event organised by a loose grouping of individuals and organisations in 2015 to protest against the outbreak of xenophobic violence saw approximately 25 000 people march through the streets of Johannesburg. Out of this the People's Coalition Against Xenophobia was launched. The coalition mobilised communities to make submissions calling for the withdrawal of the Refugees Amendment Bill (Amandla. mobi n.d.). Time frames for submissions and engagements were very short. And the process is going ahead.

RESPECT FOR HUMAN DIGNITY

Taking away the right to work for asylum seekers

Amendments to the refugee policy have been widely criticised by civil society (Botha 2016). Section 13 of the 2016 Draft Bill states that 'the right to work in the Republic may not be endorsed on the asylum seeker visa of any applicant who – (a) is able to sustain himself or herself and his or her dependants . . . is offered shelter and basic necessities by the UNHCR or any other charitable organisation or person'.[6] This is problematic on a number of levels. Both the

White Paper on International Migration and the Refugees Amendment Bill do not outline what support will be provided to asylum seekers, whose status as refugees is yet to be determined. All it states is that they will be confined to a processing centre. Asylum seekers are not supported in any way by the state and have to fend for themselves.

In a rare occurrence in court judgments, the Constitutional Court of South Africa made a ruling in 2004 on the right to work as being integrally linked to human dignity, beyond just the recognition of work linked to survival. The court ruled:

> The inherent dignity of all people is one of the foundational values of the Bill of Rights. It constitutes the basis and the inspiration for the recognition that is given to other more specific protections that are afforded by the Bill of Rights. The freedom to engage in productive work – even where that is not required in order to survive – is an important component of human dignity, for mankind is pre-eminently a social species with an instinct for meaningful associations.[7]

ESTABLISHMENT OF PROCESSING CENTRES

Consistent with what is taking place in First World countries in Europe, but also following the election of Trump, the South African government is using the narrative of risk and security threat to justify policy changes. This amounts to a justification for increased repression through arrest and deportation of predominately black foreign nationals in South Africa. The Department of Home Affairs has outlined policies that propose the closing down of all urban-based Refugee Reception Offices currently located in main cities, including the Desmond Tutu Refugee Reception Office in the city of Tshwane (Marabastad) and those in Durban and Musina. The plan is to move the Refugee Reception Offices to the border and replace them with processing centres (euphemism for enforcement in camps). This becomes a de facto detention centre. The most important characteristics of the camps are: segregation from the host population; shared facilities; a lack of privacy; overcrowding and a restricted area within which the whole compass of daily life is to be conducted. This imposes a state of dependency on refugees, and clearly signals that they have special, temporary and limited status, and are being subjected to control. In a camp set-up, human beings are stripped of agency and are reduced to being a number. The current urban-based policy of integration respects the human dignity of the refugee.

THE ALIENS ACT

The apartheid regime in South Africa ruled the country for decades under constitutionally institutionalised racism. The ideology of this regime rested on the prejudice that black people were inferior to white people and this justified the use of an entire state apparatus to keep black people in subjugation. The state declared the privileged interest of the white minority at the expense of the majority of the people who lived in South Africa. This was enforced through policy and legislation that discriminated against blacks (African, coloured and Indian people) living in the country. Instead of accepting rights as protecting everyone, they privileged the declared interests of the white minority and denied the black majority basic human rights and respect for human dignity.

The Aliens Control Act was an example of policies enforced to keep black people ('aliens') out of South Africa. This act is described as 'draconian immigration policy . . . a vestige from the apartheid era' (Hicks 1999: 394).

The Aliens Control Act (96 of 1991) is the law controlling immigration policy. Spawned during the apartheid era, the Act remains a relic of the past, in stark contrast to the ethos and vision espoused by the constitution under a democratic dispensation. Critics of the Aliens Control Act note that it is one of the most ignominious remnants of the apartheid regime, symbolising the racist and anti-Semitic sentiments inherent in past society and today institutionalises the practice of favouring whites over non-whites in immigration-related issues (Human Rights Watch 1998).

South Africa's history, for the better part of the twentieth century, reveals a variety of historical phenomena ranging from colonisation, unjust legal systems and other discriminatory practices. This bred a society of extreme imbalances and socio-economic inequalities. Post-1994, a reconstruction and development agenda became a priority (Rapatsa 2014). But the current shifts in policy, especially with respect to refugees and migrants, go against the ethos of the constitution, which embraces the principles of social justice and the bill of rights. The cornerstone of the bill of rights and the constitution is equality and respect for human dignity for all who live in South Africa and not just its citizens (Budlender 2014).

INHUMANE CONDITIONS OF DETENTION

Human rights violations, flagrant flouting of policy and disrespect for the human dignity of migrants has been the subject matter of 10 reports spanning two decades.[8] These reports provide a litany of allegations recording infringements of human rights at the Lindela Repatriation Centre.

Following an investigation into the Lindela Repatriation Centre in 1999, Judge Jodi Kollapen, then chair of the South African Human Rights Commission, stated in 2000: 'What comes across clearly is the huge gap between standards of treatment of various categories of migrants as set out in international human rights instruments and the practicalities of immigration management in our country today' (SAHRC 2000: 2).

Damning evidence is provided in all 10 reports of human rights abuses. These include testimonies of detainees who have been incarcerated for over 120 days in violation of the statute of limitations, physical abuse of detainees by Lindela guards and lack of access to medical services.

Another report was produced in 2012, following an inspection visit by Justice Edwin Cameron of the Constitutional Court of South Africa. This report specifically mentions the absence of a functioning institutional mechanism to document complaints. Without such a mechanism, the judge pointed out that there was no way to determine the reliability of the complaints made by detainees and whether they had substance. What was called for was 'functioning institutional mechanisms to determine complaints' (Cameron 2012: 3). To date there is no independent complaints mechanism in place at Lindela that has the competency to investigate complaints and address them. What happens, in fact, is that the private company that has been outsourced to manage and run the detention facility simply refutes any claims or complaints and there is no mechanism in place to hold them to account.

The report details evidence provided by the detainees of 'shells', which apparently came from sound bullets. This confirms that physical force and weapons are being used against detainees as a means of control and/or punishment. The delegation recorded repeated statements that security guards mistreated them and that they suffered assaults. But no investigation has been carried out and no measures have been taken to prevent such unlawful practices (Cameron 2012).

There is no oversight over immigration detention centres. In April 2017, LHR spoke out about another incident of extreme use of violence as a means of punishing detainees (Mzantsi 2017). LHR heard testimony of what amounts to collective isolation and punishment of asylum seekers from the Democratic Republic of Congo. Medical examination by a physician from Doctors Without Borders confirmed collective isolation, accompanied with excessive violence, by Lindela guards and functionaries. According to the detainees, this included being shot at with rubber bullets from close range and assaults with lead pipes.

LHR is concerned that the situation will get worse. The proposed changes to the policy include the establishment of detention centres at the borders, referred to as processing centres. Without independent monitoring of these detention centres, infringement of basic human rights and disrespect for human dignity through neglect and subhuman conditions will continue.

In a recent judgment handed down by the Constitutional Court, the judges made reference to current practice by the ANC-led government as being reminiscent of the apartheid era – including the practice of detention without trial. In this instance, LHR challenged the constitutionality of Section 34(1)(b) and (d) of the Immigration Act (13 of 2002).

The Constitutional Court ruled that Sections 34(1)(b) and (d) of the Immigration Act were inconsistent with the constitution and therefore invalid. Current policy for the arrest and detention of undocumented migrants allows state officials to detain a person arrested for the crime of being undocumented. This person can be kept in detention for up to 30 days without access to any form of judicial oversight.

In its introductory comments, the judgment makes the following point: 'Personal freedom was one of the rights routinely violated during the apartheid era. Arrest and detention without trial were commonly used to suppress opposition to the laws and policies of the government of that time.'[9]

CONCLUSION

The phrase 'precarious work' is a euphemism for workers being paid slave wages and is a phenomenon of outsourcing and the casualisation of work. Workers are left vulnerable and are unable to join a union to fight for decent working conditions. Discrimination and exploitation are two sides of the same coin. Undocumented workers are exploited by employers because of their vulnerability and fear of being arrested. They are paid very low wages and poor, unemployed South Africans blame foreign nationals for taking 'all the jobs'.

Trade unions face a formidable challenge today as they struggle to unionise vulnerable workers in the hospitality sector, for example. Trade unions have to build international solidarity and cannot organise along national boundaries. Circular migration is a feature of work in the so-called informal sector. Workers' rights to decent wages and working conditions must be protected. Unions need to learn from movements such as Streetnet. Pat Horn (2017: 24) speaks about 'self-organising'. In the current crisis of chronic structural unemployment in the 'formal economy', we need an international campaign on the right to decent work.

There appears to be a lack of political will by officials running and working in the Department of Home Affairs. The scapegoating of non-nationals, such as in 2015/2016 with the introduction of Operation Fiela in the wake of xenophobic violence in Gauteng and KwaZulu-Natal, saw a targeting of non-nationals by police, immigration authorities and the military. Operation 'Clean Sweep' is an example of reckless interventions and unsubstantiated statements by politicians, linking poor, working-class foreign nationals to crime and drugs and declaring them undesirable. Government officials capitalise on protecting citizens' rights against foreign nationals, who they allege come to South Africa to take all the jobs and commit crime. Instead, South Africans should be organising themselves into community structures to hold politicians and public servants to account for failing to implement policies and allocate sufficient resources as a priority to address crime, unemployment and rampant acts of violence against women and children. It is accepted that the injustices of apartheid resulted in poverty being the burden of black Africans and predominantly African women, making South Africa one of the most unequal societies in the world. This is confirmed in a recent report released by Statistics South Africa (2017). But the government has the power to allocate resources and to ensure that there is a plan to eradicate poverty.

Migrants and refugees cannot be blamed for the impoverished conditions that the majority of South Africans are living under. Africa Check (2017) refers to a report by Statistics South Africa, which found that approximately four per cent of people of working age (15 years to 64 years) across the whole of South Africa were born outside South Africa.

South Africa offers migrants and refugees the possibility of protection from real life-threatening living conditions. We have a history to be proud of. Just over two decades ago, South Africa was the poster child of the triumph of good over evil. Progressive forces internationally galvanised in a united force of solidarity against apartheid and in support of the struggle for human rights and justice for all. Today, South Africa and the rich nations of the world are shamefully failing to defend the human rights of vulnerable populations forced to flee conflict, violence and inhumane living conditions.

The movement of capital (goods, factories and industries) is made possible and is protected by trade treaties. Wars are fought over trade routes and access to land, oil, minerals and water. Respecting human dignity and protecting the basic human rights that every human is born with is a liability to the capitalist system and is the first casualty in the constant grind to reduce costs in the face of fierce competition and to feed the greed for excessive profits. We need international solidarity based on values of respect for human dignity, and we need to fight for stringent measures to hold states and multinational corporates to account. Vulnerable communities must be organised and mobilised to build international solidarity and be empowered to hold those in power to account. Why can we not aspire to noble concepts such as world citizenship?[10]

'Non-white' was an apartheid construct. White racism was also socially constructed over 350 years. One definition states that 'white South Africans are people from South Africa who are of European descent and who do not regard themselves, or are not regarded, as being part of another racial group'.[11] The unfair privilege of white people was enforced through legislation and policies and the propaganda of white superiority. Black people were oppressed and exploited and the ideological belief was that black people were inferior. Of the approximately 15 000 foreign nationals that LHR assists through the provision of legal advice on an annual basis, over 90 per cent are black Africans. The testimonies detailing the manner in which poor, vulnerable black Africans are treated as they struggle to gain access to legal documentation in South Africa reminds me of how I and fellow black people in South Africa were treated, living under the repressive apartheid regime and classified as a 'non-white'.

ACKNOWLEDGEMENT

I would like to thank Vishwas Satgar for his contribution and moral support, without which I would have given up.

NOTES

1   The South African Human Rights Commission (SAHRC) produced a detailed report based on its investigation into the violence. It makes extensive recommendations

for all relevant government departments and external role players. To date not a single recommendation has been implemented. It is an indictment on the state and reflects a lack of political will to address the root causes of xenophobia as set out in the report. See the 2010 'Report on the SAHRC investigation into issues of rule of law, justice and impunity arising out of the 2008 public violence against non-nationals', http://pmg-assets.s3-website-eu-west-1.amazonaws.com/docs/101124sahrcrep_0.pdf (accessed 2 December 2017).
2   See Amit (2012). This report reveals a department that is failing to fulfil its core mandate with respect to the asylum system – identifying individuals in need of protection under refugee law. As a result, many asylum seekers face the risk of refoulement.
3   This is according to a weekly international journal on science reports on an incidence of incorrect data issued by European Union border guards in 2015. See http://www.nature.com/news/data-on-movements-of-refugees-and-migrants-are-flawed-1.21568 (accessed 20 October 2016).
4   Directed by Andy Spitz. See https://www.tcff.org.za/films-2017/voetsek-us-brothers/ (accessed 10 December 2017).
5   These figures are referenced in an official document issued by UNHCR in South Africa. See http://unicpretoria.org.za/files/2017/07/CEoI-Legal-Assistance-EOI-ZAF-3-2017.doc (accessed 1 September 2017).
6   See Draft Refugees Amendment Bill, 2015/Refugees Amendment Bill (B12-2016), https://pmg.org.za (accessed 1 September 2017).
7   *Minister of Home Affairs v Watchenuka* (2004) (4) SA 326 (SCA), paras 25–27.
8   Reports published about the Lindela Repatriation Centre include: SAHRC, 'Lindela at the crossroads for detention and repatriation', 2000, http://www.gov.za/sites/www.gov.za/files/lindela2_0.pdf; LHR, 'Monitoring immigration detention in South Africa – 2008', 2008, www.lhr.org.za/publications/monitoring-immigration-detention-south-africa-2008; ACMS, 'Lost in the vortex: Irregularities in the detention and deportation of non-nationals in South Africa', 2010, http://www.migration.org.za/uploads/docs/report-21.pdf; LHR, 'A submission on common complaints from people detained in Lindela compiled by Lawyers for Human Rights for the UN Special Rapporteur on human rights of migrants', 2012, http://www.lhr.org.za/publications/international-detention-coalition-submission-special-rapporteur-human-rights-migrants-f; Solidarity Peace Trust and PASSOP, 'Perils and pitfalls: Migrants and deportation in South Africa', 2012, http://www.solidaritypeacetrust.org/download/report-files/Perils%20and%20Pitfalls.pdf; ACMS, 'Breaking the law, breaking the bank: The cost of Home Affairs' illegal detention practices', 2012, http://www.migration.org.za/uploads/docs/report-37.pdf; Edwin Cameron, 'Visit to Lindela Repatriation Centre, Krugersdorp: Justice Edwin Cameron, Constitutional Court of South Africa', 2012, https://www.concourt.org.za/images/phocadownload/prison_visits/cameron/Prisons-Lindela-Report-Monday-29-October-2012-FINAL.pdf (accessed 3 December 2017); SAHRC, 'Investigative report on access to health', https://www.sahrc.org.za/home/21/files/4%20SAHRC%20Investigative%20Reports%20VOLUME%20FOUR%2025062015%20to%20print.pdf (accessed 3 December 2017).
9   *Lawyers for Human Rights v Minister of Home Affairs and Others* (2017) ZACC 22.

10 The author is inspired by the lyrics and performances of artist Bob Marley (https://www.youtube.com/watch?v=loFDn94oZJ0) when he speaks about 'world citizenship'. She is also angered by how predominantly black women are abused and exploited. Violence, unpaid labour and discrimination are best described by John Lennon ('Woman is the nigger of the world', https://www.youtube.com/watch?v=OA8N0xy3hjE).
11 'White South African', *Wikipedia*, https://en.wikipedia.org/wiki/White_South_African (accessed 12 November 2017).

REFERENCES

Africa Check. 2017. 'Mayor's claim – undocumented foreigners make up 80% of Joburg inner city – "absurd"'. Accessed 20 September 2017, https://africacheck.org/reports/mayors-claim-80-joburg-inner-city-residents-undocumented-foreigners-absurd/.

Alfred, C. 2015. 'What history can teach us about the worst refugee crisis since WWII: European states were the architects of the modern refugee regime'. *Huffington Post*, 9 December. Accessed 3 December 2017, https://www.huffingtonpost.com/entry/alexander-betts-refugees-wwii_us_55f30f7ce4b077ca094edaec.

Amandla.mobi. n.d. 'More information and analysis of the Home Affairs International Migration Green Paper'. Accessed 2 August 2017, http://www.amandla.mobi/home-affairs-green-paper.

Amit, R. 2011. 'No refuge: Flawed status determination and the failures of South Africa's refugee system to provide protection', *International Journal of Refugee Law*, 23 (3): 458–488.

Amit, R. 2012. 'All roads lead to rejection: Persistent bias and incapacity in South African refugee status determination'. *ACMS Report, June 2012*. Johannesburg: African Centre for Migration and Society.

Amit, R. 2015. 'Queue here for corruption measuring irregularities in South Africa's asylum system'. Accessed 3 December 2017, http://www.lhr.org.za/publications/queue-here-corruption-measuring-irregularities-south-africa%E2%80%99s-asylum-system.

Bakewell, O. and De Haas, H. 2007. 'African migrations: Continuities, discontinuities and recent transformations'. In *African Alternatives*, edited by P. Chabal, U. Engel and L. de Haan. Leiden: Brill, pp. 95–118.

Botha, C. 2016. 'The Refugees Amendment Bill: Will it truly combat corruption?' Submission to the Portfolio Committee on Home Affairs by the Centre for Constitutional Rights, 16 September. Accessed 3 December 2017, http://www.cfcr.org.za/index.php/latest/624-article-the-refugees-amendment-bill-will-it-truly-combat-corruption.

Budlender, G. 2014. 'The annual human rights lecture'. Faculty of Law, University of Stellenbosch, 2 October. Accessed 7 June 2017, http://blogs.sun.ac.za/law/advocate-geoff-budlender-sc-delivers-annual-human-rights-lecture/.

Bush, G. 2001. 'State of the nation address'. *The Guardian*, 21 September. Accessed 20 June 2017, https://www.theguardian.com/world/2001/sep/21/september11.usa13.

Cameron, E. 2012. 'Visit to Lindela Repatriation Centre, Krugersdorp: Justice Edwin Cameron, Constitutional Court of South Africa'. Accessed 3 December 2017, https://www.concourt.org.za/images/phocadownload/prison_visits/cameron/Prisons-Lindela-Report-Monday-29-October-2012-FINAL.pdf.

DHA (Department of Home Affairs). 2017. 'White Paper on International Migration in South Africa'. Accessed 13 September 2017, http://www.dha.gov.za/WhitePaperon InternationalMigration-20170602.pdf.

Desai, A. 2015. 'An exploratory critique of the notion of social cohesion in contemporary South Africa', *Psychology in Society*, 49: 99–113.

Duponchel, M. 2009. 'Who's the alien? Xenophobia in post-apartheid South Africa'. Accessed 25 November 2017, http://citeseerx.ist.psu.edu/viewdoc/download?doi=10.1.1.438.5307&rep=rep1&type=pdf.

Ekambaram, S. 2017. 'Border camps in South Africa will not solve the asylum crisis'. *Refugees Deeply*, 26 June. Accessed 23 November 2017, https://www.newsdeeply.com/refugees/community/2017/06/21/border-camps-in-south-africa-will-not-solve-asylum-crisis.

Gunderman, D. 2014. 'Donald Trump's "big, beautiful wall" may end up being a fence'. Accessed 25 September 2017, http://www.nydailynews.com/news/politics/donald-trump-big-beautiful-wall-fence-article-1.2867648.

Hicks, T.F. 1999. 'The constitution, Aliens Control Act, and xenophobia: The struggle to protect South Africa's pariah – the undocumented immigrant', *Indiana Journal of Global Legal Studies*, 7 (1): Article 15.

Horn, P. 2017. 'Nothing for us without us! New forms of self-organisation by workers in the informal economy', *Amandla* 52 (May): 24–25.

Human Rights Watch. 1998. '"Prohibited persons": Abuse of undocumented migrants, asylum-seekers, and refugees in South Africa'. Accessed 29 May 2017, http://www.refworld.org/docid/3ae6a8430.html.

Mbembe, A. 2017. 'Scrap the borders that divide Africans'. *Mail & Guardian*, 17 March. Accessed 20 August 2017, https://mg.co.za/article/2017-03-17-00-scrap-the-borders-that-divide-africans.

Misago, J.P., Landau, L. and Monson, T. 2009. 'Towards tolerance, law and dignity: Addressing violence against foreign nationals in South Africa'. Pretoria: International Organization for Migration. Accessed 20 May 2017, https://www.atlanticphilanthropies.org/wp-content/uploads/2015/09/IOM_Addressing_Violence_Against_Foreign_Nationals.pdf.

Moseneke, D. 2014. 'Reflections on South African constitutional democracy: Transition and transformation'. Accessed 5 August 2017, https://constitutionallyspeaking.co.za/dcj-moseneke-reflections-on-south-african-constitutional-democracy-transition-and-transformation/.

Möser, R.E. 2016. 'Migration and xenophobia in the new South Africa: The rise of anti-foreigner sentiments and apartheid's inherited policy framework, 1995–2008', *Global Histories* 2 (1): 2–16.

Mzantsi, S. 2017. 'Foreign nationals hit with lead pipes claims LHR'. Accessed 30 August 2017, https://www.iol.co.za/news/crime-courts/foreign-nationals-hit-with-lead-pipes-claims-lhr-8808461.

Rapatsa, M. 2014. 'Transformative constitutionalism in South Africa: 20 years of democracy', *Mediterranean Journal of Social Sciences*, 5 (27): 887–895.

Rodney, W. 1972. *How Europe Underdeveloped Africa*. Dar es Saalam: Tanzania Publishing House.

SAHRC (South African Human Rights Commission). 2000. 'Lindela at the crossroads for detention and repatriation'. Accessed 20 September 2017, http://www.gov.za/sites/www.gov.za/files/lindela2_0.pdf.
Said, E.W. [1979] 2014. *Orientalism.* New York: Knopf Doubleday Publishing Group.
Satgar, V. 2009. 'Global capitalism and the neoliberalisation of Africa'. In *A New Scramble for Africa? Imperialism, Investment and Development*, edited by R. Southall and H. Melber. Pietermaritzburg: University of KwaZulu-Natal Press, pp. 35–55.
Statistics South Africa. 2017. 'Poverty trends in South Africa: An examination of absolute poverty between 2006 and 2015'. Accessed 2 November 2017, http://www.statssa.gov.za/publications/Report-03-10-06/Report-03-10-062015.pdf.
Tempo, C.J.B. 2015. *Americans at the Gate: United States and Refugees during the Cold War.* Princeton: Princeton University Press.
UNHCR (United Nations High Commissioner for Refugees). 2010. 'United Nations convention and protocol relating to the status of refugees'. Accessed 30 August 2017, http://www.unhcr.org/3b66c2aa10.html.
UNHCR. 2017. 'UNHCR statistics'. Accessed 10 September 2017, http://popstats.unhcr.org/en/overview.

CONCLUSION

Vishwas Satgar

In the twentieth century, anti-Semitic fascism, Jim Crow segregation, apartheid and ethnic cleansing through horrific genocides, such as in Rwanda, brought home the realities of racism in our world. Racism, as forms of violence, discrimination and oppression, found its place in capitalist societies, in some instances functional to capitalism, given the racial history of capitalism; in others informed by the complex relationship between historical racisms, nationalist ideology, racialisation, class relations and institutional power. Anti-racism triumphed in some of these struggles to dismantle systems of racial oppression. In parts of colonial Africa, anti-colonial struggles did succeed in many respects to end systems of racialised domination within their countries. African rule came to the fore. However, many of these post-colonial societies still had to face neocolonial international relations and challenges of transforming their societies beyond colonial patterns. Africa was freed, but not completely.

In other contexts, victories were scored through de-racialisation but these did not go far enough. Racism, at particular moments and in particular contexts, may not have been in the interests of capitalism while struggles against racism might have shifted common sense and political power, but also might not have had the radical impulse necessary to push for more. The struggle for civil rights in the US, while of immense historical significance, is a good example. It did not end the deep racism of US society, despite its crucial victories. In other racialised experiences and struggles, racism prevailed and has continued to do so in Israel/Palestine, for example. W.E.B. Du Bois's colour-line was broken but also continued into the twenty-first century. This volume has foregrounded the continuities of racisms but also its new expressions in the current conjuncture of a crisis-ridden capitalism. Anti-racist Marxists and non-Marxists grapple with these realities in this volume. There is a rich and fruitful dialogue but also important analytical and theoretical interventions that challenge both Marxism and anti-racism more generally. This is meant to contribute to strengthening anti-racist commitments, analysis and struggles.

RACISMS IN THE WORLD

The world of globalised capitalism and neoliberalisation has deepened racist, imperial, capitalist and modern relations. This volume demonstrates that racisms are alive and well in the world. These are racisms with historical roots but are also articulated in conjuncturally specific ways. This is more than thinking about racism as merely 'new racism', in which culture and cultural encoding of difference engenders racialised practices. In the US context, the rise of white nationalism, spurred on by Donald Trump, is a supremacist response to the Barack Obama presidency, and is part of Islamophobia and a racialised immigration politics. At the same time, racism against African Americans is starkly expressed through police violence, incarceration and inequality. In this volume, we highlight a further contradiction and relation of racial oppression in the US social formation. Indigenous peoples of the US and the world have also been victims of historical racisms and are facing a new wave of racialised dispossessions. The sovereignty of the US state is based on an exclusionary and supremacist nationalism. This is not unique for a predominantly white society, whose pre-condition for its existence as a capitalist society was white domination and genocide. This volume has brought this to the fore.

In Europe today, the 'migration crisis' reveals different levels of racism at work. While Europe was constructed on a white supremacist understanding of itself over the past few centuries, it has not completely confronted its Eurocentrism. Genocidal violence against Jews, racialised welfarist nationalisms, Islamophobia and now racist approaches to migration have come to the fore. The 'European' seems to be more important in this context than the human. A new racist right wing is on the march, increasingly expressing neo-fascist tendencies in its racial othering and exclusivist nationalist discourses. While fractions of capital might want greater migration and labour mobility, including sections of the European working class who embrace human solidarity, a neoliberalising Europe, a precarious Europe and a failing European integration project are all dynamics feeding into the racialisation of the border regime. This volume has emphasised how the Euro-American standard of liberalism is farcical in its anti-racism and is even being eclipsed by more explicit racist nationalisms.

South Africa captures the complexity of racisms in the world today. While formal apartheid has ended, race and racism are still central to the new social order. Official non-racialism, as articulated by the ruling African National Congress (ANC), has not worked. The 'race card' has also been abused in self-serving ways that takes away from more serious engagements with racism. This volume highlights the limits of how racialising practices are understood, how outmoded ANC-SACP-led national question approaches have become in confronting resurgent black and white racisms and the imperative of thinking new ways forward beyond racism, including renewing non-racialism as a radical principle. Racialising essentialism can be overcome but it has to be understood, analysed and discoursed in ways that renew anti-racist struggles and practices. South Africa can be a crucial site for constructing a twenty-first century society and world that go beyond racism. This volume has affirmed that a South Africa advancing a future beyond racism has to learn from past anti-racism but also has to break new ground.

CONFRONTING RACISM THROUGH POST-EUROCENTRIC MARXISMS

The translation of Marxism in the African context of struggles against colonialism and apartheid has spawned Marxisms that are deeply post-Eurocentric. These are Marxisms that are non-reductionist and do not seek to subsume all forms of struggle into class struggle. Neither have these Marxisms explained racism merely through the economic factor in the last instance. Such Marxisms have analysed and understood the historical specificity of racism, the lived experience of racism, racial structures of oppression and how this relates to particular forms of capitalism. The thought of Amilcar Cabral, Thomas Sankara, Frantz Fanon, Samir Amin, Ruth First, Govan Mbeki, Harold Wolpe and many others stand out in this regard. The theoretical resources of these post-Eurocentric Marxisms have to be retrieved and engaged with critically for current anti-racist struggles. The crisis of national liberation politics, the unfinished processes of transformation and anti-Marxism, even in the academy, should not occlude us from engaging these African Marxists (and others outside Africa) to think about and struggle for anti-racism. This is a crucial theme and message of this volume.

Moreover, post-Eurocentric Marxisms are also breaking new ground. In this volume, several chapters demonstrate how such Marxisms can draw on the tools of historical materialism, Marxist historiography and conceptions of anti-racist struggles to explain historical racisms, to understand its contemporary articulation and to also think about modes of resistance. Such Marxisms are engaged in actual anti-racist struggles in the world, as specified in the first chapter of this volume. A post-Eurocentric Marxism, including this Democratic Marxism series, is one example of the making and role of post-Eurocentric Marxism. It also emphasises that the Marxist canon is willing to confront epistemological Eurocentricism and white supremacy by being self-aware. This means recognising Marx's own Eurocentric moment but also how he broke with this. This epistemological and political break in Marx's thought and practice is central to a post-Eurocentric Marxism, and has been affirmed in this volume.

CHALLENGES FOR ANTI-RACISM

Is a world post-race and racism possible? This volume answers this question in different and in context-specific ways to highlight challenges for contemporary anti-racism. First, this volume does not accept race and racism as part of the natural order of society. It is not natural to discriminate, oppress and categorise based on racial attributes or group characteristics. While this phenomenon exists, various chapters highlight how capitalism, capitalist modernity, race and racial structures have been co-constitutive. In short, race and racism within capitalist societies are understood as socially constructed and therefore can be overcome. Second, we need to understand socially constituted racisms in order to overcome them. For some analysts, racisms are individual problems, ideational problems and merely expressions of extreme behaviour. These understandings of racism are really part of a continuum. This volume adds to this continuum by emphasising how racisms, as forms of genocidal violence, oppression and discrimination, relate to ideology (such as acts of signification and nationalism), to unconscious processes, social practices and institutional power. Historical and conjunctural racisms have to be analysed to understand how they are constructed, perpetuated and advanced structurally and through social agency.

Third, race and racism does not travel and manifest alone in social relations. Most theorists and analysts of racism understand that various social differences and forms of power are expressed through race and racism. This implicates class and gender. This volume did not seek to resolve the question of whether intersectional approaches to race, class and gender are the theoretical solution to these lived experiences and analytical challenges. Nonetheless, drawing on Marxist engagements with intersectionality, this volume does highlight the analytical and political weaknesses of narrow identity and individual centred approaches to intersectional analysis. The volume reinforces concerns that gender and ecological relations have to be considered in relation to various oppressions, including class, race and caste. Practically, this is also a challenge for how anti-racist struggles are thought and constituted.

Fourth, overstretching racism and related categories also has its dangers. In some contexts, racial oppression may not be the best way to understand a form of oppression. Caste is a good example, which, it is argued by some contributors to this volume, has its own distinctive historical and social structure in India. Of course, this does not make the caste system less repugnant but it does require a proper analysis as a basis of resistance. Another example would be merely using the category 'settler colonialism' to explain the historical, social and political complexities of contemporary Israel/Palestine. Such a category might highlight some features of racial oppression but might also be inadequate in terms of macro-social explanation and understanding.

Fifth, resisting racisms is necessary, possible and happening. Anti-racist struggles today have a crucial salience. In this volume, different contributors, many of whom are active in anti-racist struggles, grapple with the challenges of making anti-racist struggles more efficacious and posit ways forward. These are not the only answers and ways of strengthening anti-racist struggles but they offer crucial issues for consideration as we strive for a world post-race and post-racism. Central to this is a recognition that a post-Eurocentric Marxism is an integral part of this urgent twenty-first-century struggle.

CONTRIBUTORS

Roxanne Dunbar-Ortiz is a historian and professor emerita at California State University. She has authored and edited many books, including *Roots of Resistance: A History of Land Tenure in New Mexico* and *An Indigenous Peoples' History of the United States*. She is a veteran of anti-imperialist/colonialist and anti-capitalist movements and, over the past decade, she has participated in developing the international indigenous project and international human rights law.

Sharon S. Ekambaram works at Lawyers for Human Rights where she is the head of the Refugee and Migrant Rights Programme. She is a long-time human rights activist with extensive advocacy experience. She was a health activist with the Treatment Action Campaign and was the founding director of Médecins Sans Frontières Southern Africa office.

Fabian Georgi is a political scientist working as a research associate at the University of Marburg in Germany. His doctoral thesis was a critical history of the International Organization for Migration. His research interests include critical theory, materialist state theory and migration policy.

Ran Greenstein is an associate professor of Sociology at the University of the Witwatersrand. He works on issues of comparative history, conflict, race and political theory. Among his publications are *Genealogies of Conflict: Class,*

Identity and State in Palestine/Israel and South Africa; *Comparative Perspectives on South Africa*; and *Zionism and its Discontents: A Century of Radical Dissent in Israel/Palestine*. His most recent book is *Identity, Nationalism, and Race: Anti-Colonial Resistance in South Africa and Israel/Palestine*.

Peter Hudson worked with the National Union of South African Students' Wages Commission, the Industrial Aid Society and the Metal and Allied Workers' Union in the 1970s. He taught in the Department of Political Studies at the University of the Witwatersrand from 1982 until his retirement in 2016. He is currently an honorary senior lecturer in the School of Social Sciences at Wits University.

Khwezi Mabasa is a researcher in Political Economy at the Mapungubwe Institute for Strategic Reflection (MISTRA). He is also an adjunct lecturer in Political Science at the University of Pretoria and a research associate at the Society, Work and Development Institute (SWOP) at the University of the Witwatersrand. His research interests include the agrarian question, heterodox political economics and political sociology. He writes in his personal capacity.

Firoze Manji is an activist and public intellectual from Kenya. He founded *Pambazuka News*, Pambazuka Press and Fahamu – Networks for Social Justice, and is the publisher at Daraja Press in Montreal. He is the Richard von Weizsacker Fellow at the Richard Bosch Academy, Berlin, and adjunct professor at the Institute of African Studies at Carleton University, Ottawa. With Sokari Ekine, he co-edited *African Awakenings: The Emerging Revolutions*, and with Bill Fletcher Jnr, he co-edited *Claim No Easy Victories: The Legacy of Amilcar Cabral*.

Nivedita Menon is a professor at Jawaharlal Nehru University in Delhi and a feminist scholar and activist. Her latest book is *Seeing Like a Feminist*.

Aditya Nigam has been a left activist for over two decades before returning to academia. He works at the Centre for the Study of Developing Societies in Delhi and is author of *The Insurrection of Little Selves: The Crisis of Secular-Nationalism in India*; *Power and Contestation: India Since 1989* (co-authored with Nivedita Menon); *After Utopia: Modernity, Socialism and the Postcolony*; and *Desire Named Development*.

Vishwas Satgar is a democratic eco-socialist and has been an activist for over three decades. He is an associate professor of International Relations at the University of the Witwatersrand, and he edits the Democratic Marxism series, for which he received the distinguished contribution award from the World Association of Political Economy. He recently edited *The Climate Crisis: South African and Global Democratic Eco-Socialist Alternatives*.

INDEX

A
Achar, Gilbert 4–5, 17–18
Adams, Hank 36, 41
Adorno, T.W. 107–108
Afghanistan 99, 113n9, 126, 129, 223
African
  etymology of term 52
  as ontological concept 56
  political conception of being 20, 49–52, 55–58, 63–64, 71, 138
  as synonymous with 'non-humanity' 50, 52–54, 56, 58, 64, 71
  see also dehumanisation
African civilisations 52, 55
African-American Freedom Movement 35
African National Congress (ANC) 10–11, 23, 38, 42, 175, 197
  and Congress Alliance 196
  mythologised history of 23, 195, 213n2
African National Congress (ANC) as ruling party 11
  ANC-led Alliance 158, 195, 200–203, 207, 209
  calls for radical economic transformation 202–204
  failure of 2, 204, 210
  legitimacy crisis 2, 23, 194
  re-racialising dynamics of 204, 206
  state-centred nationalism of 194
Africanist politics 18, 64, 199–201, 205
  nativist attack on Marxism 2–3, 35n6
  Pan African Student Movement 200
  see also Black Consciousness; Economic Freedom Fighters
agrarian question 182, 185, 204–205
  and capitalist agriculture 185
Aguilar, D 14, 187
Alam, Javeed 121–122
Alexander, Neville 186, 188

Algeria 68–69, 76, 79
Althusser, L. 160–161
Ambedkar, B.R. 119–120, 127, 129, 132
  Ambedkarite movement 133n1, 134n7, 141
American Indian Movement (AIM) 35–36
  see also indigenous resistance/struggles
Amin, Samir 15, 18, 239
Amit, Roni 224–225
Anderson, Kevin 5–7, 25n10
Angola 10, 57, 68, 76
  MPLA 50
Anta Diop, Cheikh 51, 55, 65
anti-apartheid resistance 93, 195–196, 239
  global movement 2, 10
  see also national liberation struggle, South Africa
anti-capitalist resistance 3, 16, 18, 20, 182
  see also working class: struggles
anti-caste crusaders 118–119, 132
  see also Dalit revolt
anti-colonial resistance/struggles 7, 10, 18, 24, 59, 81, 93, 132
  African subjectivity as part of 20, 56–57
  see also decolonising universities; imperialism: struggle against
anti-imperialism *see* imperialism: struggle against
anti-Muslim/Islamic sentiments
  Hindu-Muslim divide 17, 125–129
  racism 22, 84, 96, 107
  see also Islamophobia
anti-racist resistance/struggles 1, 3, 9, 15–16, 23–24, 30, 56, 189, 237–239
  #BlackLivesMatter 17
  in Europe 21, 102–104, 106, 110
  see also decolonising universities; indigenous resistance/struggles; Marxist anti-racism

245

anti-racist strategies/challenges 21,
   111–112, 240–241
   practical anti-fascism 111
anti-Semitism 107, 164–165, 170, 237
apartheid 11, 19, 49, 63, 75, 88–91, 93–94,
   158, 167, 197–198, 209, 230–232
   Aliens Control Act 228
   capitalism 2, 180, 184
   legacy 217–218, 221, 239
   of a special type 1, 18, 20–21, 77, 88–89,
      92, 94, 237
Arab-Jewish conflict/divide 18, 79, 85–86,
   88, 94
   Palestinian struggle 85, 92–93, 241
   peace process 85, 87, 94
   1967 war 82, 84
Arab Spring 88, 104
Australia 16, 32, 40, 68, 76, 218
Austria 96, 98, 101
authoritarianism 2, 8, 96, 110, 124–125,
   174, 200, 204
   race-based 176, 180, 189

B
Balibar, Étienne 100–102
Basu, Tapan 121–122
Bernstein, Rusty 174, 176
Bharatiya Janata Party (BJP) 124–125, 129–130
Biko, Steve 180, 188, 198–199
Black Consciousness 2, 188, 194–195, 198–200
black economic empowerment 171n7, 178,
   195, 202
#BlackLivesMatter see under anti-racist
   resistance/struggles
black Marxist tradition 3, 11–12, 42
   see also race-relations theory: democratic
   Marxist approach
black nationalism 12, 59
   bourgeoisie/reductionist 1, 23, 174, 179,
      181, 187–189
Black Power Movement 63
Black Radical Tradition 12
Black Republic Thesis 9, 174
black trade union movement, South Africa
   89, 196–198, 203
   Congress of South African Trade Unions
      (Cosatu) 196, 203
   National Union of Metalworkers of South
      Africa 158, 213n4
Bojadžijev, M. 101, 103
Bolivia 9, 34, 43
Bond, Patrick 173, 182
Bonilla-Silva, Eduardo 101–102, 106, 108
border regimes 21, 97, 99, 105, 239

role of racism in 100, 102–103, 109–110,
   113n8, 223
see also migration, European 'crisis'
bourgeoisie/middle class 144, 180, 183, 212
   Jewish 80, 88
   black 59, 176, 178, 187–189, 199, 214n16
   Hindu 124–125, 143–144
Brown, Malcolm 13, 56
Bureau of Indian Affairs (BIA), Washington
   35–36
Burkina Faso 61, 69
Bush, George H.W. 34, 223

C
Cabral, Amilcar 18, 59, 61–62, 64, 182, 239
   on culture/history as source of liberation
      42, 55–58
   humanist approach 20, 49–51, 54, 65, 69–70
   as leader of PAIGC 42, 50
Camfield, David 13, 100–101, 106, 108–110
Canada 16, 30, 40, 68, 76
   National Indian Brotherhood of 35, 37
Cape Verde (Cabo Verde) 50, 58
capital accumulation 5–6, 15, 31, 53–54
   by dispossession 103, 177, 182–184
   primitive 5, 43–44, 181
capital-labour relations 6, 185, 202–203
   business unionism 203
   capitalist contract 147–148, 151
capitalism 6, 146
   as relation of oppression 12, 107, 112
   global 1, 11, 15, 54, 70, 103–104, 238
   neocolonial 184–185
   role of colonialism/slavery in 2, 5, 43–44,
      53, 180, 220
   symbolic 163–164, 168
   see also neoliberalism; racialised capitalism
capitalist exploitation 19, 50, 57, 61, 70–71,
   109, 181, 187, 218
   of nature 152
   of resources 31–32, 221
   wage/labour 8, 14, 66, 89, 92, 110, 143,
      148, 176, 180, 182, 185–186, 221
capitalist modes of production 2, 4–5, 13, 43,
   101, 112, 120, 158, 170, 175, 214n23
capitalist relations of production 21, 147,
   162, 166, 168–169, 171n4, 174, 182,
   184–185, 187
   de-racialisation of 176, 184, 201–202, 204
   see also non-racialism
Caribbean 37, 57, 63
   CARECOM 42
Chibber, Vivek 6, 24n1
China 8, 12

Christian Doctrine of Discovery *see under* dispossession of indigenous peoples
citizenship 7, 50, 54, 57, 59, 65, 67, 98, 112, 145
  as basis for exclusion 108–110, 219
  Palestinian rights 81–83, 85–86, 88–91
  women's 143
class 7
  'caste-cum-class oppression' 141
  exploitation 85, 184
  formation 175, 178, 183, 209
  intersection between nationalism and 175
  intersectionality of race, gender and 2, 9, 14–15, 25n8, 178, 199, 241
  see also working class: exploitation of
class reductionism 2, 7, 9, 12, 170
  non-reductionist approach 210, 239
class struggle/antagonism 6, 9, 162–163, 166, 168, 175, 180, 200
climate change 24, 68, 103, 109, 206, 208, 210–212
climate crisis, South African perspective 195
  and eco-cidal logic of capitalism 8, 19, 23–24, 195, 198, 206–208, 210–212
  see also eco-socialism, democratic
climate justice politics 17, 208
cold war 24, 35, 109, 220, 223
colonial liberation struggles *see* anti-colonial resistance struggles
colonial subjectivity 20, 22, 43, 161–162
colonial symbolic 164, 167, 171n3
colonial unconscious 22, 159, 161, 168
  inertia theory 22, 158–159, 167, 170
  link with capitalist unconscious 22, 162–163, 165–170
  link with liberal democracy 23, 163, 168, 170, 173
  see also colonialism of a special type thesis
colonialism 2, 5, 13, 42
  British 7, 32, 43, 63, 76, 80, 126
  civilisation myths 4, 221
  Dutch 43
  French 32, 43, 180
  genocide/violence under 19, 31, 33, 37, 55, 71, 94, 212, 221
  impact on psyche 41–42
  Portuguese 31, 50–51, 55, 58, 61, 76
  racial antagonism/division and 7, 63, 162–164, 171n3, 221
  Russian 43
  Spanish 30–34, 43–44
  see also capitalist exploitation; dispossession of indigenous peoples; settler colonialism; underdevelopment: colonial

colonialism in contemporary South Africa 158–159, 163
  link with capitalist practice 159, 162, 166–168, 170n4, 184
  see also colonial unconscious
colonialism of a special type (CST) thesis 23, 165, 174, 209
  shortcomings of 175–178
Columbus celebrations 30–31, 33–34
communalism 121–122, 124, 131
Communist Party of South Africa (CPSA) 8, 10, 174, 197–198, 209
Communist Party of the USA 10
corruption 2, 23, 66, 144n4, 196, 200, 202, 204, 208, 225
Couldthard, Glen 17, 44–45

D
Dalit Bahujan castes 19, 153n1
  agential autonomy/assertiveness of 21–22, 137–139, 141–142, 144, 146, 149, 151–152
  discrimination against/exclusion of 21, 119, 128, 130, 132, 134n7, 153
  feminist perspective 21, 132–133, 139, 141, 151, 153
  queer politics 146
  'untouchable' experience 119–120, 133n1&2, 141, 145, 153n1
  sacred prostitution among 149
  see also under Hindutva
Dalit revolt 129, 132–133
  conflict with cow gangs 128–129, 131
  Mahishasura controversy 128–130, 135n9
Datta, Pradip Kumar 121–122
Davis, Angela 63, 75
decolonisation 13, 15, 41, 60
  fundamental transformations after 60–61
  of immigration policy 221
decolonising universities 18, 199
  #FeesMustFall 56, 199
  #RhodesMustFall 56, 199
dehumanisation 20, 56, 58, 60, 64, 67, 69–71, 201
  slavery as encapsulation of 50, 53–54, 71
  see also under Hindu caste system
democracy 19, 31, 54, 70, 132, 152, 223
  ethnic 77
  social 9–10, 143
  in South Africa 2, 22, 158–159, 162, 163, 166, 176, 202–203
  see also eco-socialism, democratic; Israel: Jewish democracy in

247

Department of Home Affairs, South Africa 217–218, 224–227
devadasi communities 148–149, 151
development impasse in South Africa 173, 202
developmentalism 59–60, 62, 66–67
   neoliberal 184, 186
Dietrich, Gabriele 152–153
displacement of populations 78, 81, 152, 153
dispossession of indigenous peoples 1, 16, 55, 93–94, 103, 238
   Christian Doctrine of Discovery 19, 30–33
   Israeli 80, 93–94
   land claims 19, 33, 35
   racialised 30, 54, 109
   Treaty of Tordesillas 31
   see also ethnic cleansing; land dispossession, South Africa
Du Bois, W.B.E. 1, 12, 53, 63, 190n3, 237

E
eco-cide *see under* climate crisis South African perspective
eco-feminism in India 139
   environmental feminism 152
   masculinist perspective 151–153
   socialist analysis of ecology 152–153
economic development
   concept of Africa rising 67–69
Economic Freedom Fighters (EFF) 158, 200
eco-socialism, democratic 17, 24, 152–153
   through deep just transitions 24, 211–213
   Democratic Eco-Socialist Project 24
   nation-building project 211, 213
Egypt 4, 55, 69, 70, 86–87
elites
   African 10, 59–61
   Ashkenazi 87–88
   elite pact, South Africa 173, 178, 187
   Hindu 129
   liberal Israeli 87–88
emancipatory freedoms 20, 57–59, 62–65, 71
Engels, F. 181, 185
ethnic cleansing 80, 237
   1948 Nakba 78, 80–82, 84, 86, 92
ethnocentrism 4–5, 8, 18
ethno-nationalism 8, 16, 20, 84, 89
Eurocentrism 18–19, 69, 181, 238, 240
   Marxist 3–5, 8, 11–12, 15, 25n6
   see also Marxism: post-Eurocentric
European Enlightenment 4, 53–54
European Union (EU) 85, 97–99, 103–105, 109–110
   refugee policy 97–99, 104–106, 113n5, 219
   see also border regimes; migration, European 'crisis'
exclusion 8, 11, 13, 37, 103, 108, 112
   see also under Israel

F
Fanon, Frantz 15, 17–18, 22, 51, 63, 65, 137–138, 170n2, 182, 199, 239
   on the black non-subject 137–138, 161, 163, 170n2, 171n3
   post-colonial critique 177–178
fascism 8, 10, 124–126
   Euro-Marxist debates on 121
   new/neo 1, 16
   proto 22, 129
feminist engagement with Marxism 138–139, 153
   on domestic labour 142–143
   on commodification of female body 146–148
   on sexuality 22, 139, 145–146
   see also eco-feminism in India; Indian feminist perspectives on caste-based labour; labour: gendered division of
   see also labour
fetishism 160
   homo economicus as form of 162–163, 166, 171n4
First, Ruth 18, 239
First World War 9–10, 78, 80, 86
food security/sovereignty 103, 186, 205, 208, 212
foreign nationals *see* refugees and foreign nationals post-apartheid state policy on
fracking 16, 19, 42, 207
France 10, 49, 52, 69, 97, 143
   Paris terrorist attacks 99
Freedom Charter 175, 196–197, 201, 210, 213n3&4
French Front National 96–97, 110

G
Gabon 68–69
Gandhi 127, 143n2
Gauthier, Florence 49, 52
Gaza Strip *see* Israeli occupied territories
gender 11, 138
   inequality/oppression 9, 187, 195
   see also class: intersectionality of race, gender and; eco-feminism in India; feminist engagement with Marxism; Indian feminist perspectives on

caste-based labour; labour: gendered division of;
geopolitics, changing 24, 39, 220
Germany 57, 78, 97–98, 101, 103, 105–107, 111, 143
   Alternative for Germany (AfD) party 96, 110
   PEGIDA-movement 96
global North 18, 207, 220
global South 15, 18, 103, 219
   Marxism 174, 182
   racialised hierarchy of 11
globalisation 62
   deep capitalist 1, 23, 195, 200, 203–205 of labour 84
   neoliberal 208, 218–219, 221–222, 238
Gopal, Meena 139, 141
Greece 15, 78, 98–99
Guha, S. 119–120
Guinea/Guinea-Bissau 42, 50, 55, 68, 70

H
Haiti
   San Domingue uprising 12, 57, 69
Hall, Stuart 25n9, 101, 178, 180, 214n12
Hensman, Rohini 143–144
heteronormativity 100, 145–146
Hindu caste system 21–22, 118, 125–127, 133, 241
   Arya Samaj stance 126–127
   caste-class coalition 127
   dehumanisation under 21
   feminist perspective 21–22, 137, 141
   Sanatani stance 126–127
   see also Indian Marxists: elision of caste by; modern Indian self
Hindu right *see* Hindutva
Hinduism 141
   Brahminical/upper caste hegemony in 119, 127–130, 132–133, 154
   Manuvadi elite 128–129
   and question of disunity 126–127
   Vedic religion 126, 130
Hindutva 118, 120–122, 124–126
   Hindu Rashtra project 129, 131
   problematic relationship with Dalit Bahujan 123, 127–131
   Sanghism 125, 129, 134n5
   'theory' of 126
   see also Rashtriya Swayamsevak Sangh
historical materialism 6–7, 14, 21, 25n9, 41, 43, 96, 100–101, 103–104, 108, 209, 240
Holocaust 80, 84, 219, 238

human emancipation 6–7, 12, 20, 49–50, 62, 71
   re-Africanisation as part of 56–58, 64, 71
human rights 24, 38–39, 60, 66, 83, 88, 111, 219
   and respect for human dignity 217–218, 225–230, 232
   violations 229–231
   see also indigenous rights; UN Commission on Human Rights
humanism *see* universal humanism
Hungary 96, 98, 143

I
identity 15
   Arab 87, 89
   black 12, 63, 138, 199
   class 41, 138
   community 145
   indigenous/pre-colonial 33, 41, 76
   Jewish 84, 86–87
   Marxist 3, 9, 11
   see also whiteness
identity, depoliticisation of 62–63, 65–66, 71
identity politics 3, 11, 16, 20, 57, 138, 181
   anti-Marxist 2, 13, 240
   chauvinistic 187–189, 205
   in modern India 119, 126–127, 130, 133&n1
   individualistic 14, 50
   see also African, political conception of being; modern Indian self; racial essentialism
immigration 13, 24, 77, 81
   Jewish 78–79, 81, 83–84, 86, 91
   racialised regimes 16–17, 75
   see also migration/migrancy
imperialism 11, 54–55, 57, 59–60, 79, 124, 146, 177, 220–221
   centrality of race in 109, 175, 179
   global capitalist 177, 179–180, 206, 238
   neo-imperialism 183
   struggle against 61–62, 65, 70, 111–112, 148, 176–177
   US 10–11, 15–18, 61, 201, 220
India 4–6, 10, 12, 52
   Indian National Congress 11, 124, 134n4
   Muslim League (ML) 127
   1947 Partition 78, 127, 129
   see also Hindu caste system; Hindutva
India, left politics in 129, 132–133, 134n4
   Communist Party of India 134n3
   Communist Party of India (Marxist) (CPI(M)) 123–124, 134n3&4

249

Indian feminist perspectives on caste-based labour 21–22, 137–139, 141–142, 144–145, 153
   sex work 22, 139–141, 148–151
Indian Marxists 22, 118, 123–124
   elision of caste by 120–122, 133
   see also modern Indian self
Indian Termination Act 35
indigenising of Marxism 9, 15, 19, 40–45
   calls for 'nationalising' of 43
   Native Study Group 42
   Red Power activism 42
indigenous resistance/struggles 9, 16–17, 19, 32, 34, 39–42, 44–45n5, 75–76, 94
   1977 Geneva conference 35, 37–38
   Trail of Broken Treaties 35–36
   Wounded Knee 36–37
indigenous rights 35
   citizenship 82–83, 89–90
   land/property 16, 19, 31–35, 37
   Marxism and 40–41
   self-determination/sovereignty 8, 16, 19, 32, 35, 37–39, 41–42, 44
industrialisation 8, 60, 126, 152–153, 204, 207
   deindustrialisation 182
   racial 94
inequality 2, 231
   and crisis of social reproduction 185–187, 205
   non-racial 199
   racial/colonial 93, 166–170, 184, 188–189, 238
   socio-economic/income 23, 85, 186, 202, 214n14, 222
International Indian Treaty Council (IITC) 37–39
International Indigenous Peoples' Movement 30
International Organization for Migration (IOM) 98–99, 102, 104–105
internationalism 21, 111, 174
Iraq 86–87, 99, 113n9, 223
Islamisation 18, 96
Islamophobia 1, 17–18, 84, 222, 238
   see also anti-Muslim/Islamic sentiments
Israel 20, 77–78
   exclusion of non-Jewish people in 79, 81–84, 89, 92, 94
   Jewish democracy in 20, 82–83, 90
Israel/Palestine apartheid see apartheid: of a special type
Israeli Communist Party 83

Israeli occupied territories 82–85, 89–90, 92
   Green Line 82, 84–86, 90, 93–94
   Palestine Intifada 87, 92
Italy 10
   Lampedusa disaster 98–99

J
James, C.L.R. 12, 25n7, 53, 63, 180, 182
Jim Crow segregation 10, 17, 237
John, Mary 144–145
Jordan 82, 84

K
Karakayali, S. 98, 103
Karat, Prakash 123–125, 134n4
Kenya 69, 76, 79

L
labour
   gendered division of 141–144, 146, 185
   mobility 222
   see also migrant labour
   stigma theory of 144–145
   women's 14, 139–140, 143–145, 149–150, 185
   see also migrant labour
labour market 21, 82, 105–106, 110, 148–150, 202
   informal/precarious 139, 182, 202, 230–231
land dispossession, South Africa 94, 177, 180, 182–183, 203–204
   among black working class 184–185, 187
land question, South Africa 204–205
Latin America 15, 37, 42–43, 61
Lawyers for Human Rights (LHR) 24, 223, 225, 229–230, 232
Lenin, Vladimir 8–9, 44, 176, 209
liberalism 20, 54, 239
liberation politics 2–3
Libya 55, 68, 99
Losurdo, Domenico 53–54

M
Magubane, Bernard 180, 182, 184
Malema, Julius 200, 205
Maloka, E. 173–174
Mamdani, M. 63, 65, 76
Mandela, Nelson 195, 197, 201
Marx, Karl 3–5, 12, 240
   approach to temporality 5–6
   Capital 5, 162

on commodity 147–148
Manifesto of the Communist Party 5, 7, 181, 185
concept of production modes 43
transition from unilinear to multilinear path 5–6
Marxism 19, 25n12, 44, 170, 181–182
post-Eurocentric 12, 13, 15, 18–19, 111, 239–241
racially essentialised approach to 11–13
see also Eurocentricism: Marxist; Indian Marxists; indigenising of Marxism
Marxist anti-racism 1–3, 7–13, 15, 19, 25n9, 238–240
Marxist feminist theory 3, 14, 25n10, 137, 142, 185
see also feminist engagement with Marxism
Marxism-Leninism 8, 10
Masondo, David 175–176
Mbeki, Govan 18, 239
Mbeki, Thabo 195
African Renaissance 67
Merkel, Angela 98, 106
migrant labour 77
in Europe 21, 96, 103, 105–106, 110
migrant labour system, South Africa 14, 24, 91, 186, 218, 221, 231
migration, European 'crisis'
Long Summer of Migration 21, 97–99, 103, 111–112n4
and resurgence of racism 96–97, 99–100, 102, 106–110, 220, 238
role of neoliberal actors in 104–110, 112
and welfare chauvinism 96, 105–106, 108–110, 124, 238
see also border regimes
migration/migrancy 77, 91, 94, 105
relational autonomy of 103–104
see also immigration; post-migrant societies; refugees; refugees and foreign nationals, post-apartheid state policy on
minerals-energy complex, South Africa 184, 207, 210
Mizrahim 81, 86–87, 89
support for Likud 87
modern Indian self 118, 122, 131
national unconscious of 22, 118
modernisation 5, 59, 62, 139, 181, 183–185, 204
agricultural 182, 203–204
socialist 8, 209

modernism 130, 137, 153
modernity 5, 8, 11, 15, 122, 151, 223
capitalist/carbon-driven 16, 151, 208, 211, 240
Modi, Narendra 124–125, 129, 131, 134n4&6
Morocco 69, 105
Mozambique 10, 69, 76, 217
Frelimo 50

N
Nakba *see under* ethnic cleansing
Namibia 38, 69, 76
nation building, South Africa 195–196, 200–201, 204
see also under eco-socialism, democratic
national democratic revolution (NDR) 176, 210
see also national liberation struggle, South Africa
national liberation movements/ struggles 2, 10–11, 32, 37–38, 42, 50, 76
failure of 61–63
national liberation struggle, South Africa 20–21, 38, 57, 196, 198, 203, 218–219
internal contradictions 176–177, 210
mass resistance 196–197, 201
multi-class alliances within 175, 196–197
two-stage theory 175–177
see also African National Congress; Communist Party of South Africa; United Democratic Front
national question, South Africa 23, 195, 209
class-race power nexus and 24, 174, 178–183, 186–189, 209
climate determinism and 210–211
Marxist approach to 2, 8, 174, 178–179, 183, 185, 189, 207, 209–210
and persistence of racism 173–174, 184–185, 189, 201, 239
see also black nationalism: bourgeoise/ reductionist; colonialism of a special type thesis; identity politics: chauvinistic; racialised capitalism: South Africa
nationalism 2, 19, 237
African 9, 175, 202, 205, 208
Arab 86
chauvinistic 8, 11–12, 97, 99, 102, 105–106, 109–110, 239
class/race links with 7, 23–24, 174, 178–179
exclusionary/narrow 1, 10, 108, 200, 222, 238, 241
Indian/Hindu 126–129, 131

251

nationalism (cont.)
  neo-fascist white 1, 17
  racialised 9, 13, 96
  rainbow *see under* non-racialism in South Africa
  resource 194, 196
  see also black nationalism; ethno-nationalism
Navajo nation 42–44
Negritude 56, 64–65, 138
neocolonialism 20, 50, 58, 60, 62, 237
  and rhetoric of independence 59–60
  see also capitalism: neocolonial
Neocosmos, Michael 57, 59, 65, 176
neoliberalism 10, 21, 50, 107, 179, 183, 201
  Afro- 11, 194–195, 200–204, 208
  mass mobilisations against 69–70, 183
  racialised/racist 10–11, 15–16, 24, 66, 109–112, 218–219, 222
  structural adjustment policies 66, 222
  transnational 66, 68–69, 109, 201, 222
  see also developmentalism
Netherlands 97, 107, 112n2
New Mexico 42–43
New Partnership for Africa's Development (NEPAD) 67
Non-Aligned Movement (NAM) 10, 37, 39
non-racialism in South Africa 2, 159, 167, 169, 176, 199, 209
  ANC rainbow nationalism 23, 173, 194–195, 200–204, 239
  see also radical non-racialism

O
O'Hanlon, R. 119–120
orientalism 4, 120
  racism of 17
Ottoman Empire 79–80, 86

P
Pakistan 78, 113n9
Palestine 1, 17–18, 55, 77
  Jewish settlement project in 78–81, 84, 87
  militarisation/Palestine Liberation Organization 20, 38
  see also ethnic cleansing; Israeli occupied territories
Pandian, M.S.S. 119, 135
Patel, Surendra 60–61, 142
patriarchy 9, 43, 70, 140, 145–146, 148
peasantry 19, 175, 177, 181–182, 212
Periyar (E.V. Ramasamy) 118–119, 132

Phule, Jyotiba 118, 132
Pithouse R, 51, 57
political agency 20, 98
  impact of dehumanisation on 67
  revolutionary 23, 176–177, 179, 181–183, 189
populism 2, 32, 96–97, 110, 199–200, 203–205, 226
post-migrant societies 21, 102, 104, 106, 109
privatisation 35, 66, 182, 222
prostitution 140
  as commodification 146, 148, 151

R
race 1–2, 49, 76, 94, 145, 183, 239–241
  biological/pseudo-scientific concept of 4, 49, 53, 56–57, 63–64, 101, 119–120
  conflation with caste 21–22, 118–120, 123, 137–138
  Marxist theorising on 3, 9, 11–13
  as social construct
  taxonomy of 71
race-relations theory 23
  democratic Marxist approach 174, 178–179, 183, 185, 189, 209
  liberal tradition 173, 176
race theory, critical 23, 63–64, 119–120
  insights for caste 137–138, 141, 153
racial essentialism 12, 20, 23, 24, 100, 188–189, 199–200
racial oppression *see under* racism
racialisation 10, 12, 14, 16, 21, 24, 63, 101, 109
  of history 65
  of labour 91, 110
racialised capitalism 2, 4, 9, 12–13, 16–17, 19–20, 32, 53–54, 220–221, 237–238
  impact of unpaid labour on 142–144, 185–187
  in South Africa 14, 23–24, 174, 176, 179–180, 184–189, 197, 209
racism 1, 4, 9, 12–13, 21, 54, 56, 103, 232, 237
  conjunctural 1, 3, 13, 21, 23–24, 97, 101–102, 106, 109, 179, 181, 203 *see also* xenophobia
  ethnic-based 7
  historical 2, 9, 13, 19, 65–66, 112, 179, 237
  ontological 56, 113n7, 161, 167, 171n3, 174
  as relation of oppression 9, 13–15, 21, 50, 100–102, 107, 110, 175, 187, 197, 201, 204, 232, 237–238, 241

right-wing national-social 21, 97, 99, 104, 106–111, 238
systemic/institutionalised 1–2, 54, 65, 173–174, 179
see also apartheid; anti-Muslim/Islamic sentiments; Jim Crow segregation; migration, European 'crisis'; white supremacy
racism, struggle against *see* anti-racist resistance/struggles
see also Marxist anti-racism
racist mobilisations 106–107
radical non-racialism 23, 194–195, 199, 202, 205, 239
  anti-capitalist/anti-racist 23, 197–198
  centrality of working class to 203
  challenge to white supremacy 195, 197–199
  and climate crisis 24, 211–212
  intersectionality of 199–201, 212
  in people's history of struggle 23, 195–198, 201, 213n2
'rainbowism' *see under* non-racialism in South Africa
Raj, Rekha 141–142
Rashtriya Swayamsevak Sangh (RSS) 125, 127
  attack on JNU 129–130
  mobilisation of women in 121
refugees
  on African continent 219–220
  in Europe 96, 102–103, 108, 111
  Palestinian 81–82, 84, 86–87, 89
  in US 222–223
  see also European Union: refugee policy; migration/migrancy; UNHCR; xenophobia
refugees and foreign nationals, post-apartheid state policy on 24, 217
  failed asylum system 218, 224–226, 232
  Lindela Repatriation Centre 229–230
  narrative of risk/security threat 218–219, 227
  Refugees Amendment Bill 218, 225–227
  White Paper on International Immigration 218, 221, 225–227
  see also xenophobic violence, post-apartheid
renewable energy 208, 213
Reno, Philip 41–42
Robinson, Cedric 12–13, 32, 52, 181–182
Rodney, Walter 51–52, 180, 221
Russia 43–44, 220
  see also Soviet Union
Russian commune 6
Russian Revolution 10

S
Sahni, R. 149–150
Said, Edward 4, 223
Sankara, Thomas 69, 239
Sarkar, Sumit 120–121
Sarkar, Tanika 121–122
Sartre, Jean-Paul 137–138
Savarkar, V.D. 126–127
Second World War 35, 57, 78, 80, 219–220
secularism 18, 87, 107, 121–124, 132, 137
Sen, S. 121–122
settler colonialism 20, 31–32, 88, 93, 241
  indigenous-settler relations 75–77, 79
Shankar, V.K. 149–150
Shiva, Vandana 151–153
Sioux nation 36–37
slavery/slave trade 2, 5, 13–14, 17, 20, 30–31, 33, 43, 50, 52, 55, 71, 77, 181, 212
  abolition of/uprisings against 7, 32, 57
  chattel 31, 52–53, 70
  see also dehumanisation: as encapsulation of slavery
socialist struggle 9, 15, 175–177, 187
South Africa 69
  democratic transition in 173, 177–178
  renewed left politics in 195, 198
  social protest/civic struggles in 203
South African Communist Party (SACP) 175, 177, 209–210, 239
South African Constitution 24, 194, 201–203
  Bill of Rights 218, 225–228
  Constitutional Court 227, 229–230
Southall, Roger 68, 178
Soviet Union 8–9, 39, 41, 84, 197, 209
Stalin, Joseph 8, 209
Stavenhagen, Rodolfo 41, 46n17
Sudan 63, 69
Sudras 119, 133n1, 149, 153n1
supremacism, Western/Euro-American 4–5, 11, 16–17
  see also white supremacy
Sweeny, Robert 65–66
Syria 55, 98–99, 113n9

T
Third World Solidarity 10–11
Tomsic, Samo 160–161, 170n1
trade unions 66, 102, 144, 182, 231
  unionisation of women workers 140, 143–144
  see also black trade union movement, South Africa
Trump, Donald 207, 223, 227, 238

Tunisia 52, 69–70
Turkey 78, 98–99
Turok, B. 158–159

U

UN Commission on Human Rights 38–40, 46n13
  Sub-Commission on Racism 38, 40
UN Council on Human Rights *see* UN Commission on Human Rights
UN Declaration on the Rights of Indigenous Peoples 16, 33–34, 36, 39–40
UN High Commissioner for Refugees (UNHCR) 219, 226
UN World Conference Against Racism, Racial Discrimination, Xenophobia and Related Intolerances 119
unconscious, psychoanalytic concept of 159–160, 164–165
  see also colonial unconscious
underdevelopment 50, 66, 181, 184
  colonial 41, 59, 174, 220–221
unemployment 19, 107, 182, 202, 205, 214n14, 230
  structural 231
United Democratic Front (UDF) 196–198, 213n5
universal humanism 20, 50, 57, 69–71, 198
US 17, 34–35, 85
  Civil Rights Movement 145n5, 237
  Red Scare 42
  undermining of indigenous rights 19, 30–33, 37, 39–40, 238
  war on terror 17, 223
  see also cold war; imperialism: US

V

Vatican 30, 33–34
Vemula, Rohith 128, 130, 134n7
Vietnam War 35, 37

W

West Bank *see* Israeli occupied territories
western welfare states 10, 108, 110
white supremacy 17, 64, 174, 180–181, 188, 195, 197–199, 212, 221, 238, 240
  economic underpinnings of 175
  opposition to 49, 52, 56
  see also supremacism, Western/Euro-American
whiteness 2, 17, 106, 161, 167, 197, 212
  colonial 169, 171n5
Wilders, Geert 96, 112n2
Winant, H. 90, 104, 109
Wolpe, Harold 158, 170, 175, 185, 239
working class 41, 108, 162, 181, 183, 188, 238
  exploitation of 143, 179–180, 182, 184
  organised 196, 203, 205
  struggles 176–177, 182–183
  survivalist activities 182
  see also labour
working class solidarity 5–6, 12, 17, 20, 238
  fragmentation/division of 7, 16, 205
World Conference on Indigenous Peoples 34
World Conference against Racism 21, 119
World Council of Indigenous Peoples (WCIP) 16, 37–38
Working Group on Indigenous Populations (WGIP) 38–40, 46n13

X

xenophobia 1, 81, 87, 119, 205, 221–222
  among Arab nationalists 81, 87
xenophobic violence, post-apartheid 2, 24, 205, 217–218, 223–224, 231–232n1
  People's Coalition Against Xenophobia 226

Z

Zimbabwe 69, 205, 217, 224
  Great 52
Zionism 18, 79–81, 86, 90
  anti-Zionist orthodox Jews 90
Zionist Movement *see* Zionism
Zizek, Slavoj 164–165, 168
Zuma, Jacob 23, 196, 200, 202, 204

www.ingramcontent.com/pod-product-compliance
Lightning Source LLC
Chambersburg PA
CBHW020249030426
42336CB00010B/693